Legendary

Logic Puzzles

kurt smith,
Norman D. willis,
and Mark zegarelli

PUZZLE
WRIGHT
PRESS
New York

PUZZLE WRIGHT PRESS

New York

An Imprint of Sterling Publishing
387 Park Avenue South
New York, NY 10016

The puzzles in this book come from the following Sterling titles:
"Logic Puzzles to Bend Your Brain" © 2003 by Kurt Smith
"Poker Logic Puzzles" © 2005 by Mark Zegarelli
"False Logic Puzzles" © 1997 by Norman D. Willis
"Mystifying Logic Puzzles" © 1998 by Norman D. Willis

© 2010 by Sterling Publishing Co., Inc.
This edition published 2014

ISBN 978-1-4549-1094-7

Distributed in Canada by Sterling Publishing
^{c}/o Canadian Manda Group, 165 Dufferin Street
Toronto, Ontario, Canada M6K 3H6
Distributed in the United Kingdom by GMC Distribution Services
Castle Place, 166 High Street, Lewes, East Sussex, England BN7 1XU
Distributed in Australia by Capricorn Link (Australia) Pty. Ltd.
P.O. Box 704, Windsor, NSW 2756, Australia

For information about custom editions, special sales, and premium and corporate purchases,
please contact Sterling Special Sales at 800-805-5489 or specialsales@sterlingpublishing.com.

Manufactured in the United States of America

2   4   6   8   10   9   7   5   3   1

www.puzzlewright.com

CONTENTS

PART I   Brainbender Puzzles

CONTENTS continued

PART II   Poker Logic Puzzles

CONTENTS continued

PART III   False Logic Puzzles

CONTENTS continued

CONTENTS continued

PART IV   Mystifying Logic Puzzles

CONTENTS continued

PART I
Brainbender Puzzles

Stephanie's Water Bottle

Stephanie brought a filled water bottle to class. Several of her students wanted a drink from it, so Stephanie got paper cups and offered some. The first person, Teresa, took $1/4$ of the total. Brady then took $1/5$ of what remained. After that, Keith took $1/3$ of what was left. The next person, Cathy, took $1/2$ of what was remaining. Kent then took two ounces, leaving Stephanie with the remaining two ounces. How many ounces of water did Stephanie start with?

See answer on page 288.

My Favorite Class

Eighty students were surveyed about their favorite class. Using this pie chart, record the responses of the correct number of students (percentages have been rounded off to the nearest whole number).

_____ Art

_____ Biology

_____ English

_____ Math

_____ PE

_____ Social Studies

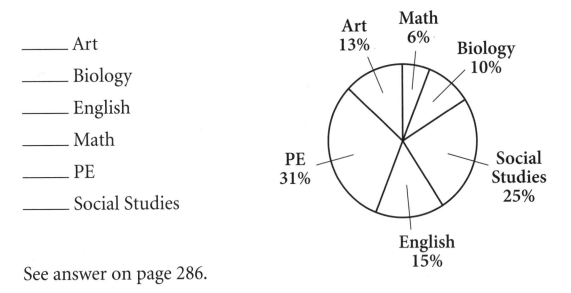

See answer on page 286.

At the Zoo

Five animals at the zoo (one each of ages 10 to 14) get into an argument about their ages because the oldest gets fed first and they're all ravenous. See if you can figure out how old each animal is.

1. The otter is older than the leopard.
2. The emu is younger than the otter.
3. The leopard is older than the hippopotamus.
4. The hippo is older than the emu and the lion.
5. The lion is older than the emu.

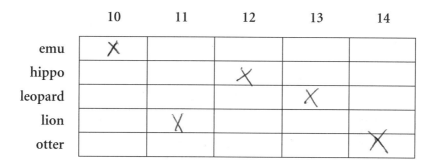

	10	11	12	13	14
emu	X				
hippo			X		
leopard				X	
lion		X			
otter					X

See answer on page 275.

Cornivores

In Tristan's Video Arcade, the Corn Eaters from the *Cornivores* game got out and started eating some of the creatures from the other games. When Tristan opened his arcade the next morning he discovered, to his horror, that several creatures were missing. Using these clues, figure out exactly how many of each kind are missing and which games they belong in.

1. There were 21 more Grabbers taken than Wombats.
2. A total of 115 creatures were eaten in the night.
3. Some of the Iguanidae from *Lizard Lair* were eaten, 10 fewer than the Trocta from the *Trout School.*
4. All of the Wombats are gone! There were 11. Poor little fuzzy critters.
5. 44 Slimeballs are gone.

Body Grabbers	Lagoon Slimeballs	Lizard Lair	Trout School	Wombat Willies
32	44	9	19	11

WAIT! In an unexpected turn of events, the *Cornivore* denizens admitted that all the creatures were simply creature-napped, not eaten, and they have all been returned to their games. Whew! That was a close one, eh, Tristan?

See answers on page 278.

Beverly's Yard Sale

Beverly decided to have a yard sale to get rid of a bunch of yards—and some feet and inches, too—that had been piling up in her den. She advertised this way:

Yard Sale

Yards and other assorted lengths.

MUST GO!   **Cheap!**

By noon she had sold almost everything. Just a few items were left, all of which Beverly plans to send to be recycled. Using the following information, figure out how much Beverly made on her yard sale and how many feet she will donate to recycling.

started with	sold	price	earned	left over to recycle (in feet)
13 yards	11 yards	.20 per foot		
27 feet	8 yards	.03 per inch		
216 inches	186 inches	.24 per foot		
		Totals		

See answer on page 276.

How Far?

Five people each put a gallon of gasoline in their vehicles to see who could go the farthest. Using the clues, including the conversion information below, figure out the distance each vehicle traveled, who drove it, and what color it was.

1 mile = 1.6 kilometers

1. The red motorcycle traveled 12 kilometers farther than the SUV.
2. One vehicle, not the SUV, went 34.5 miles.
3. The old woman drove 55.2 kilometers.
4. The person driving the motorcycle wore a green coat and traveled 48 kilometers.
5. The referee traveled 19.2 kilometers fewer than the one in tennis shoes and 4.5 miles fewer than the green station wagon.
6. The one in ski boots traveled at a rate of 27 miles per gallon.
7. The driver of the blue sports car wore gold earrings.
8. The orange vehicle traveled 22.5 miles.
9. The five vehicles traveled a total of 150 miles.

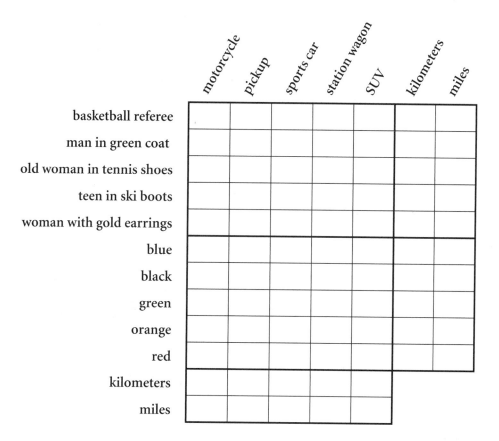

	motorcycle	pickup	sports car	station wagon	SUV	kilometers	miles
basketball referee							
man in green coat							
old woman in tennis shoes							
teen in ski boots							
woman with gold earrings							
blue							
black							
green							
orange							
red							
kilometers							
miles							

See answer on page 282.

Vanilla Swirl

How much ice cream could you eat in five minutes? Six kids had a little contest to see who could eat the most. They all went to Leo's Ice Cream Palace and told Leo to "bring it on," meaning, of course, to serve them a lot of ice cream. See if you can figure out who ate the most, how much, and what kind. Have fun dreaming of being in a contest like this!

1. Sara ate half as many scoops as Caleb.
2. Neither Joey nor Loren likes raspberry.
3. The one who ate peach ice cream won the contest.
4. Dakota doesn't like rocky road.
5. Loren ate more than twice as much as Sara.
6. The one who ate four scoops chose vanilla swirl.
7. Sydney, who chose rocky road, ate three more scoops than Joey.
8. Loren ate three more scoops than Dakota.
9. Sydney ate two fewer scoops than Loren.
10. The one who chose chocolate ate two more scoops than the one who chose vanilla swirl.

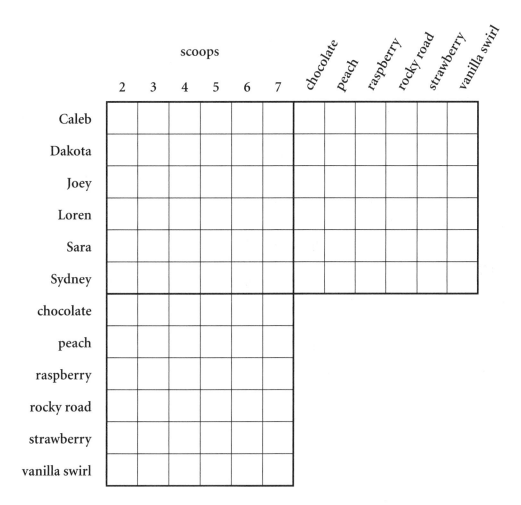

See answer on page 290.

Paper Clips

A total of 303 whole paper clips are in 12 boxes. The box with the fewest has four. Another box has 39. Based on the following, how many paper clips are in each box?

Box C contains half as many as Box J.
Box F contains $1/10$ as many as Box D.
Box L contains $1/5$ as many as Box E.
Box H contains five times more than Box F.
Box L contains two fewer than Box C.
Box I contains three times as many as Box C.
Box A contains half as many as Box K.
Box K contains one fewer than Box I.
Box B contains four times as many as Box F.
Box G contains twice that of Box L.

A	B	C	D	E	F

G	H	I	J	K	L

See answer on page 287.

Four Football Fans and Four Pizzas

Four guys are watching a football game. Four frozen pizzas are waiting in the freezer. By the end of the first quarter, all four pizzas are ready to eat. (Yes, the guys did cook them first.) Because not all the guys like the same kinds of pizza, they slice the four pizzas this way:

> 3 pepperoni pizza slices
> 5 cheese pizza slices
> 4 sausage pizza slices
> 4 vegetarian pizza slices

Using the clues below, answer these questions: Which guy ate which kinds of pizza, and how many slices of each? Note: All four guys had four slices.

1. No one ate more than three slices of any one kind.
2. One of the pizza slices, a pepperoni one, was chosen by Hank. Another one that he had was vegetarian.
3. Three of Peter's choices were just one kind. One was vegetarian.
4. Two of the guys ate one of each kind.
5. Jason does not like cheese pizza.

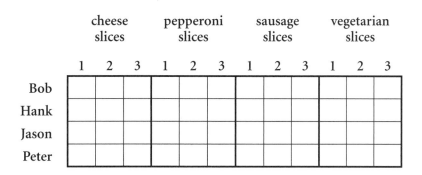

See answer on page 280.

Babysitting

Five young people (three boys—Barry, Dylan, and Elvis—and two girls) have been babysitting to earn extra money. Each one is saving for something special. Using the clues given, figure out how much each makes per hour, how much each has earned so far, and what each is saving to buy.

1. Dylan has earned the most so far, although he makes the least per hour.
2. Carson has worked 19 hours, 23 fewer than Wills.
3. Gray makes $4.75 and has worked 35 hours so far. She's saving for the bicycle.
4. The person saving for a computer (not Ellison) earns $5.25 per hour and has earned $99.75 so far.
5. The one saving for the clothes is not Elvis.
6. Sands has worked 66 hours so far and is saving to go on a trip.
7. The person saving for college has worked 38 hours so far; the one saving for clothes has worked 42.

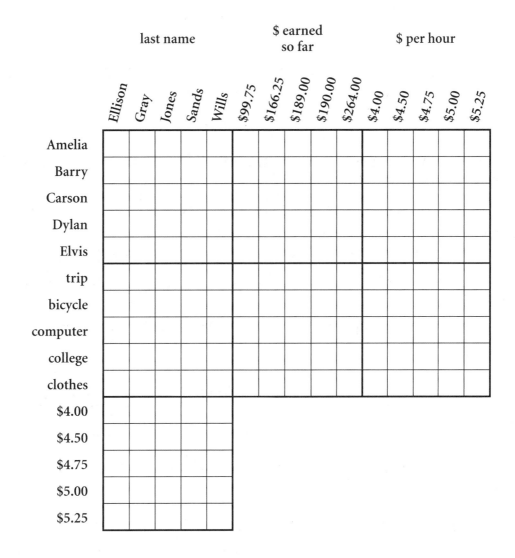

See answer on page 275.

Berry Streets Bus

The last five students to get off the school bus in the afternoon are Diana, Bruce, Tracy, Danny, and Justin. Each lives on the street where he or she leaves the bus. Using these six clues, determine the order the students get off the bus and the street each lives on.

1. Danny gets off the bus before Justin and Tracy; Justin leaves before Diana.
2. Huckleberry Avenue is between Cherry Street and Elderberry Road.
3. Tracy leaves the bus after Bruce.
4. The name of the second person off the bus doesn't begin with "D."
5. Diana gets off the bus between Huckleberry and Mulberry Street, both of which are before Blueberry Street.
6. The person who gets off the bus next to last lives between Elderberry and Blueberry.

	Bruce	Danny	Diana	Justin	Tracy	1st	2nd	3rd	4th	5th
Blueberry										
Cherry										
Elderberry										
Huckleberry										
Mulberry										
1st						
2nd						
3rd						
4th						
5th						

leaves bus

See answer on page 276.

Check!

Bob and Al play a lot of chess. Al is better than Bob, so when they wagered on a 50-game series (the loser had to wash the winner's car) they agreed to the following point system:

	checkmates	draws	stalemates
Bob	$3\frac{1}{2}$ points	$3/4$ point	$1/4$ point
Al	$1\frac{1}{2}$ points	$1/2$ point	$1/8$ point

Who won after 50 games? (Try doing this one without using a calculator!)

	checkmates	draws	stalemates	total
Bob	12	8	2	
Al	28	8	2	

See answer on page 277.

Hogs in a Fog

Five hog farmers were taking their hogs to the Annual County Fair when a sudden fog came up at an intersection at exactly the time all five were crossing, causing everyone to run into each other. No one was injured, but all the hogs—a total of 336—got loose and ran into the fog. From the clues, how many hogs were in each truck?

1. The Dodge carried four times as many hogs as the Chevrolet.
2. The largest load, $1/3$ of the hogs, had been in the Mack.
3. The smallest load, 24 hogs, was not from the Ford.
4. The Ford carried 24 fewer hogs than the GMC.

Chevrolet	Dodge	Ford	GMC	Mack

See answer on page 282.

Mr. Clark's PE Storage Room

Mr. Clark cleaned out his PE room the other day and found a bunch of balls for various sports, in the five amounts shown below. Given the following clues, how many of each kind of ball did he find?

1. There were six more tetherballs than footballs.
2. There were fewer footballs than soccer balls.
3. There were half as many soccer balls as softballs.

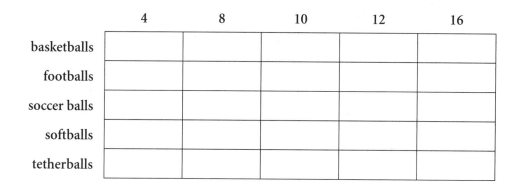

	4	8	10	12	16
basketballs					
footballs					
soccer balls					
softballs					
tetherballs					

See answer on page 285.

Sit-ups

These guys are crazy! About sit-ups, that is. Every morning before school they meet in the gym for a sit-up race. This morning, how many sit-ups did each boy do?

1. Logan did half as many as Leo.
2. Nicky did twice as many as Zack.
3. Chan did $1/3$ as many as Axel.
4. Dale did three times more than Andy.
5. Leo did half as many as Dale.
6. Chan did three times as many as Zack.
7. Andy did $2/3$ as many as Leo.
8. Logan did three times more than Nicky.
9. The smallest number of sit-ups was five.
10. One of the boys did 60 sit-ups.

_____ Andy _____ Axel _____ Chan _____ Dale
_____ Leo _____ Logan _____ Nicky _____ Zack

See answer on page 288.

Bogmen

As holidays approach, cranberry bogs are busy places as pounds of berries are shipped all over. Which bog shipped the most?

1. Billy's Berries shipped one-fifth fewer berries than Miles O'Bogs.
2. Grand Cranberries Ltd. shipped twice the amount of berries than Cranberries, Inc. did.
3. Tiny's Bog Co. shipped a third as many pounds as Grand Cranberries Ltd.

pounds of cranberries

	600	900	1,200	1,500	1,800	2,100
Billy's Berries						
Bog by the Bay						
Cranberries, Inc.						
Grand Cranberries Ltd.						
Miles o' Bogs						
Tiny's Bog Co.						

See answer on page 276.

Bobcats

The Bobcats basketball team is very good. They shoot like crazy and are great rebounders. Using all the clues below, see if you can determine the full name of each Bobcat varsity player, how tall each is, and their scoring averages.

1. Jon is not the tallest, but he's taller than Aaron.
2. Ben and Lien are the two shortest.
3. Blum played in 12 games and scored a total of 228 points.
4. Dan is taller than Delg, who is taller than Ross.
5. The one who scored 132 in 15 games is not Katz or Sid.
6. Ben is 3″ shorter than Sid.
7. Ross, who scored a total of 219 points in 15 games, is 6′3″.
8. The shortest player does not have the lowest shooting average.
9. Delg is 7″ taller than Lien.
10. The tallest player has the highest average.

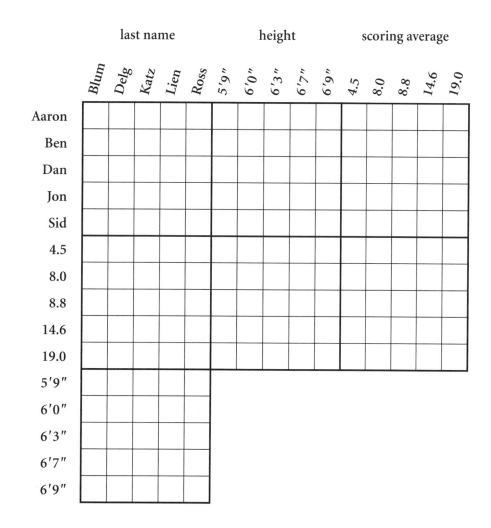

See answer on page 276.

Misplaced Numbers

It seems that a number of numbers have been misplaced. Your task is to put them all back in their correct boxes, in order from lowest to highest, according to these rules:

Box A contains even numbers larger than 12.

Box B contains odd numbers smaller than 40.

Box C contains multiples of 9.

Box D contains multiples of 7.

Box E contains all other numbers.

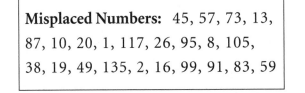

Misplaced Numbers: 45, 57, 73, 13, 87, 10, 20, 1, 117, 26, 95, 8, 105, 38, 19, 49, 135, 2, 16, 99, 91, 83, 59

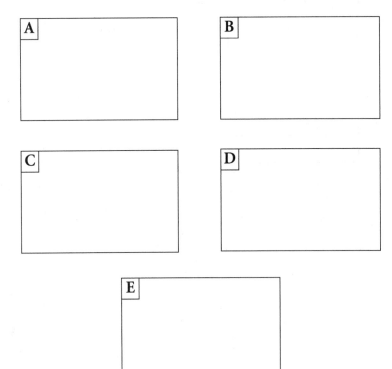

A

B

C

D

E

See answer on page 284.

Corn Dogs

Dwight sells hot dogs, corn dogs, and bags of pretzels, peanuts, and popcorn at baseball games. Today he sold everything he had (the numbers he had of each item he sold are below). How much did he sell?

1. He had four times as many hot dogs as bags of popcorn.
2. He had more corn dogs than bags of pretzels and popcorn combined.
3. He had three times as many bags of peanuts as bags of popcorn.

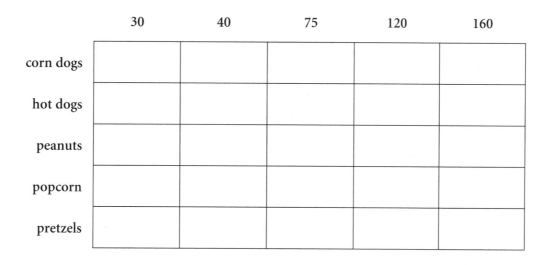

	30	40	75	120	160
corn dogs					
hot dogs					
peanuts					
popcorn					
pretzels					

See answer on page 278.

Five Boxes

1. Each box has a whole number in it.
2. The number in Box A is 12 times larger than Box B.
3. Box D is $1/2$ as large as Box A, and is the product of Boxes B and C.
4. Box E, containing the middle-sized number, is the sum of Box C and another box.
5. Box C is Box A divided by 8.
6. One of the boxes contains the number 4.

A	B	C	D	E

See answer on page 279.

Magazine Drive

Three classrooms sold magazine subscriptions as a fund-raiser over the months of October, November, and December. Using the information about the magazine drive in the chart at right, fill in the blanks in the statements below.

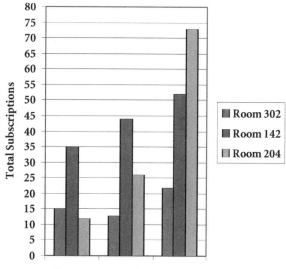

1. Room _____ sold twice as many subscriptions in November as Room _____ did in December.
2. In October, total sales were _____.
3. The best selling month was _____, with _____ subscriptions.
4. The best selling room was _____, with _____ subscriptions.
5. Room _____ sold twice as many subscriptions in November as Room _____.
6. Total sales for the month of _____ were more than the other two months combined.
7. Room _____ sold eight more subscriptions than the other two combined in the month of _____.
8. The largest difference in sales occurred in the month of _____, between Room _____ and Room _____.
9. Only Room _____ failed to make a gain each month.
10. Room _____ made the biggest gain in one month, from _____ in the month of _____ to _____ in the month of _____.

See answer on page 284.

Dale's Trip

Dale took a little time off from his deli to do some traveling by car. Using the given clues, see if you can tell how many gallons of gas he used, how much he spent on gas, the average amount he paid per gallon of gas, and how many miles per gallon he averaged.

Dale set his trip indicator at zero and filled his empty tank with 14 gallons of gas at $1.90 per gallon. He traveled 210 miles and added 8 gallons at a place that sold it for $1.99 per gallon. At the next stop, which he reached after traveling 225 miles, he filled up again for $1.89 per gallon, buying 12 gallons. The next time he stopped for gas, he had driven 199 miles and bought 6 gallons at a price of $1.78 each. His last stop was after driving 230 miles at a place that sold gas for $2.09 per gallon, where he filled his tank with a purchase of 11 gallons.

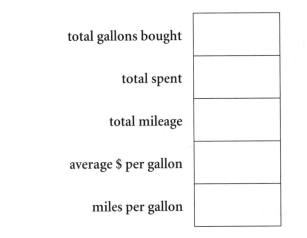

total gallons bought

total spent

total mileage

average $ per gallon

miles per gallon

See answer on page 278.

Farmer Bob's Barn

Bob sent Little Bob out to the barn one night to count the animals there. There are 2, 4, 6, 8, and 10 of the five different animal types. Can you figure out the numbers with just three clues?

1. There are twice as many cows as horses.
2. There are two more chickens than goats.
3. There are six more goats than horses.

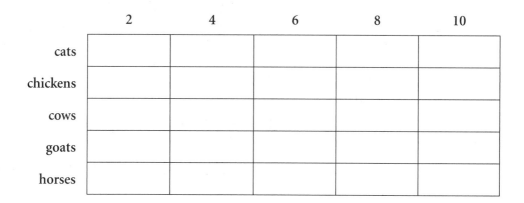

See answer on page 279.

Halloween Party

IT'S A PARTY! Candy. Cider. Costumes. Tons of sugar. You know the drill. Anyway, figure out who wore the witch's costume, who won the pumpkin-carving contest, who won the apple-bobbing contest, how many glasses of cider each drank, who got sick (yuk!), who broke their mother's dish in the apple-bobbing bucket, and who helped the teacher clean up afterward.

1. The one who broke the dish drank three glasses of cider.
2. Emily drank two more glasses of cider than Katie.
3. The one who wore the witch's costume drank six glasses of cider.
4. The one who helped clean up after drank four glasses of cider.
5. The one who drank one glass of cider won the pumpkin-carving contest.
6. Sam drank half as many glasses of cider as Emily.
7. Donny drank three more glasses of cider than Erin.
8. The person who got sick drank two glasses of cider. (I guess whoever it was didn't like it that much.)
9. The one who wore the witch's costume (not Donny) drank five more glasses of cider than Dina.

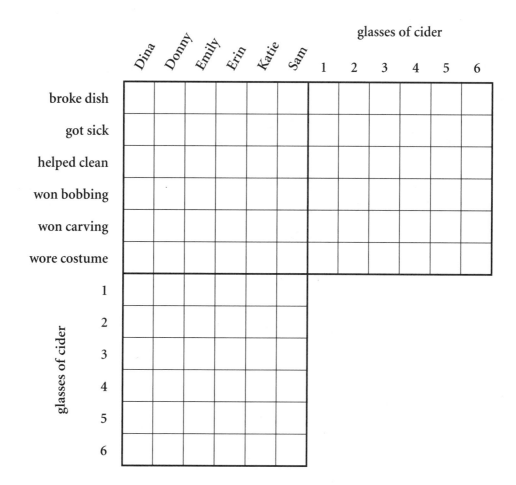

See answer on page 281.

Martha's Books

Martha loves books! She has books all over the place ... on her bookshelves, on the windowsill, under her bed, on shelves in the dining room, in the hallway, in closets. Her mother asked her to put some of her books into five boxes. Using these clues, figure out how many books she put into each box. *Hint: There are actually two different answers to this one, both correct!*

1. Martha was able to stuff 180 books into the five boxes.
2. The box with the most books has 12 more than the second largest.
3. The box with the fewest books, not A or D, has $1/15$ of the total number of books.
4. Box D has twice as many books as B.
5. $1/3$ of the books are in one of the boxes.
6. Box C has 24 fewer books than E.

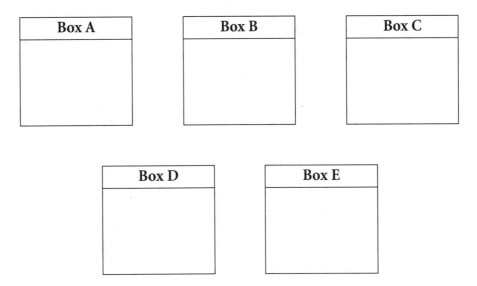

See answer on page 284.

The Dalton Express

Poor Engineer Jones ... he lost his train schedule! Seems it must have fallen out of his engineer's vest pocket while he was having an espresso at Half-Off Dale's Deli. All he remembers is that he leaves Dalton at 7:15 this morning, stops at several cities on the way to Reedville, then comes back to Dalton, nonstop, at the end of the day. From years of experience, he knows that the train waits exactly six minutes from the time it arrives at each station until it departs. He also knows that the train averages 48 miles per hour during the trip to Reedville and 56 miles per hour on the nonstop trip back to Dalton. Can you help him recreate his schedule?

Mileage from Dalton	
Carroll	96
Farmington	12
Newton	24
Portsmouth	156
Reedville	168

City	Arrive	Depart
Dalton	—	7:15
Farmington		
Newton		
Carroll		
Portsmouth		
Reedville		
Dalton		—

See answer on page 278.

Double Bogey

Eagle	= 2 strokes under par
Birdie	= 1 stroke under par
Par	= same score as the scorecard
Bogey	= 1 stroke over par
Double Bogey	= two strokes over par

Four friends played nine holes of golf. They all shot par on each hole except the following. What were their scores?

Hole 1: Smith had an eagle, Munro had a double bogey, and Dyment had a birdie.

Hole 2: Horn had a bogey, Munro had a birdie.

Hole 3: Smith had a birdie, Dyment had a double bogey, Horn had a bogey.

Hole 4: Munro had a birdie.

Hole 5: Dyment had a double bogey, Smith had a birdie, Horn had an eagle.

Hole 6: Horn had a double bogey, Smith had a birdie, Munro had a bogey.

Hole 7: Smith had another eagle, Horn had a birdie, Dyment had a bogey.

Hole 8: Munro had a birdie.

Hole 9: Dyment had a birdie, Horn had a double bogey, Smith had a bogey.

Scorecard

Par	4	5	3	4	4	3	5	4	4	36
Hole	1	2	3	4	5	6	7	8	9	Total
Dyment										
Horn										
Munro										
Smith										

See answer on page 279.

Warm-ups

Mr. Clark is at it again—pushing his students to work hard! Use this chart to determine how many points each student earned in PE class during warm-ups.

Push-ups	=	4 points each
Laps	=	8 points each
Sit-ups	=	3 points each

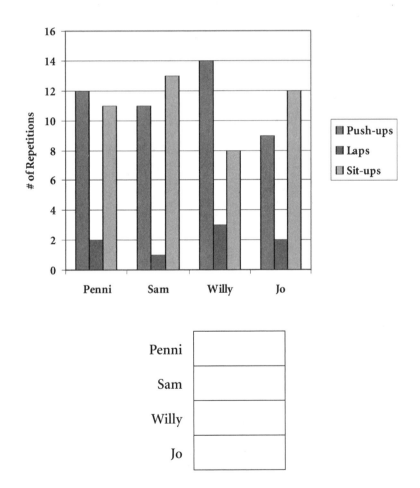

Penni	
Sam	
Willy	
Jo	

See answer on page 290.

Odometer

Five people drove their cars from Seattle to Portland, a distance of 185 miles. To check the accuracy of their odometers, they each set their mileage indicators to zero in a parking lot at Safeco Field. They each drive a differently colored car. Using the clues below, figure out the full names of all the drivers, the colors of the cars they drive, and the reading of their odometers as they cross the I-5 bridge into Portland three hours later.

1. Shepard is not Roberta, nor is his car green.
2. The odometer of the white car reads 6.9 miles fewer than the black car.
3. Rudy is neither Fisher nor Delphino.
4. The car driven by Swank is tan and the mileage is 2.2 more than Delphino's black car.
5. Lester's green car has 5.8 more miles than Roberta's red one.
6. Willy's tan car has .8 more miles than Curley's.

	Delphino	Fisher	Lester	Shepard	Swank	179.4	181.9	186.3	187.7	188.5
Curley										
Danny										
Roberta										
Rudy										
Willy										
black										
green										
red										
tan										
white										
179.4					
181.9					
186.3					
187.7					
188.5					

See answer on page 286.

Fraction Match

Your job here is to match the pictures with the fractions (put the letters of the matching pictures in the spaces at the bottom).

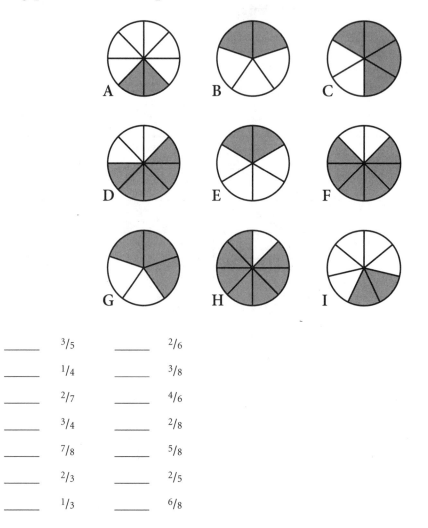

_____	3/5	_____	2/6
_____	1/4	_____	3/8
_____	2/7	_____	4/6
_____	3/4	_____	2/8
_____	7/8	_____	5/8
_____	2/3	_____	2/5
_____	1/3	_____	6/8

See answer on page 280.

Big hint #1: There is more than one answer for some of the pictures.
Big hint #2: There is one answer that has no picture representing it. Draw a circle around it.

Paul's Guppies

Paul had a bowl of guppies for sale. Four customers were milling around in his store.

1. Rod told Paul, "I'll take half of the guppies in the bowl, plus half a guppy."
2. Heather, the second customer, then said, "I'll take half of what you have left, plus half a guppy."
3. The third customer, Nancy, then said, "I'll take half of what you have left, plus half a guppy."
4. Michele, the fourth customer, then said, "I'll take half of what you have left, plus half a guppy."

All four of the customers left the store with only live guppies, and Paul was happy to have sold all his fish. How many guppies were there in the bowl when he started? How many did each customer take?

customer	guppies bought
Heather	
Michele	
Nancy	
Rod	
total in bowl	

See answer on page 287.

Half-Off Dale's Deli

Dale offers his customers a half-order of any item on his menu (except drinks) for 40% off. Seven people just walked into Dale's Deli and ordered from this menu:

Hungarian Mushroom Soup..... $3.00
Black Forest Ham Sandwich $6.00
Roast Beef Sandwich $6.00
Smoked Turkey Sandwich......... $6.00
Chili.. $2.50
Tuna Sandwich $5.50
Cinnamon Roll $2.00
Espresso..................................... $2.25
All soft drinks $1.25

Using the following clues, figure out how much each person's lunch cost, and who got stuck with the bill.

1. No one ordered both espresso and a soft drink, and no two people ordered the same kind of sandwich.
2. Neither Ginger, C.J., nor Beverly ordered a sandwich.

	sandwich		soup		chili		
	full	¹/₂	full	¹/₂	full	¹/₂	
Beverly							
C.J.							
Geri							
Ginger							
Kelsey							
Ted							
Tristan							

3. Three people ordered the mushroom soup; two of them ordered $1/2$ a bowl.

4. Kelsey ordered four items totaling $7.85. Her food items were $1/2$ orders.

5. C.J. and Ginger later figured that if they had split a cinnamon roll instead of ordering two halves they'd have saved money. Neither of them had anything but the $1/2$ cinnamon roll.

6. Three people ordered soft drinks (not Geri), and two ordered espressos (not Ted).

7. Tristan's lunch cost $11.25. He was the only one to have a full bowl of chili.

8. Four people ordered sandwiches: one was Tristan's tuna, and two were $1/2$ orders.

9. Geri had four items including half a sandwich and half a bowl of chili. Her total was $9.35.

10. Ted, Tristan, and Kelsey each had a soft drink.

11. The one who paid the total bill of $47.15 (not Beverly or Ted) had four items including a bowl of chili and a soft drink.

12. Ted was the only one who didn't have any cinnamon roll. Why not, Ted?

13. Just two people had chili and just two had espresso. One of the people had both.

14. Beverly ordered three items, including a full bowl of soup. Her total was $7.25.

	cinnamon roll		espresso	soft drinks	lunch cost
	full	$1/2$			
				total	
				paid by	

See answer on page 281.

B-r-r-r-r-r

Using the chart, answer the following (to the nearest tenth):

1. The average median temperature for the week was ____ degrees.
2. The coldest median was below the average by ____ degrees.
3. The warmest median was above the average by ____ degrees.
4. The day closest to the average median temperature was ____.
5. The biggest change from one day's median to the next was ____ degrees.
6. On three different days, the median temperature was the same: ____ degrees.
7. The median temperature was (warmer / colder) on the weekend than the rest of the week. By how much (average)? ____.

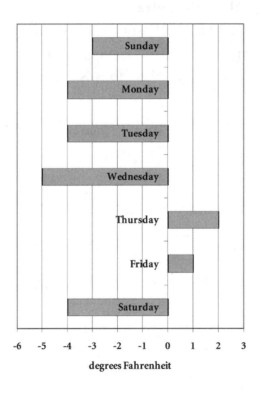

See answer on page 277.

Kids and Cars

The kids in Mrs. Flapdoodle's class were asked what kind of car they would buy if they were old enough. Twenty-two kids filled out the survey. Given that percentages have been rounded to the nearest whole number, how many chose which kind of car?

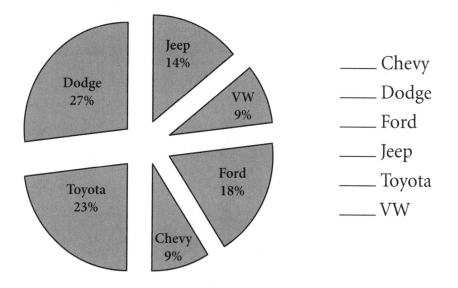

_____ Chevy

_____ Dodge

_____ Ford

_____ Jeep

_____ Toyota

_____ VW

See answer on page 282.

Jessica

Jessica got a new computer and she's driving her friends crazy with her questions. She charts the information she gets from them on her computer. Using her latest graph derived from birth dates, fill in the blanks below. (Assume that a month is equal to four weeks.)

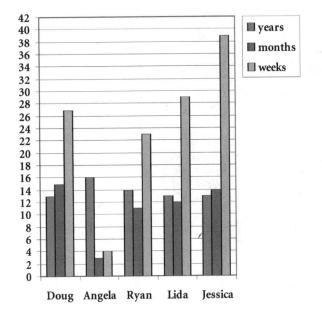

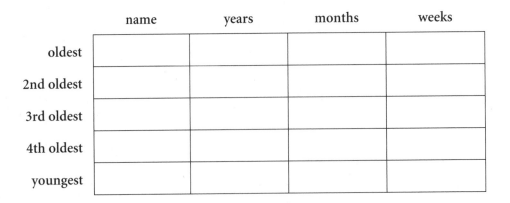

	name	years	months	weeks
oldest				
2nd oldest				
3rd oldest				
4th oldest				
youngest				

See answer on page 282.

Woody's Tires

A temperature change put the tire pressure in Woody's car out of whack. A tire place he went to uses gauges with kPa (kilopascals) rather than psi (pounds per square inch). To find kPa when you have psi, you have to multiply psi by 6.89. Woody is ready to either put air in his tires or let some out. Can you tell him how much?

	current tire pressure	desired pressure	add kPa's	subtract kPa's
right front	166.30 kPa	26 psi		
left front	184.98 kPa	26 psi		
right rear	199.32 kPa	28 psi		
left rear	147.86 kPa	28 psi		
spare	213.44 kPa	30 psi		

See answer on page 291.

Wholesome Decimals

By adding or subtracting the decimals inside the box, create seven whole numbers. (For example, 5.21 + 1.604 + .186 = 7, a whole number.) *Hints: Don't mix operations in the same problem, and use each number only once.*

6.09+.91=7
5.47+.53=6
9.25-.25=9
7.997+.003=8
4.78+.22=5
3.96+.04=4
.878+.121+.001=1

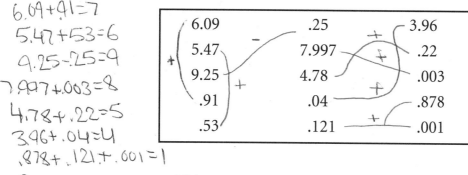

```
6.09        .25    +   3.96
5.47   -  7.997    +    .22
9.25      4.78          .003
 .91       .04    +    .878
 .53       .121   +    .001
```

See answer on page 291.

Kookaburra Stew

Four kookaburras are planning a stew for dinner. Each one likes different ingredients. Using these clues, determine which ingredient each kookaburra prefers and how much of it. Also, figure out the name of each bird, and where each is from.

Conversion Chart
1 pint   = .47 liters
1 quart = .94 liters
1 gallon = 3.76 liters

1. The stew calls for a pint more scampi than perch.
2. The kookaburra from Wollongong prefers sardines.
3. The kookaburra from Wagga Wagga prefers scampi.
4. The recipe calls for 1.175 liters more perch than angleworm.
5. The kookaburra that likes angleworm in his stew is from Kangaroo Island.
6. Plato likes perch.
7. Neither the bird from Wollongong, nor Augustus, prefers angleworm. They eat it on occasion, but it's not their first choice.
8. The kookaburra from Wollongong recommends 2.585 liters more of his ingredient than Caesar does of his.

	kookaburra				liters			
	Augustus	Caesar	Plato	Pluto	.235	1.41	1.88	2.82
angleworm								
perch								
sardine								
scampi								
3 pints								
3 quarts								
half a gallon								
half a pint								
Gympie								
Kangaroo Island								
Wagga Wagga								
Wollongong								

See answer on page 283.

Mr. Lockety's New Carpet

Four classrooms in Old Stewball School are getting new carpet, and Mr. Lockety is in charge. But, dashing to class, he lost all his requests. He's even forgotten what he needs in his own room! Which teacher gets which color, and how many square feet of carpet is needed for each? All measurements are in feet—no inches.

1. Room 168 is square.
2. Mrs. Eddy does not like sage.
3. Mr. Lockety's room is 27 feet long.
4. One of the dimensions of the room getting navy is 25 feet.
5. Mrs. Ebuley's room, 22 feet wide, will not have taupe carpet.
6. Just two rooms, 194 and the one getting taupe carpet, have a one-foot difference between length and width.
7. Room 186 (not the one getting mauve carpet) is 22 feet wide.
8. Ms. Stalk isn't fond of taupe.

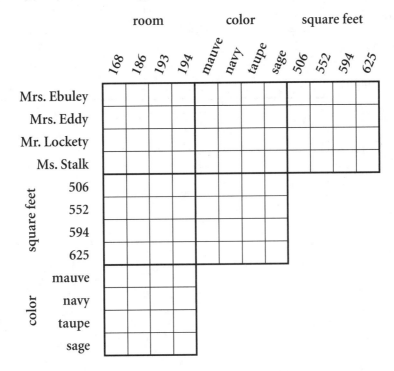

See answer on page 285.

Catapult

Four kittens weigh four pounds together, but they don't weigh one pound each. No, no, that would make this puzzle too easy for a person as smart as yourself. Two of the kittens weigh less than a pound and two of them weigh more than a pound. (The actual weights are shown below.) Four kids come along and take the four kittens. Makes sense, the kittens being really cute and all. So see if you can figure out which kid takes which kitten and how much each one weighs (no, not the kids ... the kittens).

1. Catapult weighs more than the kitten taken by Martha.
2. The kitten that weighs 17 oz. is not Bandit.
3. Codi weighs just under a pound but is not the lightest.
4. Kurt's kitten is not Bandit.
5. Ted's kitten is not the largest, but weighs over a pound.
6. Hallie weighs less than Codi.
7. Martha's kitten weighs 14 oz.

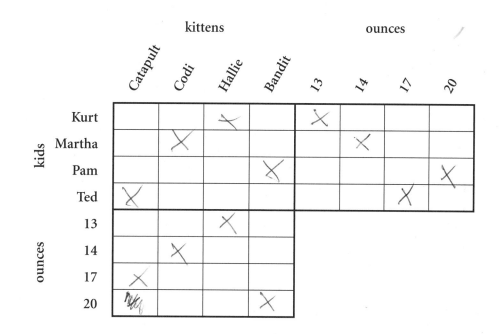

See answer on page 277.

Kurt's Bicycle Ride

Kurt rode his bicycle from Otis Junction, Oregon, to Baltimore, Maryland, in 40 days. He kept a log of the distance between several cities, but he neglected to keep a total. He is curious about the distances he traveled and his averages, but the only map he can find has kilometers only. Can you help? Remember: One mile is equal to 1.6 kilometers.

days	distance between cities	kilometers	miles	miles per day (nearest tenth)
7	Otis Junction, Oregon, to Boise, Idaho	838.4		
4	Boise to Ogden, Utah	528.0		
7	Ogden to Cheyenne, Wyoming	713.6		
6	Cheyenne to Omaha, Nebraska	811.2		
2	Omaha to Des Moines, Iowa	217.6		
6	Des Moines to Indianapolis, Indiana	764.8		
8	Indianapolis to Baltimore, Maryland	939.2		
	Total			

See answer on page 283.

Lily Claire and the Pirates

Team Captain Lily Claire and four other girls on one of two Pirates teams (varsity and junior varsity) compared their results from a recent game. See if you can tell how many baskets and free throws each made, which team each played on, and the total points for each player.

1. Rachel made three times as many free throws as the player who made four baskets.
2. Three players, including the one who made four free throws, are on the varsity team.
3. The player who made one basket and no free throws (not Teresa) is on the varsity team.
4. Tina made fewer free throws than Teresa, but more than Julia.
5. Teresa, who is on the varsity team, made half as many free throws as the player who made twice as many baskets as she did.
6. Lily Claire made two more baskets than Rachel, but Rachel made two more free throws than Lily Claire.

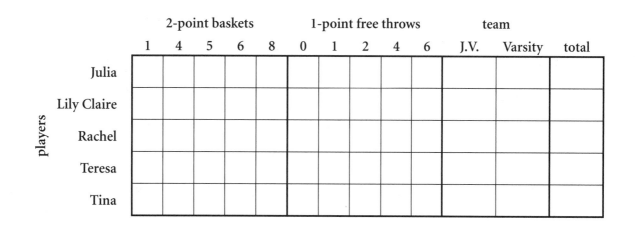

players	2-point baskets					1-point free throws					team		total
	1	4	5	6	8	0	1	2	4	6	J.V.	Varsity	
Julia													
Lily Claire													
Rachel													
Teresa													
Tina													

See answers on pages 283.

Wildcats

Five members of the Wildcats baseball team are listed, complete with their batting averages and current number of stolen bases. Determine who plays which position and their stats by using these hints.

1. The catcher, not Billsly or Lewis, has fewer stolen bases than the player batting .309.
2. Lewis's batting average is 20 points higher than the shortstop's.
3. The player batting .240 has the most stolen bases.
4. Atkins has fewer stolen bases than Johnston, but neither has three.
5. The center fielder leads in one statistic and is second in the other.
6. Lewis, who has a higher batting average than Billsly and Downey, has stolen seven bases so far this year.
7. Downey, the pitcher, is last in one statistic and next to last in the other.

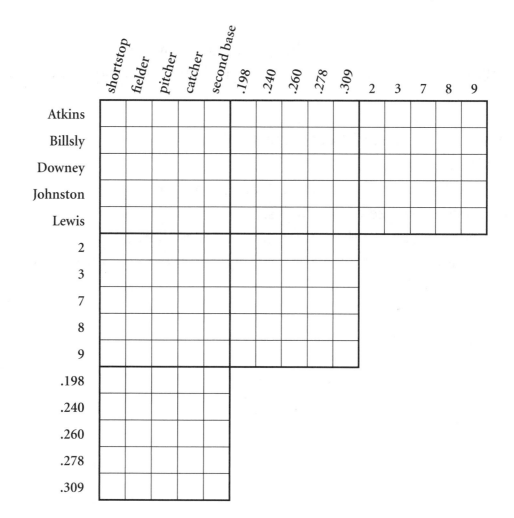

See answer on page 291.

N & G

The five top readers at the middle school are shown in this puzzle. It's your job to figure out how many books each student read, their initials, and their room numbers.

1. B, who is not L, read $^3/_4$ as many books as S.
2. G is in Room 103.
3. M read four more books than N and two more than P.
4. L's room is between N's and G's.
5. V read more books than N, who read more than L.
6. The student from Room 104 read eight books fewer than the student in Room 101.
7. T's classroom is 102.

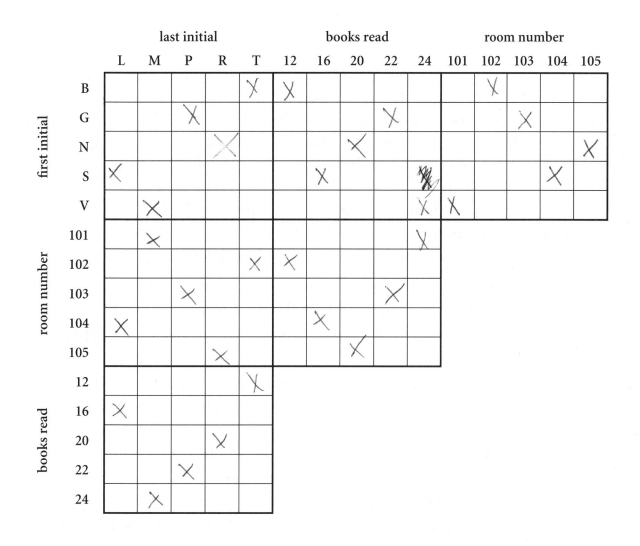

See answer on page 286.

Grandpa Willard's Applesauce

Grandpa Willard says he knows how to make the best applesauce in town. So he's down at Half-Off Dale's Deli telling his pals about it, and pretty soon there's a big argument over which apples and which ingredients make the best applesauce. At one point Dale had to ask them to be quiet because they were scaring off the other customers. So, using the following clues, see if you can tell which apples and which key ingredients go with which grandpa.

1. Cooper hates Northern Spy apples and horseradish.
2. Neither Smith nor Ted would allow lemon in his applesauce.
3. McGee uses twice as many apples as John Willard.
4. Neither Dick nor Cooper likes almond.
5. Neil and Cooper can't stand Granny Smith apples.
6. The one using almond extract, not Rod or McGee, uses 1 lb. apples.
7. Grandpa John uses .5 lb. more apples than Grandpa Frandsen.
8. The grandpa using 2.5 lbs. does not care for cinnamon.
9. The one using three teaspoons of horseradish also uses Northern Spy apples.
10. The grandpa using brown sugar (2 c.) uses 1.5 lbs more apples than the one using Granny Smith apples.
11. Ted and Cooper both disdain Yellow Transparents.
12. Neil likes Northern Spy. He uses three times as many as the one who uses almond.
13. Delicious apples and brown sugar go together, claims Rod.
14. Grandpa Smith uses 4 oz. of flavoring with his Gravenstein sauce, 3 oz. more than Ted.

pounds of apples   amount of flavoring

	1	1.5	2	2.5	3	Dick	John	Neil	Rod	Ted	1 oz.	2 c.	2 tbsp.	3 tsp.	4 oz.
almond extract															
brown sugar															
cinnamon															
horseradish															
lemon extract															
Delicious															
Granny Smith															
Gravenstein															
Northern Spy															
Yellow Transparent															
Cooper															
Frandsen															
McGee															
Smith															
Willard															

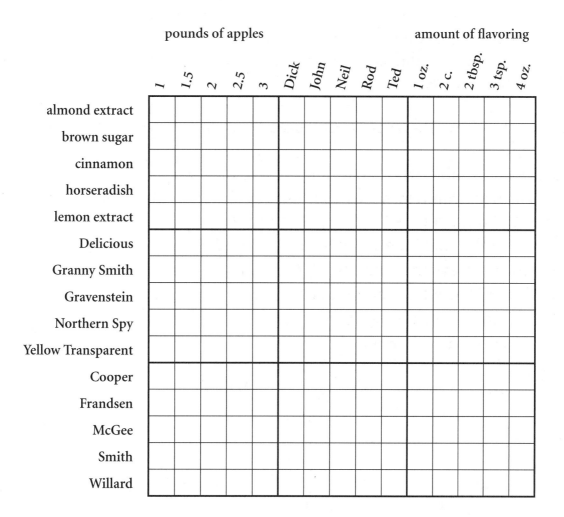

See answer on page 281.

Mustardville

Mustardville—that's the town where farmers deliver their hot dog supplies: onions, cucumbers, dill, etc. Determine which driver drives which truck and what he delivers there.

1. Hiram drove his truck from Pickelton to Mustardville, a total of 32 miles.
2. The cucumber truck is slower than the blue truck.
3. The trip from Relish City to Mustardville, the route of the dill truck, is 4.5 miles. It took the driver 15 minutes.
4. Cucumber Gap to Mustardville is 4 miles.
5. Townes drove the onion truck faster than the red truck.
6. The red truck traveled for two hours.
7. The onion truck drove for 12 minutes.
8. Vance did not drive the blue truck.

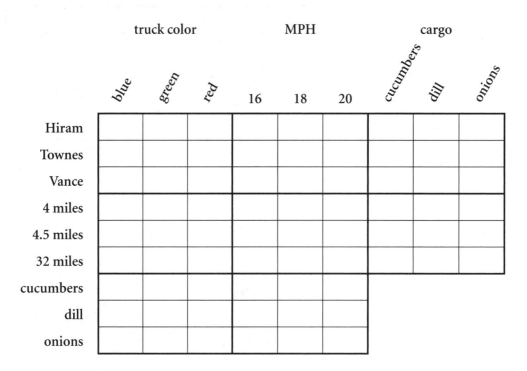

See answer on page 285.

Flapdoodle

A loggerhead shrike, a cattle egret, a black oystercatcher, a red-breasted merganser, and a roseate spoonbill are in a shouting match over who gets to be first going down the waterslide. They finally take a vote and agree that they will slide in order of height, with the shortest first. Can you figure out who's who and the order of their turns?

1. Jake is five inches shorter than the cattle egret.
2. The shrike and Sal combined are as tall as the spoonbill.
3. Tony gets to go first, the black oystercatcher third.
4. Milly is shorter than Willy by 25 inches.

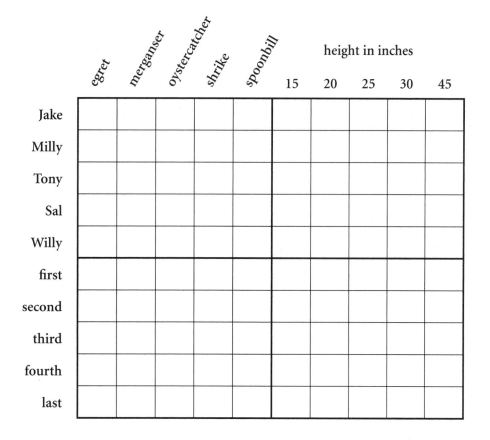

See answer on page 280.

Bone Hunters

Four big dogs went on a bone search. They dug up six bones all together. One dog found three. Another dog found two. A third dog found one, and one dog found none. You are to help figure out which dog (by name) found how many bones and what breed of dog each is.

1. Baggy is the Dalmatian.
2. The dog who found two bones wasn't the boxer or Muffin.
3. The German shepherd found more bones than Blue.
4. Muffin isn't the Labrador.
5. The Lab didn't find as many bones as Blue.

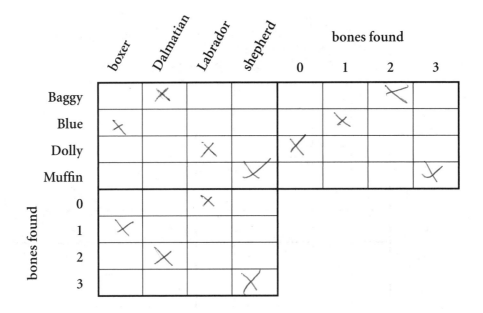

See answer on page 277.

Do the Math

Match the operations in Graphs A and B, do the math, and chart the four answers in Graph C.

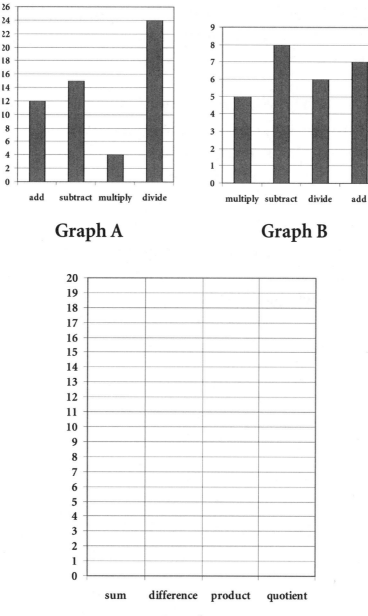

Graph A

Graph B

Graph C

See answer on page 279.

Nico's Algebra Test

Nico is sure he aced the last algebra test and has the highest average in the class. To give him some much-needed practice, his teacher gave him all the scores and asked him to calculate sums and averages. Columns A to I represent scores on tests taken by Nico and eight of his classmates. Help Nico with the calculations, and match the sum/average of each column to a name. Round averages to the nearest tenth.

1. The person with the highest sum is not Max or Nico.
2. Liz has the lowest average but not the lowest sum.
3. Zane's average of 22.8 is second highest.
4. Ruby's sum/average is in column B or D.
5. Shaw's sum of scores is 149.
6. Nico's sum is nine fewer than Liz's.
7. The highest sum has the highest average, but the lowest sum has an average 1.1 higher than the lowest average.
8. Column G is neither Max nor Moss.
9. Tyne is not B or D.
10. The combined sum for Max and Tyne is 193.

	A	B	C	D	E	F	G	H	I
	11	6	11	2	24	10	17	15	15
	6	9	4	19	26	24	9	13	23
	7	10	13	6	13	26	21	14	5
	4	5	8	14	32	13		16	17
	11	15	3	9	19	32		12	2
	8	1	4	12		44		9	41
	7		7	7				17	9
	2			4				5	19
	3							11	
								6	
								2	
sum									
average									
Liz									
Max									
Moss									
Nico									
Rob									
Ruby									
Shaw									
Tyne									
Zane									

See answer on page 286.

Really Exotic Aliens

We are:

Really	**G**athered
Exotic	**R**andomly
Aliens	**O**utside
Dancing	**U**ncle
In	**P**ete's!
Night	
Gowns	

Mrs. Tyee's reading group named themselves this year. Can you tell? Despite the weird name they came up with, these students love to read! Figure out how many words per line (average, no rounding necessary) each student in the group read in a recent timed test. Here are some clues to help you solve:

1. Noah read 20 more words than the one who read 11 lines.
2. Stacie read nine lines.
3. Alex read the fewest words.
4. Leah read two more lines than the one who read 108 total words.
5. Dennis read 126 words.
6. Derrick had the lowest average, but read the most lines.

	lines read							total words							average words per line
	9	10	11	12	14	16	19	84	108	110	114	126	128	130	
Alex															
Dennis															
Derrick															
Leah															
Noah															
Ryan															
Stacie															

See answer on page 287.

Saturday Jobs

Mrs. Scatterbones hired four young people to work for her at $10.00 per hour. She needed five things done: wash the car, rake the leaves, weed the garden, trim the hedge, and mow the lawn. Using the following clues, determine who did which jobs (three did more than one job), their last names, how much time it took, and how much each earned.

1. White earned $5.00 trimming and another $5.00 in a different job. Those were her only two jobs.
2. Sarah raked 15 fewer minutes than Gray, who earned the most.
3. The most earned was $17.50, the least $2.50 by Blue.
4. Joey is not Gray.
5. Jered weeded for 15 minutes.
6. Green did three jobs.
7. The four worked a total of 270 minutes: 15 washing, 75 trimming, 90 mowing, 75 raking, 15 weeding.
8. Jered and Gray earned $20.00 between them.
9. Green washed the car in 15 minutes. Joey and Sarah trimmed the hedge.
10. It took Green and Kim 90 minutes to mow the lawn. Kim mowed $\frac{2}{3}$ of the time.

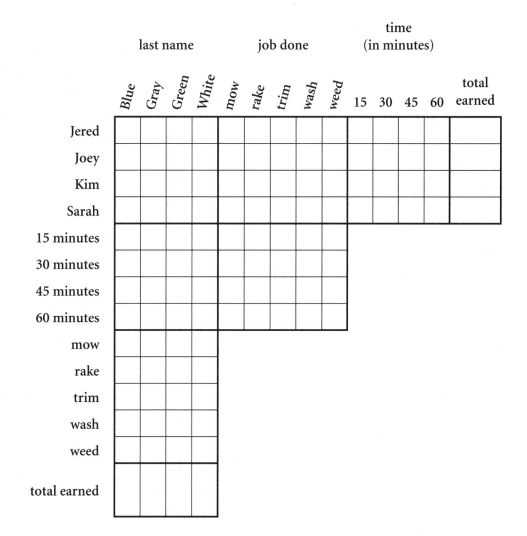

See answer on page 287.

WES Favorites

Mr. Bodle, Mrs. Clark, and Mrs. Olson just surveyed their 3rd graders at Waldport Elementary School to see what some of their favorites might be. The students were asked to list their favorite in each of these three categories: school lunches, holidays, and playground games. Every student voted once in each category, and every category got at least one vote in every class.

Use these clues to assist you to in determining how many students in each class voted in each category and their room numbers.

1. 28 of the students choosing Christmas are from Bodle's and Clark's classes.
2. Five of Mrs. Olson's students chose soccer.
3. Mrs. Clark has just 12 third graders in her class. 75% of them chose Christmas.
4. 31 of the students selecting pizza are from Mr. Bodle's and Mrs. Olson's classes, not Room 191.
5. $1/3$ of Mrs. Clark's students chose soccer.
6. Mrs. Olson has 26 students. Five chose chicken; four picked a corn dog.
7. All classes had 2 students choose Thanksgiving.
8. Of the students choosing 4-square, Mr. Bodle had two more than Mrs. Olson, who had 12 more than Mrs. Clark.
9. 3 students from Room 196 chose soccer.

	room			favorite lunch			favorite game			favorite holiday		
	190	191	196	chicken	corn dog	pizza	4-square	soccer	tetherball	Halloween	Thanksgiving	Christmas
Mr. Bodle												
Mrs. Clark												
Mrs. Olson												

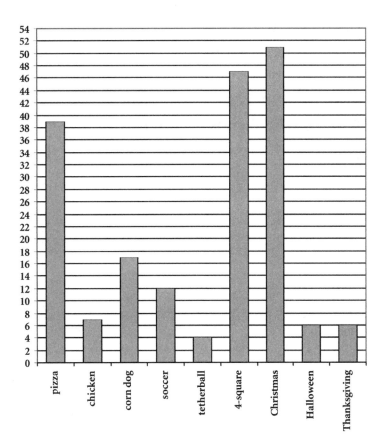

See answer on page 291.

Summer Birthdays

Most of the students attending Heartwood Middle School have birthdays during the school year. For those who don't, they have a special birthday party on the last day of school. This year there are five. Your job is to figure out the five students' birthdays, their full names, and their ages at the end of the school year.

1. Iris is younger than Elliott, who was born on August 6th.
2. Avery is at least one month older than Ken.
3. Amy, older than Scott and Elliott, has a birthday on the 16th.
4. The youngest person was born in June.
5. Wyatt and Eli are the two oldest.
6. Ada and Scott have the first and last birthdays in summer.
7. The student who will be turning 15 has a July 3rd birthday.
8. The birthday on the 19th is in August.
9. Eli will be 14 when school ends on June 8th.
10. Scott is the youngest.
11. Ken is younger than Amy by just 21 days.

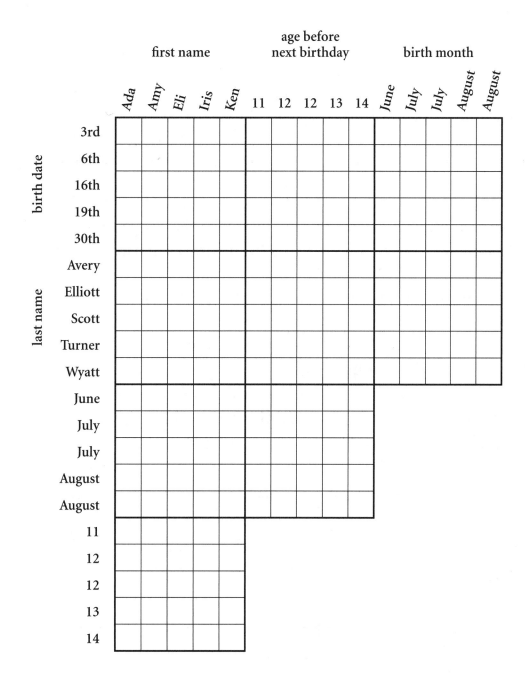

See answer on page 288.

Traffic Flow

One of the ways the Department of Transportation studies traffic flow is by counting cars in a given stretch of highway during a given time. This particular study counts all the southbound cars from 7:00 to 8:30 a.m., and all the northbound cars from 4:00 to 5:30 p.m., for five days. Your job is to figure out the number of cars going both directions, the average number of cars traveling each day, and the overall southbound and northbound averages for the week. Get out your pencils and erasers!

1. The total number of cars counted for the week was 12,200.
2. The total for Tuesday was 2,334, with northbound carrying 264 more.
3. The southbound carried 870 fewer than the northbound for the week.
4. Friday's southbound was 194 more than Tuesday's.
5. Wednesday's northbound count was 83 fewer than Friday's.
6. Thursday's average was 85 less than Tuesday's.
7. Monday's count was 2,606. Northbound had 122 more cars.
8. Thursday's southbound was 147 below Thursday's average.

	southbound	northbound	total	average
Monday				
Tuesday				
Wednesday				
Thursday				
Friday				
total				
average				

See answer on page 289.

Sweaty Cities

A study of the nation's most sunny cities shows these six as having the most sunny days per year.

Bakersfield, California
El Paso, Texas
Las Vegas, Nevada
Phoenix, Arizona
Sacramento, California
Tucson, Arizona

With just four clues to work with, match the city with the number of cloudless days each enjoys.

1. Phoenix has 16 more sunny days than Tucson.
2. El Paso has four days fewer than an Arizona city, which has four days fewer than one of the California cities.
3. The greatest difference is between a California city and Las Vegas.
4. Fourteen days separate Bakersfield and a city in a different state.

	193	194	198	202	214	216
Bakersfield				X		
El Paso		X				
Las Vegas						X
Phoenix					X	
Sacramento	X					
Tucson			X			

See answer on page 289.

Soccer Schedule

The Central League soccer season is being planned. The coaches want each of the six teams to play each other team once in the first five games of the season. Help them make a schedule so that this can happen.

1. The Panthers will host the Spartans for the 4th game.
2. The Rockets will play the Bobcats in the 1st game.
3. One of the teams plays four of their games in this order: Panthers, Spartans, Bobcats, Rockets.
4. In the 3rd game, the Panthers will play a team starting with the letter "B."
5. The Buffaloes play the Spartans first.
6. The Cyclones and the Buffaloes meet after the Spartans play the Panthers.

opponents

	1st game	2nd game	3rd game	4th game	5th game
Bobcats					
Buffaloes					
Cyclones					
Rockets					
Panthers					
Spartans					

See answer on page 288.

Slapjack

Two girls and two boys stayed in from recess and played four games of slapjack. Each person won one game (last one in) and each person lost one game (first one out). See if you can figure out who won and lost which games, and the full names of each player.

1. One of the boys lost the first game and won the second game.
2. Jones won a game before Brown, who won a game before he lost one.
3. Mary won before Sam lost.
4. Moore, who isn't Mary, won the game that Lisa lost.

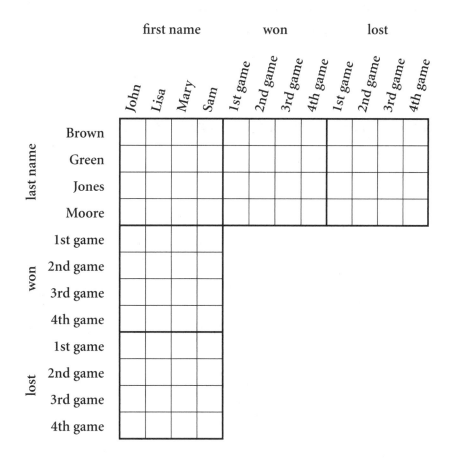

See answer on page 288.

At the Shoulder

The following animals stand anywhere from three feet to over five feet tall at the shoulder. Using the clues, figure out each animal's name and height.

1. Louie is taller than all but two others.
2. Lars is five inches taller than the shortest.
3. The moose is 11 inches taller than Paco.
4. Max is eight inches taller than Milly and 16 inches taller than the llama.
5. Paulo, the shortest, is not a vicuna.
6. The guanaco is exactly the same height as the group average.
7. The antelope is 14 inches taller than the elk.
8. Milly is 11 inches above average, and the reindeer is eight inches under.
9. Sofia is 16 inches taller than the alpaca and 2 inches shorter than Louie.
10. The vicuna is three inches shorter than José.

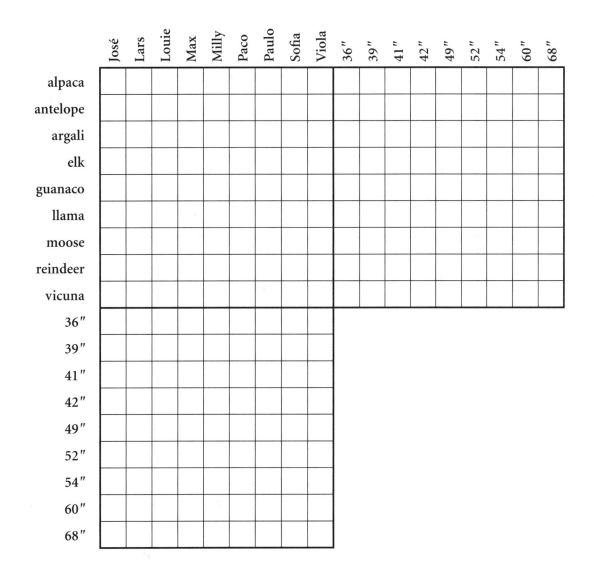

See answer on page 275.

Flying Wool Ranch

Four ranchers are raising sheep like crazy. And dogs! Using all the clues you can find, match the name of the owners with the ranch each owns, the number of sheep on the ranch, its acreage, and the main dog's name. Oh, yeah, also how much each dog weighs!

1. Clark's ranch has $1/5$ more sheep than the ranch where Joey lives.
2. The B-Baa-B ranch has 300 more acres than the Sullivan ranch, but 600 fewer than Clark's.
3. Dingo weighs 11 pounds less than the Flying Wool Ranch dog.
4. Medici's acreage is 300 fewer than the Merino Ranch.
5. The heaviest dog, not Skip nor Sullivan's dog, lives on the ranch with the most sheep.
6. The Hunter ranch has $1/3$ more sheep than the Merino ranch.
7. Joey weighs $1/4$ more than Skip, who lives on 2400 acres.

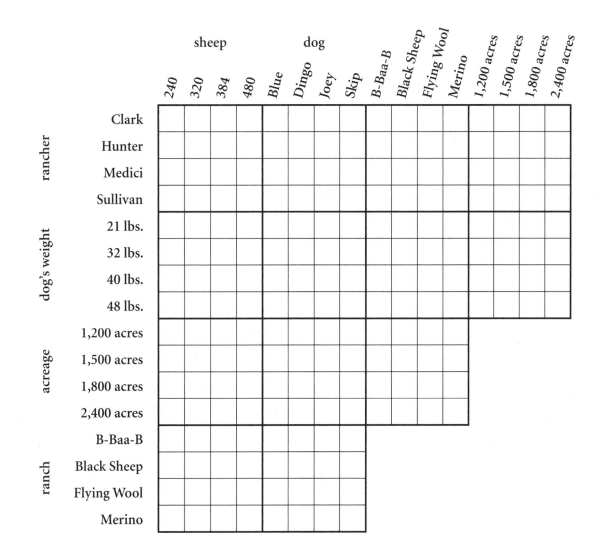

See answer on page 280.

Mrs. Wilcox's Challenge

Mrs. Wilcox, a local recycling center volunteer, challenged four high school classes to see which could recycle the most newspapers in a month, to be judged by weight. The winning class gets milkshakes paid for by the losing class. You have to figure out which class won, the name of the teacher, the room number, and how many pounds of newspaper they each turned in.

1. Room 201 turned in 200 pounds fewer than Mrs. Wilcox's class.
2. Mrs. Lindly's class is on the same floor as the biology room.
3. Ms. St. John does not teach the English class.
4. Room 210 is the French class.
5. Mrs. Williams's class turned in 200 pounds more than the biology class and 200 pounds fewer than Room 210.
6. Room 110 buys the milkshakes for the French class.
7. The algebra class turned in 100 pounds fewer than Room 201.

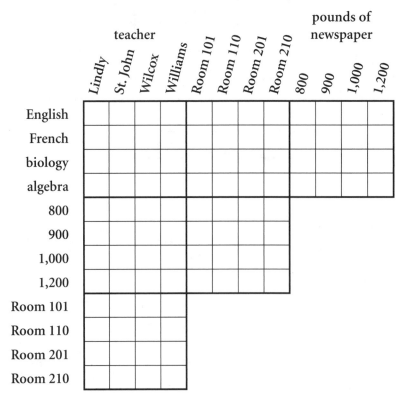

See answer on page 285.

Walking for Wilma

Mrs. Olson's many birds, rats, and frogs are hungry! Even Wilma, her Walking Stick, is eager for more crickets. So some of Mrs. Olson's students decided to organize a fundraiser to buy food for the class menagerie. They got pledges for walking: $2.50 per mile. Using the clues below, figure out how far each person walked, how much each earned, and the total raised. Only the two people who made it all the way walked the same distance.

1. Kim walked 1.5 miles farther than Ira.
2. Ian walked 2.5 miles fewer than Luc.
3. Joy walked farther than everyone but two others.
4. Fay walked 4.5 miles farther than Ian.
5. Von went farther than Liv.
6. Eve went .5 fewer miles than Ian.
7. Ada walked 3 miles more than Ira.

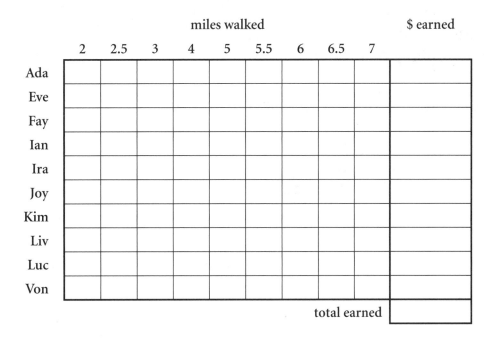

	2	2.5	3	4	5	5.5	6	6.5	7	$ earned
Ada										
Eve										
Fay										
Ian										
Ira										
Joy										
Kim										
Liv										
Luc										
Von										
total earned										

miles walked

See answer on page 290.

Ten-Pin Alley

"Hey, let's go bowling! You keep score."

Here's how you bowl. You roll a ball down the lane and try to knock over all the pins. There are ten of them.

If you knock them all down with one ball, it's called a **strike**. If you knock them all down in two tries, it's called a **spare**. If you don't knock all ten down with two balls, you count the total number of pins knocked down. You get ten tries (frames) all together.

Here are the scoring rules for bowling:

1. If you knock down a total of nine pins with both balls, for example, you get a score of 9. Seven pins, you earn 7. Six, 6. And so on.
2. If you knock all ten pins down with two balls (spare) you earn 10 points plus the number of pins you knock down with the next ball.
3. If you knock all ten down with one ball (strike) you earn 10 points plus the number of pins you knock down with the next two balls.
4. Instead of putting each frame's individual score in the corresponding box, you keep a running total.

Sound confusing? Here's an example to help you.

Frame	Ball	Max's Total	
1	first	10	16
	second		
2	first	4	22
	second	2	
3	first	8	31
	second	1	

Now try this. Three people went bowling and here is how each did. Using these numbers, figure out each person's total score.

Frame	Ball	Jeremy's Total		Wynona's Total		Jill's Total	
1	first	10	20	4	9	6	19
	second			5		4	
2	first	9	40	7	29	9	28
	second	1		3		0	
3	first	10	54	10	49	9	48
	second					1	
4	first	8	68	7	66	10	77
	second	1		3			
5	first	9	88	7	75	10	46
	second	1		2			
6	first	10	107	10	95	9	105
	second					0	
7	first	8	116	9	111	9	123
	second	1		1		1	
8	first	9	136	6	120	8	143
	second	1		3		2	
9	first	10	155	8	139	10	162
	second			2			
10	first	8	164	9	148	7	171
	second	1		0		2	
	Total		164		148		171

See answer on page 289.

PART II

Poker Logic Puzzles

Dreams and Nightmares

Recently, three friends who are poker fanatics found that they all share something in common. Each man has both a recurring dream (one dreams of owning his own casino resort) and recurring nightmare involving poker. See if you can discover each man's poker dream and poker nightmare.

1. Adam's nightmare is that he has a nut hand in a high stakes game of Texas hold'em and his wife won't give him money for the final bet.
2. Geoff isn't the one whose nightmare is that he's betting four kings and suddenly realizes that the game is California Lowball.
3. The man who dreams of winning the World Series of Poker has a nightmare that he's at the table and suddenly can't remember what hands beat what.
4. Pete isn't the man who dreams of playing poker at the Flamingo with the Rat Pack in the early '60s.

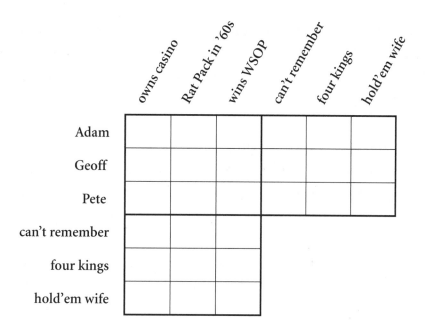

See answer on page 292.

Poker Blogs

Websites devoted to poker have sprung up in record numbers during the last few years. Four avid poker players have recently started their own weblogs—or blogs—each focusing on a different aspect of poker (one site features advice on how to bet). See if you can figure out the name of each person's blog (one is called floptoriver.com) and its specialty.

1. Maureen's blog is 1eyedjill.com.
2. Terence didn't start aloneinreno.com or queen-of-spades.com.
3. queen-of-spades.com features poker celebrity gossip.
4. Either Lizzie or Terence started the blog that posts tournament schedules.
5. aloneinreno.com (which isn't Alexander's site) doesn't specialize in poker variations or tournament schedules.

	leyedjill	aloneinreno	floptoriver	queen-of-spades	betting	celebrities	tournaments	variations
Alexander								
Lizzie								
Maureen								
Terence								
betting								
celebrities								
tournaments								
variations								

See answer on page 292.

Don't Quit Your Day Job

Inspired by Greg Raymer's unexpected $5 million win at the 2004 World Series of Poker, Biff thought that he, too, might join the ranks of the pros. He got himself invited into five local games (one at a nearby firehouse), on five consecutive days (Wednesday through Sunday). Unfortunately, with each group he lost a different amount of money (including $24 and $177). Figure out which group Biff played poker with on each day and how much he lost.

1. Biff lost $82 to his college fraternity brothers.
2. He lost $31 three days earlier in the week than he lost to the local Elks order.
3. He lost $57 the day after playing a game at the local Marine base.
4. Biff lost more money on Wednesday than on Friday.
5. His humiliating defeat against his grandmother's garden club friends on Sunday finally finished off Biff's aspirations at Binion's.

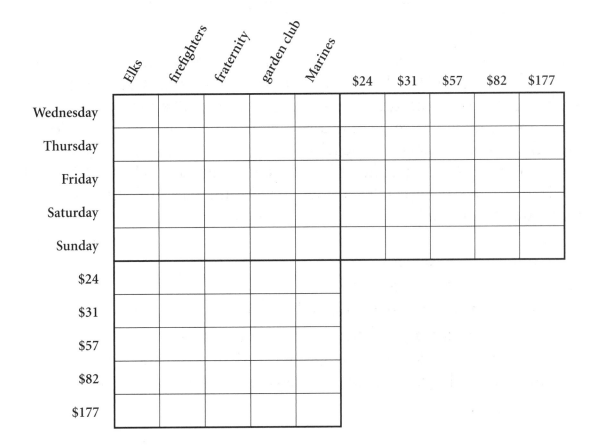

	Elks	firefighters	fraternity	garden club	Marines		$24	$31	$57	$82	$177
Wednesday											
Thursday											
Friday											
Saturday											
Sunday											
$24											
$31											
$57											
$82											
$177											

See answer on page 293.

The Road to Monte Carlo, Part 1: Planning the Trip

Three couples (surnamed Renaldi, Stormgren, and Tanner)—poker players one and all—decided to take a vacation together to Monte Carlo for their first-ever poker tournament, the Monte Carlo Millions. The men (Chip, Bill, and Evan) and women (Alice, Diana, and Fawn) agreed that each couple would research a different aspect of the trip. See if you can figure out who is married to whom, their last name, and what each couple agreed to handle. Note: This is Part 1 of a five-part puzzle. You will need information from this puzzle to solve Parts 2 through 5.

1. Chip isn't Mr. Renaldi.
2. Alice isn't Mrs. Stormgren.
3. Diana and her husband arranged for all transportation.
4. The Tanners arranged for the group's accommodations.
5. The three couples are: Fawn and her husband, Bill and his wife, and the couple who researched activities for the group.

	Bill	Chip	Evan	Renaldi	Stormgren	Tanner	accommodations	activities	transportation
Alice									
Diana									
Fawn									
accommodations									
activities									
transportation									
Renaldi									
Stormgren									
Tanner									

See answer on page 293.

Lionus Interruptus and Other Stories

On a busy night at the casino, four strangers got to know each other during a half-hour wait for space at the table. To kill time, they traded poker stories that they had either heard or read. Can you discover the order in which the four told their stories and who told each?

1. The first person told a story about a high-stakes poker game that was interrupted mid-hand by a lion that had escaped from a nearby zoo.
2. Either Kathleen or Marjanne told the second story.
3. Kathleen isn't the one who told the story about the bluffer who avoided turning over his cards by tearing them into little pieces and eating them.
4. Marjanne told a story about a woman who won the deed to the house in a game of poker with her husband.
5. Dirk didn't tell the third story.
6. Neither Cyrus nor Kathleen told the story about a poker game between Winston Churchill and Charles De Gaulle.

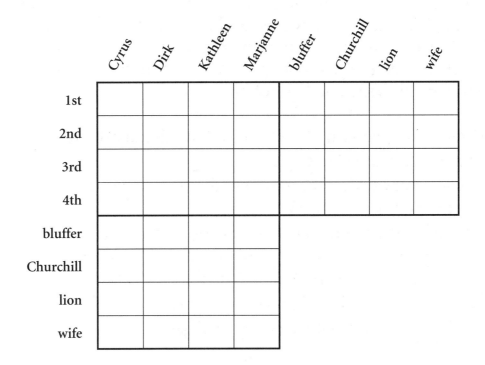

See answer on pages 293–294.

Poker Widows

If you're going to be married to an inveterate poker player, you better have a high boiling point and something you like to do that's all your own. At least, that's what five poker widows have told me. All of them are married to men who play poker constantly. Rather than despair, they've all taken to spending time together doing something on their own. Can you find out the name of each woman's husband and her hobby?

1. Drew's wife (who isn't Laverne) isn't the aikido brown belt.
2. Annie isn't married to George.
3. The woman who has taken up photography (who isn't Paulette) isn't married to Drew or Tiger.
4. The competitive Scrabble player isn't married to Tiger.
5. The five women are: Annie, Paulette, Marvin's wife, and the women whose hobbies are karaoke and Scrabble.
6. Edna's hobby is either aikido or horseback riding.
7. Susan is married to either Kenny or Tiger.

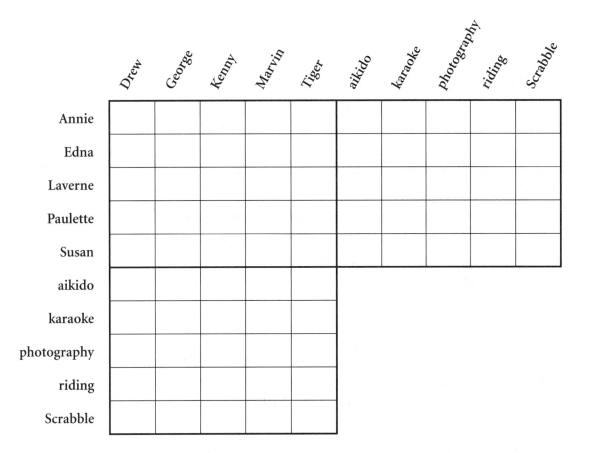

See answer on page 294.

King Arthur and the Round Table

Here's how my friend Arthur got his nickname, King Arthur, in a memorable hand of the game Texas hold'em. The flop showed three aces, and three players who held pairs started raising and re-raising furiously, while Arthur just hung in there and called. See if you can piece together who held which cards, each player's full name (one man's last name is Forrest), and what each man held.

1. The Fourth Street card, a lowly three, helped no one, and the man holding the pair of nines got out.
2. The Fifth Street card—the remaining ace—floored everyone at the table, and the man holding a pair of queens bailed out.
3. Arthur bet the maximum and Havermeyer, now nervously holding a pair of jacks, just called.
4. Arthur revealed the king and six he was holding, and scooped in the pot.
5. James said to the man whom Arthur beat, "You had to figure him for it."
6. Freddy said, "Glad I folded when I did."
7. The man who had held the lowest pair and dropped out said, "Well, James, you have to admit the man got lucky."
8. Lipkin said, "Roy had me beat no matter what."
9. Washington said, "Looks like that king is a sign—we've now gotta start calling you King Arthur."

	Forrest	Havermeyer	Lipkin	Washington	king and six	pair of nines	pair of jacks	pair of queens
Arthur								
Freddy								
James								
Roy								
king and six								
pair of nines								
pair of jacks								
pair of queens								

See answer on pages 294–295.

There Oughtta Be a Law

The poker table isn't necessarily the place for Miss Manners, but most poker players agree to a certain standard of etiquette. Six seasoned players were recently discussing the matter. It turned out that each of them had a different pet peeve that drove them crazy when someone did it. Can you figure out the order in which the six friends spoke up and the behavior that each of them finds unacceptable?

1. The first person who spoke complained about long post mortems after each hand.
2. The people who spoke about splashing the pot and taking too long to bet are of opposite sexes.
3. Larry spoke just after Jill and just before Kevin.
4. The thing that drives Doris nuts is either misdealing or splashing the pot while betting.
5. A woman talked about how annoying it can be when people bet out of turn.
6. Trisha spoke sometime before the person who can't stand when a player splashes the pot.
7. The person who doesn't stand for other players peeking at discards spoke either second or third.
8. Larry didn't complain about misdealing.
9. Either Norm or Trisha spoke third.

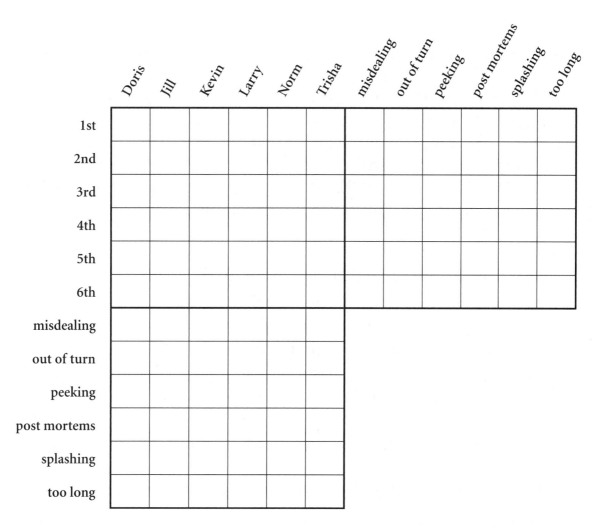

	Doris	Jill	Kevin	Larry	Norm	Trisha	misdealing	out of turn	peeking	post mortems	splashing	too long
1st												
2nd												
3rd												
4th												
5th												
6th												
misdealing												
out of turn												
peeking												
post mortems												
splashing												
too long												

See answer on page 295.

Tidy Profits

After she retired as a bookkeeper, Eloise began playing the slots. It was her way of having fun, and she didn't mind losing money as long as it wasn't too much, so she kept a careful accounting of her losses over time. Then a friend suggested that she try her hand at poker, where the competition is the other players at the table rather than the casino, and she's never looked back. Now, her bookkeeping is in black rather than red ink. In fact, over the last six years (1999 through 2004), she's made a different sum of money ($800, $1100, $1200, $1400, $1500, and $1800), allowing her to visit six places she's always wanted to see. Figure out how much money Eloise won in each year and the place she visited as a result.

1. Eloise traveled to Spain in either 2001 or 2004.
2. She earned $400 less in 2000 than she did the year she went to Japan.
3. She didn't go to Denmark in 2004.
4. Eloise won $1500 sometime after the year she went to Australia and sometime before the year she won $1400.
5. She won more money in 2003 than she won in 2002.
6. She traveled to Japan sometime before she went to Brazil.
7. Her earnings of $1800 allowed her to take a trip to either Australia or Denmark.
8. Eloise earned $800 sometime after she took a cruise to Greece.
9. She went to Brazil the year she earned either $1100 or $1400.

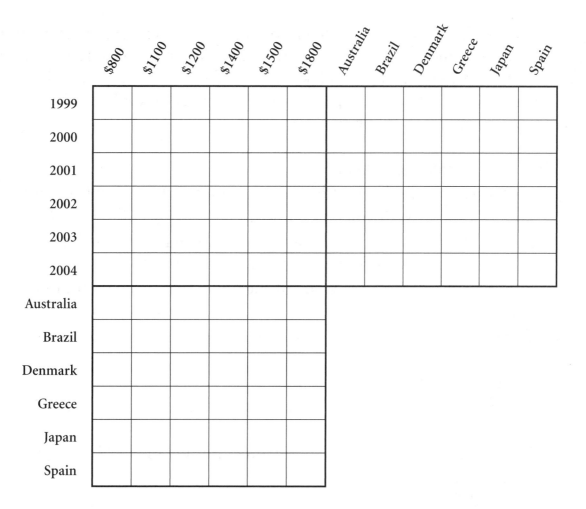

	$800	$1100	$1200	$1400	$1500	$1800	Australia	Brazil	Denmark	Greece	Japan	Spain
1999												
2000												
2001												
2002												
2003												
2004												
Australia												
Brazil												
Denmark												
Greece												
Japan												
Spain												

See answer on pages 295–296.

Sidling up to Seidel

When you live in Hollywood, you don't have to go to Paramount Studios to see a movie star. Similarly, when you live in Las Vegas, you can meet a famous poker player almost anywhere. Six friends were sharing stories of recent poker star sightings. Each friend had met a different famous poker player in a different place. Match up each person with the poker player he or she met and where the encounter took place.

1. A woman met Eric Seidel.
2. Someone met Phil Hellmuth in either a supermarket or a toy store.
3. Either Lottie or Wally met Stu Ungar.
4. Rita (who met either Doyle Brunson or Phil Hellmuth) had her encounter in either a flower shop or a supermarket.
5. Either Chuck or Harry saw one of the poker players at a plumbing supply store.
6. The people who met Johnny Chan and Stu Ungar are of opposite sexes.
7. A man met someone at an ice cream parlor.
8. Either Doyle Brunson or Johnny Chan was spotted at a wedding chapel.
9. Jasmine met one of the two men named Johnny in either a flower shop or a supermarket.
10. Chuck didn't meet Johnny Moss or Phil Hellmuth.

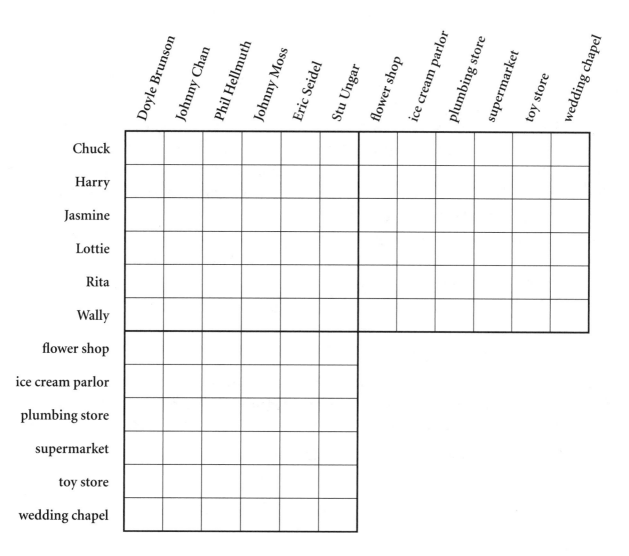

See answer on page 296.

The Road to Monte Carlo,
Part 2: The Flight

Once on the airplane, our intrepid travelers (Alice, Bill, Chip, Diana, Evan, and Fawn) were not content to wait to play poker. They sat in a single row on either side of the aisle (as shown below) and managed to get in one complete round before the flight attendants began to serve dinner. Each person won one hand of the round. Figure out where each person sat and which of the six hands he or she won. Note: This is Part 2 of a five-part puzzle. To solve it, you will need information from Part 1.

1. One couple sat in seats A and B, another in C and D, and the remaining couple in E and F.
2. Nobody sat in a seat with the same letter as his or her initial.
3. A person in an aisle seat won the first hand.
4. Bill didn't have a window seat.
5. Fawn won a hand sometime after the person in seat E.
6. Mrs. Renaldi won a hand sometime before her husband.
7. Chip sat in either seat D or seat E.
8. A woman in a window seat won the third hand.
9. One of the Stormgrens won the fifth hand.

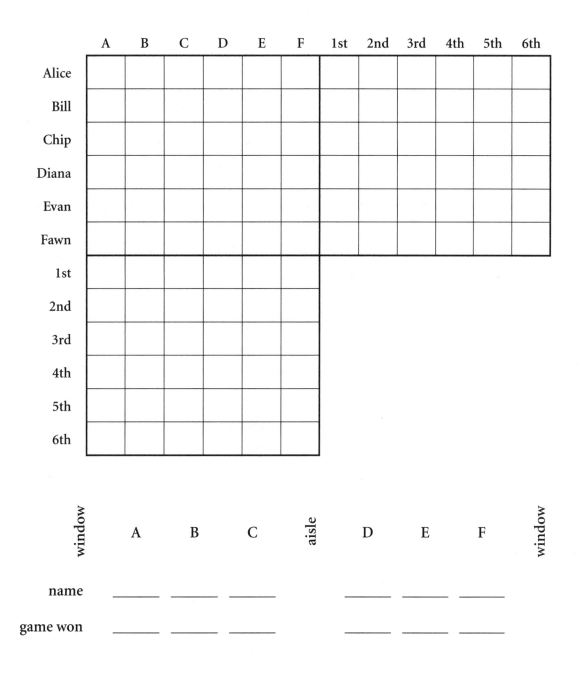

	A	B	C	D	E	F	1st	2nd	3rd	4th	5th	6th
Alice												
Bill												
Chip												
Diana												
Evan												
Fawn												
1st												
2nd												
3rd												
4th												
5th												
6th												

window	A	B	C	aisle	D	E	F	window
name	_____	_____	_____		_____	_____	_____	
game won	_____	_____	_____		_____	_____	_____	

See answer on pages 296–297.

You Wear It Well

Nadine sells jewelry for a living. Since she also plays poker regularly at the Bicycle Casino in Los Angeles, her two interests have naturally overlapped. Six of Nadine's friends from the casino have bought different types of jewelry, each with a different poker-related design. Link up each of Nadine's friends with the type of jewelry she wears and its design.

1. The jewelry with the queen of diamonds on it isn't the anklet or the ring.
2. Sophy's jewelry depicts either the Bicycle logo or the queen of hearts.
3. The necklace bears an image of the Binion's horseshoe.
4. Talese's sister wears the ring.
5. Either Maura or Sophy wears the bracelet.
6. Amelia's jewelry either has the Bicycle logo or the words "lady luck."
7. Either Laney or Talese wears the anklet.
8. Veronica wears either the pendant or the ring.
9. The earrings depict a royal flush in spades.
10. Amelia and the woman who wears the necklace aren't related.
11. Laney's jewelry has one of the two red queens on it.

	anklet	bracelet	earrings	necklace	pendant	ring	Bicycle logo	Binion's horseshoe	"lady luck"	royal flush	queen of diamonds	queen of hearts
Amelia												
Laney												
Maura												
Sophy												
Talese												
Veronica												
Bicycle logo							
Binion's horseshoe							
"lady luck"							
royal flush							
queen of diamonds							
queen of hearts							

See answer on page 297.

Don't Try This at Home

At the Pi Omega fraternity house, the brothers play their Saturday night poker game with a twist. Once a night, a player holding the two of clubs has the opportunity to turn it into a wild card by performing a crazy stunt. This semester, four brothers have successfully performed four different stunts, in each case using the wild card he earned to complete a different hand and win a pot of a different amount ($45, $88, $91, $129). See if you can figure out who performed each stunt, the poker hand that he completed, and how much money was in the pot.

1. The person who filled in four of a kind won a pot of $91.
2. Jason won a larger pot than Philip, but neither of these brothers was the one who walked a distance of ten feet on his hands.
3. In order to complete a full house, one young man walked to the corner store and bought beer for the house wearing only a hand towel.
4. The person who filled in a flush won more money than Matthew.
5. Anton held his breath for three minutes.
6. Philip isn't the one who ate two dozen hardboiled eggs in five minutes.
7. The person who completed a straight flush didn't hold his breath or walk on his hands.

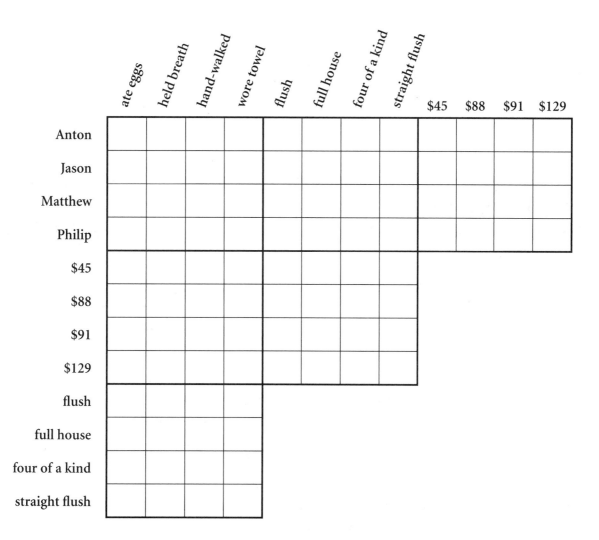

See answer on page 298.

Family Circle

Dennis taught all four of his children to play poker when they were very small. Now that they are a little older, he's teaching them the finer points of the game. At a recent hand of seven-card stud, Dennis was showing the eight of hearts, nine of clubs, ten of hearts, and ten of spades. He couldn't better his pair, but bluffed all four kids out of the pot. Afterwards, Dennis discussed the hand with them, asking each child what he or she thought he had made. Each child gave a different answer, and their father then pointed out clues that might have tipped them off otherwise. Can you figure out where each person sat, each child's age, and the hand that each child thought his father had?

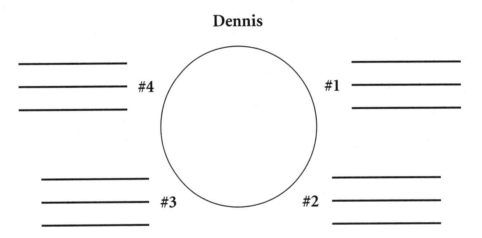

1. The child who sat in seat #2 is one year younger than the child who sat in seat #4; one of them is Randall.
2. Wendy sat next to the sibling who thought their father held two pairs.
3. The three males at the table (including Dennis) are: the child who sat in seat #2, a person who sat next to Randall, and a person who sat next to the person who believed that Dennis had three of a kind.
4. Audrey, who isn't the oldest or the youngest child, sat between Travis and the child who thought their father had made a flush.
5. The 14-year-old thought that their father had made a straight.
6. Travis is three years younger than Wendy.

See answer on page 298.

Women of Poker

As more women are playing the game, more have risen to the top ranks of poker and become famous names. Recently, four players were discussing these great players. Each woman in turn made a case for a different professional player whom she thinks is the best female poker player in the game (in some order: Annie Duke, Barbara Enright, Jennifer Harman, and Kathy Liebert). By an interesting coincidence, the four women who were speaking have the same first names as the four professional players whom they were discussing. See if you can figure out the order in which these four women spoke and which player she likes best.

1. The first woman who spoke is the only one who has the same first name as her favorite player.
2. The second woman who spoke has the same first name as Jennifer's heroine.
3. Barbara's favorite player isn't Annie Duke.
4. The Barbara Enright fan spoke sometime after the woman whose favorite player is Annie Duke and sometime before Kathy.

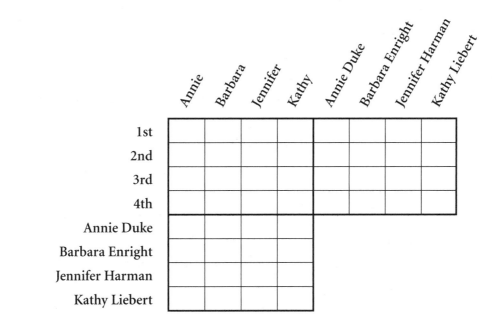

See answer on page 299.

Night of the Eagle

At our last monthly game, a regular player brought along a new acquaintance, a semi-pro who went by the nickname Eagle. True to his name, the guy never missed a thing. By the end of the night, he had taken us for everything we cared to give him. In exchange, he told us free of charge how he had known. In the first hour, he noticed that each of us had two tells—unconscious habits that tipped him off as to what we were up to. One tell let him know when each of us thought we had a winner (one man speaks in a higher-than-normal voice), and the other told him when we were bluffing. Can you match up each of my six friends with his two tells? (As for what Eagle said were my two tells—well, that I'll never tell!)

1. Eagle spotted Joey for either aggressive betting or counting chips when he was bluffing.
2. He noticed that either Drew or Mel smiles uncontrollably when he's holding good cards.
3. For either Trevor or Walt, the twitching nose is a dead giveaway that a bluff is being perpetrated.
4. The man whose hands shake when he has a winner also chats nervously when he's bluffing.
5. The man whose breathing increases when he connects isn't Joey or Walt.
6. Eagle found shaking hands to be a strong indication that one man, either Aaron or Drew, had a winner.
7. He noticed that when Trevor catches the fifth card of either a straight or a flush, either a vein appears on his forehead or he rechecks his hole card.
8. When Walt bluffs, either his nose twitches or he bets out of turn.
9. The man who rechecks his hole card when he has the cards doesn't have a problem with aggressive betting or a twitching nose when he bluffs.
10. The man who averts his eyes when he bluffs doesn't smile or breathe more heavily when he actually has the cards.

11. Either Aaron or Walt bets out of turn when he bluffs.
12. The man who bets aggressively when he bluffs (who isn't Mel) isn't the man with a vein that pops out on his forehead when he has good cards.

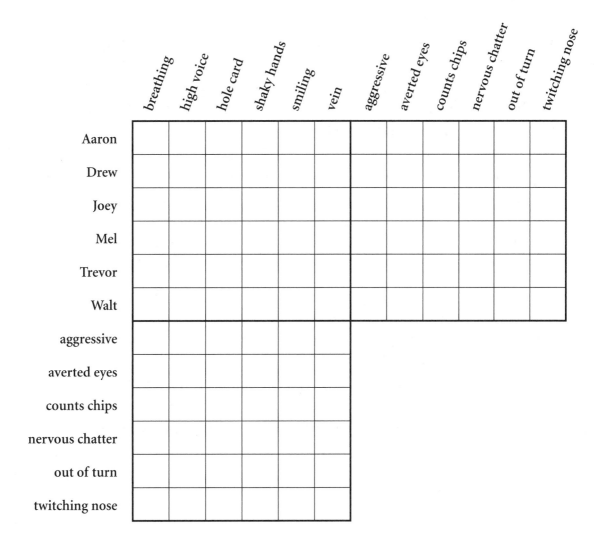

See answer on pages 299–300.

Reading, Writing, and Poker

Fran, a high school math teacher, is always being asked by her students when they will use what she teaches them. When she began a chapter on probability, she put them to a set of useful problems: calculating the odds in poker! Six students (including Mary) calculated the probability of drawing a different poker hand (from two pairs to four of a kind) from a random five cards. Fran went on to explain to them that the lower the probability, the higher the value of the hand. Find out the order in which the six students went to the blackboard and the poker hand each one worked with.

1. Jake went up to the blackboard just before the student who showed the class how to calculate the probability of getting two pairs.
2. The three girls are: the student who calculated the probability of getting a flush, the student who went to the board fourth, and a student who went to the board sometime after Eliza.
3. The probability of the hand that Bart calculated is higher than that of the hand that Alyssa calculated.
4. The student who went to the board third calculated the probability of either three of a kind or a flush.
5. Lance was the third student to go to the blackboard after the one who figured out the probability of getting a full house.
6. The probability of the hand that Eliza calculated is higher than that of the hand that Jake calculated.

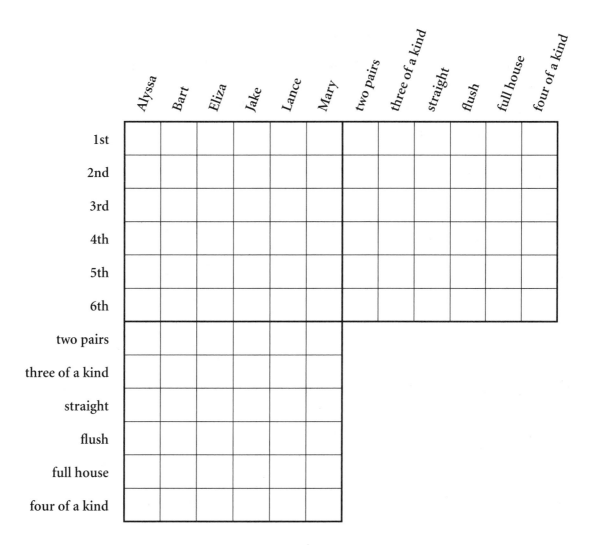

See answer on page 300.

Stardust Memories

Five people playing poker at the Stardust Casino in Las Vegas got to talking about when they first learned how to play the game as children. Each person recalled learning poker at a different age (from eight to twelve), in each case from a different person who taught him or her to play using something other than chips. Figure out the age at which person learned to play, who taught each, and what they used for chips.

1. The person who first played poker with an older sister used either buttons or cookies for chips.
2. Claude learned to play when he was three years older than the person who first learned from his or her grandfather.
3. Either Renee or Willis used jellybeans to play.
4. The person who learned the game from his or her babysitter was older than the person who first played using buttons for chips.
5. The person who first played poker with checkers was at least two years older than Virgil.
6. Willis didn't learn from his uncle.
7. The person who learned the game using matchsticks was at least two years older than the person who learned from his or her scout leader.
8. The person who learned at nine years old learned from either a babysitter or an uncle.
9. Jasper learned to play the game at a younger age than Renee did.

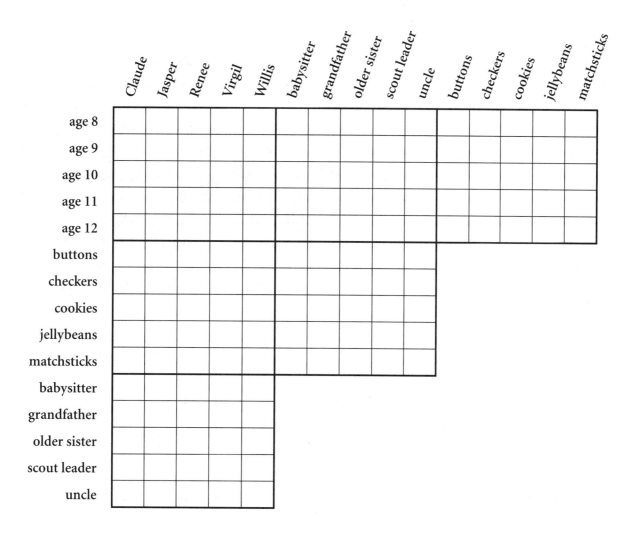

See answer on pages 300–301.

The Road to Monte Carlo,
Part 3: First Night at the Casino

Once they had checked into their hotel and had dinner, the six travelers (Alice, Bill, Chip, Diana, Evan, and Fawn) wasted no time getting to the poker tables. They headed to the casino and broke up into three pairs, each pair playing one of three types of poker (hold'em, seven-card hi-lo, or seven-card stud). After poker, each also tried out a different game of chance. Between games, they met for drinks, each person partaking of something different, including gin and tonic. Jet lag caught up with all of them eventually, and each went back to the hotel at a different time (12:30, 1:00, 1:30, 2:00, 2:30, and 3:00). Figure out the type of poker and non-poker game each person played, what he or she drank, and what time each person left the casino. Note: This is Part 3 of a five-part puzzle. To solve it, you will need information from Parts 1 and 2.

1. The person who sat in seat A on the flight to Monaco left the casino at least an hour before the person who drank Manhattans.
2. The first of the three men to leave drank vodka martinis.
3. Evan and his wife played at the same poker table.
4. Bill and the person who left the casino half an hour after him played at the same poker table.
5. The person who played English roulette left half an hour before the person who played European roulette.
6. The man who helped plan the transportation aspect of the trip left the casino at 1:30.
7. The people who drank margaritas and tequila sunrises are of opposite sexes.
8. The person who played blackjack left sometime after his or her spouse.
9. The six people are: Mrs. Renaldi, Mr. Tanner, a person who played seven-card hi-lo, the woman who played chemin de fer, the person who drank Manhattans, and the person who left at 2:30.

10. The person who drank black Russians didn't play seven-card stud.
11. Alice left the casino either an hour before or after the person who played craps.
12. The first three people to leave the casino were, in some order: the person who played trente et quarante, the person who drank margaritas, and a person who played hold'em.

name	poker game	other game	drink	time left

See answer on pages 301–302.

Wild Times

One poker group I know invented a very "wild" wild card variation. Every time they meet, they play one round of seven-card stud that they call their "progressive round." The dealer who calls the round names a wild card, which remains wild for the entire round. The next dealer names a second wild card, the third names a third wild card, and so on. By the end of the round, the sixth player deals a hand with six wild cards. Too much of a good thing? Maybe so. See if you can figure out the order in which the six players dealt this game, each person's full name, and the card each named.

1. Tanslye dealt three hands before the person who made fives wild.
2. Alexander (Alex for short) didn't make nines wild.
3. Either Chambers or Freeman dealt the third hand.
4. The person who dealt the fourth hand named a wild card of a higher value than the card that Rachel named wild.
5. The fifth dealer named either sixes or tens wild.
6. Laughlin and the person who dealt first are of opposite sexes.
7. Richter didn't make fives or tens wild.
8. Tina didn't deal just before Freeman.
9. The person who dealt sixth named a higher-valued wild card than Freeman and a lower-valued wild card than Saunders. Jimmy, however, named a wild card of a higher value than all of these.
10. Hank made either threes or queens wild.
11. Betty isn't surnamed Richter or Saunders.

order	first name	last name	wild card

See answer on page 302.

Someday the Moon

My friend Elmer wins the award for playing poker in some of the strangest places you could ever imagine. Over the last five years (2000–2004), he's played poker in five unlikely locales. Even more unlikely were the people he got to participate in each case. "And someday," he says, "I'll play poker on the Moon!" Till then, try to figure out the year in which Elmer played poker in each unusual place, and who played with him.

1. Elmer played poker on top of the Eiffel Tower the year before he played in an unusual setting with a U.N. ambassador.

2. He didn't play poker at the Taj Mahal the year after he played with a nun.

3. He played atop the Great Wall of China two years after he played with the Buddhist monk.

4. He didn't play with the Nascar driver in the submarine.

5. The five places Elmer played poker are: the Monorail at Disneyworld, the Taj Mahal, the place where he played with the Buddhist monk, the place he played the year after he played atop the Great Wall of China, and the place he played two years before he played with the cub scout.

year	place	person

See answer on page 303.

Lowball

Figuring out how to bet in Lowball can be especially tricky. I remember watching a recent hand where five people stayed in all the way to the river. Each ended up with a different lowest hand, as designated by its two highest cards (8-4, 7-6, 7-5, 7-4, and 6-5). But since most of the higher cards were hole cards and the lower cards were showing, it was hard to tell who had what, so betting remained strong. Figure out the rotation order of the five players, each person's full name (one surname is Signorelli), and all five cards of his or her lowest hand. Note: Aces are low and suits do not matter in Lowball.

1. On the last round of betting, the first person in rotation, who wasn't Epstein, checked but then called all subsequent bets.
2. The second person, who wasn't holding a 4, checked then folded.
3. The third in rotation, who had the 7-6, made a strong bet but then folded when the going got tough.
4. The fourth raised and then re-raised.
5. The fifth in rotation, who was either Benjamin or Lou, also raised, but then called when re-raised.
6. Lopez had a better hand than at least one player who checked.
7. Artie and Maxine had the same second-highest card.
8. Neither Lou nor Epstein held both a six and an ace.
9. Ernie stayed in till the end.
10. Epstein's hand was better than Trager's.
11. Maxine wasn't dealt both a five and an ace.
12. Artie was in rotation just before Lopez.
13. Pollock wasn't dealt both a deuce and an ace.

order	first name	last name	hand	actions

See answer on pages 303–304.

Lending Library

At their most recent home game, six friends, including Jason, brought along poker books that they had just finished reading. Each lent his or her book—one was *Poker for Dummies*—to one of the other five in the group, and borrowed a book from one of the remaining four people. Figure out each person's full name, the book he or she owns, and the book he or she borrowed.

1. Anthony lent a book to the owner of *Sklansky on Poker* and borrowed a book from Dawson.

2. Marya lent a book to Gracie.

3. The six people are: Theo, Dawson, the woman who owns *Super System*, the person who borrowed *Sklansky on Poker*, the person who owns and borrowed (in some order) *Hold'Em Excellence* and *The Fundamentals of Poker*, and a person who either owns or borrowed *Zen and the Art of Poker*.

4. Slattery borrowed a book from Harmon and lent one to Crawford.

5. The three women are: the person who lent a book to Gallagher, a person who either owns or borrowed *Sklansky on Poker*, and a person who either borrowed a book from or lent a book to Anthony.

6. The person who owns *The Fundamentals of Poker* (who isn't Natasha) isn't Zebatinsky.

first name	last name	book owned	book borrowed

See answer on pages 304–305.

Insomniac's Heaven

A recent retiree, Monty used to hate those nights when he just couldn't get to sleep. But ever since he discovered poker on television, he looks forward to them. On five consecutive nights last week (Monday through Friday), he stayed up late watching a different show (including *2004 World Series of Poker*). Each show aired on a different channel on a different day (Monday through Friday), in each case at a different time (2:00, 2:30, 3:00, 3:30, 4:00). Figure out the day and time each show aired and the channel that ran it.

1. Monty watched *Ultimate Poker Challenge* earlier in the week than when he watched the show that aired at 4:00 a.m.
2. *Poker Superstars Invitational* wasn't on channel 64.
3. The show on Thursday began an hour and a half later in the day than the show on channel 27.
4. Monty watched *World Poker Tour* sometime earlier in the week than he watched *Celebrity Poker Showdown*.
5. The show that began at 3:00 a.m. was three days after the show on channel 67.
6. *Celebrity Poker Showdown* aired on a lower-numbered channel than *Ultimate Poker Challenge*.
7. *World Poker Tour* began either half an hour earlier or half an hour later in the day than the show on channel 88.
8. The show on channel 45 began at 2:30 a.m.

day	time	show	channel

See answer on page 305.

Poker School

The Five-Diamonds Poker School is a small but thriving business that offers weekly classes in various aspects of poker strategy. Currently, six classes are in progress, each taught by a different person and meeting on a different day, and each with a different number of students. Can you find out the day on which each person teaches, the class he or she teaches, and the enrollment size?

1. The smallest class has five people and the largest has 15.
2. Tina's class is among the three classes with the most students.
3. Poker 101 is on Wednesday nights.
4. The class with eight students doesn't meet on Tuesday nights.
5. Angela's class has twice as many people as Hi-Lo Strategy.
6. Money Management (which has more than six people) meets later in the week than Figuring the Odds.
7. A woman teaches Reading Your Opponents.
8. No-Limit Poker meets either on Tuesday or Thursday nights.
9. Isaiah's class has more people than the class that meets the day before Angela's class.
10. Peter's class meets on Tuesday nights.
11. Victor's meets sometime earlier in the week than Hi-Lo Strategy.
12. Brandon's class has twice as many people as the Friday night class.

day	teacher	class	number of students

See answer on page 306.

Dealers' Choice

At their monthly Dealers' Choice game, eight players started off the night's play by dealing eight different games. Four were wild-card games—Baseball, Follow the Queen, Low Hole, and Woolworth—and four were non-wild-card games—Anaconda, Lowball, Omaha, and Pineapple. Can you figure out the order in which the eight people dealt, each person's full name, and the game he or she played?

1. Latham dealt just before Nielsen.
2. Four people who dealt consecutively and in order are: Jeannie, the person who dealt Anaconda, Maggie, and the person who dealt Lowball.
3. A woman dealt Woolworth.
4. Samuel dealt sometime before Karl.
5. The four people who played wild card games are: Adam, Coleridge, the sixth dealer, and a person who dealt sometime after Fiorentino.
6. Either Nielsen or Huang dealt Follow the Queen.
7. Gregg didn't deal just before or just after the person who dealt Low Hole.
8. The four men are: Ostroff, the fourth dealer, a person who dealt sometime before McGraw, and a person who dealt either just before or just after Williamson.
9. Regina dealt a hand of Pineapple.
10. The second, fourth, sixth, and eighth dealers were, in some order: Naomi, Williamson, the person who dealt Baseball, and the person who dealt Omaha.

order	first name	last name	game

See answer on pages 306–307.

The Deli Game

After hours on Thursday nights, Frank's Kosher Deli on 38th Street becomes home to a friendly neighborhood game of long standing. Last week, the six regulars (including Frank) sat at their usual circular table (see below). Each, of course, was treated to a sandwich of generous proportions (one was roast beef) each on a different type of bread. Figure out each man's position at the table, his best hand of the evening, and the sandwich he ate.

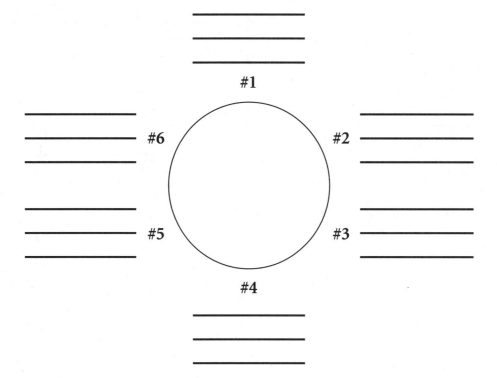

1. The man in seat #1 was one of the two men whose highest hands all night were straights.
2. One man ate a tuna sandwich on white bread.
3. The six men are: Ira, the man who ate the turkey sandwich, the man who ate the sandwich made on a Kaiser roll, the man who sat in seat #3, the man who sat directly across from Larry, and the man who sat on Larry's immediate right.
4. The man in seat #4 got a lower best hand than the man who ate the sandwich on whole wheat bread.

5. Ralph, who didn't sit in #5, didn't have the corned beef sandwich.
6. Miklos sat directly across from the man whose sandwich was on pumpernickel, and next to the man who had a liverwurst sandwich.
7. The men whose best hands were all flushes are: Larry, the man who ate the turkey sandwich, and the man whose sandwich was on a bagel.
8. Donnie sat directly across from the man who had the bologna sandwich.
9. The man who ate the turkey sandwich sat directly across from the man who ate the sandwich on rye bread.
10. Ira, who didn't eat the sandwich on a bagel, sat directly across from the only man to get a full house.

seat number	name	high hand	meat	bread

See answer on pages 307–308.

The Road to Monte Carlo, Part 4: Sightseeing Excursions

Although Monte Carlo is known for its nightlife, there is also a lot to see during the day. Our six traveling companions (Alice, Bill, Chip, Diana, Evan, and Fawn) wanted to get in as much sightseeing as they could. On six consecutive days of the trip (Monday through Saturday), they decided upon a morning and an afternoon activity. In some cases, however, one or more people opted out of the planned activity. For each day, determine the morning and afternoon activities and which people participated in each. Note: This is Part 4 of a five-part puzzle. To solve it, you will need information from Parts 1 through 3.

1. Only two people, a pair of women, went to the Wax Museum. Each of the remaining activities was attended by one of the following four groups of people: all three couples, two couples, all the men, or all the women.
2. The same group went on the trip to the Exotic Garden, the Wednesday morning outing, and the Friday afternoon outing.
3. The person who played blackjack on the first night at the casino joined neither the group that went to the National Museum nor the one that went out on Tuesday morning.
4. The person who won the first hand of poker on the flight to Europe went on only one of the following excursions: the trip to Fontvielle Park, the trip to the Oceanographic Museum, the Monday morning trip.
5. The same group that went to the Museum of Antique Automobiles also went on at least one other excursion.
6. Mrs. Renaldi attended the Wednesday afternoon outing.
7. The person who drank Manhattans on the first night at the casino either visited both Church Saint-Nicolas and the Oceanographic Museum or went to neither place.
8. Three consecutive outings, in order, were to: Church Saint-Nicolas, the National Museum, and the Zoological Terraces.

9. At least one woman went to the Prince's Palace.

10. Only once did Mrs. Stormgren go on two outings the same day; her husband didn't join her for either of these.

11. The person who played trente et quarante on the first night at the casino didn't go on either of the two Wednesday outings, one of which was to the Princess Grace Rose Garden.

12. The trips to the Exotic Garden and the Oceanographic Museum were, in some order, on Tuesday afternoon and Friday morning.

13. The person who won the last hand of poker on the plane didn't join the group for the Wednesday afternoon excursion or for the outing that was just after the one to Fontvielle Park.

14. All six people went to see a show at the Fort Antoine Theater and then, sometime later in the week, to watch a soccer game at the Louis II stadium; these were both afternoon excursions.

	place visited	sightseers
Monday morning		
Monday afternoon		
Tuesday morning		
Tuesday afternoon		
Wednesday morning		
Wednesday afternoon		
Thursday morning		
Thursday afternoon		
Friday morning		
Friday afternoon		
Saturday morning		
Saturday afternoon		

See answer on pages 308–309.

Luck Be a Lady

For the great poker players, luck doesn't enter into it. As for the rest of us, we need all the help we can get. At least, that's the attitude five of my friends take. Each man has a different lucky item that he had with him when he got the best hand of his life. Each man had received the item from a different woman (including Julie). In each case, the event took place in a different year (1996, 1997, 1999, 2001, or 2002). See if you can match up the year that each man got his best hand, the item to which he attributes his luck, and the woman who gave it to him.

1. Matt didn't receive his lucky charm from either Peggy or Yvonne.
2. Ernie got his highest hand two years before the man whose highest hand was four aces.
3. Gregg's best hand was higher than of the man who always wears his lucky ring.
4. One pair of men are brothers, the elder of whom got his highest hand sometime before his younger brother.
5. The man who got a nine-high straight flush stakes his game on either a gold coin or a ring.
6. Peggy dated the youngest of the five men.
7. The man with the lucky keychain got his highest hand the year after the man who caught the queen-high straight flush.
8. The younger of the two brothers is the man whose highest hand was four kings.
9. The man who never joins a table without his rabbit's foot, who is either Howard or Matt, never played a game of poker before 1997.
10. Suzanne gave a man either the money clip or the ring.
11. The three men who are unrelated to any of the other men are: Louis, the man who carries a lucky money clip, and the man who got his lucky charm from Cassie.
12. Suzanne's boyfriend got a better high hand than Peggy's.

13. Howard and the man who carries the gold coin aren't related.

14. One man got a royal flush in 1999.

year	man	high hand	lucky item	woman

See answer on page 310.

Eight Movies in Eight Nights

As a flight attendant, Jennifer travels for a living, so her ideal vacation was a week at home. She rented eight movies, all centering on her favorite pastime, poker. She watched one every night for eight days (from Sunday to the following Sunday), in each case with a different friend (including Stan). On each night, she and her friend ordered a different type of food to be delivered. Can you figure out the day on which Jennifer saw each friend, the movie they watched, and what they ate?

1. Jennifer spent time with Zach on one of the two Sundays.
2. She watched *House of Games* either the day before or the day after she saw Marianne.
3. On Tuesday, when Jennifer didn't see Olivia, she didn't watch *Five Card Stud*.
4. She saw Tyrone either the day before or the day after she watched *Rounders*.
5. Jennifer watched *The Odd Couple* with Rosie.
6. She watched *Loaded Pistols* the day before she ate fish and chips.
7. She ate falafel with a woman.
8. She watched a movie with Victor either the day before or the day after she ate beef potpies.
9. On Saturday, Jennifer ate either chicken wings or pizza.
10. Jennifer and her friend Olivia watched either *Luckytown* or *Rounders* while munching on either sushi or beef potpies.
11. The four men are: the person who watched *House of Games* with Jennifer, the person who ate tacos with her, the person who watched a movie with her on Monday, and the person who watched a movie with her the day before she saw *Kaleidoscope*.
12. Jennifer watched the movie *Five Card Stud* two days after she watched a movie with Pamela and two days before she and a friend shared a pu pu platter.

13. She ate sushi either three or four days before she ate pizza.
14. Jennifer watched *The Cincinnati Kid* on either Thursday or Friday.

day	friend	movie	food

See answer on pages 310–311.

Friendly Game

Poker is a very friendly game that often brings together people with very different types of jobs. At a certain regular circle, the six participants all bring something different to the table—including the table (see diagram below). Three bring refreshments—beer, potato chips, and soft drinks—and the other three bring different poker accessories—cards, poker chips, and the table. Find out where each player sat, his or her job, and what he or she brought.

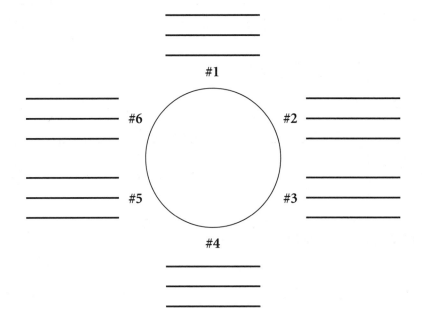

1. The chiropractor sat in either seat #1 or seat #5.
2. Raphael sat in either seat #2 or seat #4.
3. Eddie sat in seat #3.
4. Eddie's cousin, who isn't the realtor, sat directly across from the person who brought the cards.
5. Stephanie and the person to her left brought the two types of chips.
6. Either James or Tara sat in #6.
7. The surfing instructor didn't bring the soft drinks.
8. Alison sat directly across from the person who brought the table.
9. The sculptor brought the poker chips.
10. Either Alison or Raphael is the dog walker.

11. Stephanie, who sat directly across from the history professor, isn't related to anyone at the table.

12. James sat between the people who brought soft drinks and the beer.

seat number	name	profession	brought

See answer on pages 311–312.

Hawaiian Holidays

If you like to play poker and you live in Hawaii, where casinos are still prohibited, you're going to have to travel to play in poker tournaments. Last year, seven Hawaiian residents (three women named Helene, Monica, and Nancy, and four men named Keith, Michael, Nat, and Oliver), each from a different island (Hawaii, Kauai, Lanai, Maui, Molokai, Niihau, Oahu), did just that. Each participated this year in one U.S. poker tournament (California State Poker Championship, L.A. Poker Classic, Five Diamond, Orleans Open, Shooting Star, Showdown at Sands, or World Poker Finals) and one European tournament (British Open, Euro Finals of Poker, Grosvenor Open, Helsinki Freezeout, Irish Open, Poker Million, or Vienna Spring Festival). Can you find out the island where each person lives and the two poker tournaments in which he or she participated?

1. The initial of the person who played at the Vienna Spring Festival is the same as the initial of the island where Nat lives.
2. The person who played at the British Open also played at either the World Poker Finals or Shooting Star.
3. The person who played at the L.A. Poker Classic didn't also play at the Grosvenor Open.
4. Three people whose names have the same initial as the island they live on are: the person who played at the Five Diamond, the person who played at the Helsinki Freezeout, and the woman who played at the Irish Open.
5. The initial of the person who lives on Lanai is the same as the initial of the island where the person who played at the Orleans Open lives.
6. Keith didn't play at Poker Million.
7. The initial of the person who played at the L.A. Poker Classic is the same as the initial of the island where the person who played at the Vienna Spring Festival lives.
8. Monica is one of the few residents of the "forbidden island" of Niihau.
9. The people who played at the World Poker Finals and the Grosvenor Open are of opposite sexes.

10. The person who played at the Five Diamond didn't also play Euro Finals of Poker.

11. The person from Kauai didn't play at the California State Poker Championship.

12. The three women are: the person who lives on Molokai, the person who played at the Showdown at Sands, and the person who played at the Vienna Spring Festival.

13. The first initial of the person who played at Shooting Star is the same as the initial of the island where the person who played at the Grosvenor Open played.

14. Michael didn't play at the World Poker Finals.

name	island	U.S. tournament	European tournament

See answer on page 313.

Atlantic City Express

Every evening, the Atlantic City Shuttle transports New Yorkers to the casinos. Last night, eight women (including Ilene) representing all five New York boroughs rode the bus. Four were headed to the Taj Mahal, in each case to a different poker table (seven-card stud, seven-card hi-lo, Omaha, and Texas hold'em), while the other four were going to play the poker slots at four different casinos (Caesar's, the Hilton, the Tropicana, and Wild Wild West). See if you can sort out each woman's full name, the borough where she lives, the casino she played at, and which game she played.

1. The four women who played poker at the Taj Mahal are: Cathy, Ms. Schaefer, a woman who lives in a borough whose initial is B, and a woman who lives in the same borough as Ms. Fordi.

2. Anita and Ms. Kandelman are, in some order, the woman who played at the Hilton and a woman from Brooklyn.

3. Ms. Nussbaum played the poker slots.

4. The four women in the group, who are from either the Bronx or Queens, are: Francie, Ms. Brody, the woman who played at Caesar's, and a woman who played at the Taj Mahal.

5. The woman who played hold'em isn't from Queens.

6. Ms. Lawford and the woman who played at Wild Wild West are both from the same borough.

7. Beverly and the woman who played at Hilton are from different boroughs.

8. Five women who all live in different boroughs are: Patrice, Ms. Kandelman, the women who played hold'em and Omaha, and the woman who played at the Tropicana.

9. Ms. Woods, who is either Anita or Cathy, and the woman who played at the Hilton don't live in the same borough.

10. Ms. Gardiner didn't play Omaha.

11. Either Denise or Trudy played seven card stud.

12. The woman who played seven-card hi-lo is the only one from Staten Island.

13. Beverly is either Ms. Kandelman or Ms. Schaefer.
14. Trudy is from Manhattan, but Anita isn't from there.

first name	last name	borough	played	casino

See answer on pages 314–315.

Queens of Las Vegas

Five women from five different places in Maine (including Lewiston) made a recent excursion to Las Vegas. On each night of their trip (Wednesday through Sunday) they went to a different poker room (including the Stardust). In each location, one of them was the biggest winner among the group. Each won a different amount, in whole $100 increments, though no one won less than $300 or more than $1200. Can you discover which night each woman won big, her full name, the town where she lives, the casino where she won, and the amount?

1. The woman who won at the Bellagio did so on Wednesday.
2. Polly won sometime before the woman who had the second-highest winnings.
3. The woman from Presque Isle won less than $1200.
4. The woman from Brewer won more than Alyssa and less than Ms. Reynolds.
5. Either Polly or Roberta won exactly $400.
6. Three of the five women are: Jillian, Ms. Starks, and the woman who won $900.
7. Roberta won less than the woman who won at Circus Circus.
8. The woman from Arundel won on Saturday.
9. Ms. Starks won exactly half as much as the woman who won on Friday.
10. Ms. Lowell won either more or less than $1000.
11. Jillian won either three days before or three days after Ms. Reynolds.
12. Margie won more than the woman from Scarborough.
13. Ms. Haritel won the day before the woman who won at the Mirage.
14. Ms. Trower won on Sunday.
15. Either Alyssa or Margie won at Binion's Horseshoe.
16. The woman from Scarborough won either three days before or three days after the woman who won $800.

day	first name	last name	town	casino	amount

See answer on pages 315–316.

The Road to Monte Carlo, Part 5: Mini Millions

On their last night in Monte Carlo, our six travelers (Alice, Bill, Chip, Diana, Evan, and Fawn) participated in Mini Millions, a poker tournament sponsored by their hotel. For a buy-in of only 100 Euros, each person started at a different table. Five of the six lost the first round, each dropping out of the race in a different position at their table (from sixth to second place), while one took first place at his or her table and went on to win the Mini Millions prize of 2000 Euros. Win or lose, all six were glad of the experience, because each met an interesting European, each of whom has a different job in a different city. Figure out the name of the table where each person sat, the order in which he or she finished at his or her table, the person each met, that person's job and home city. Note: This is Part 5 of a five-part puzzle. To solve it, you will need information from Parts 1 through 4.

1. The person who won the Mini Millions was among the sightseeing group on Monday afternoon.
2. The three Europeans from Budapest, Copenhagen, and Paris were: a person whom an American man met, the European who sat at the Prince Rainier table, and a woman.
3. The nurse sat at the Mediterranean table.
4. The only American who met a European of the opposite sex finished at least one place ahead of the person who met the linguist.
5. The person from Madrid is either a historian or a teacher.
6. The top three finishers at their respective tables were, in some order: the person who sat at the Prince Rainier table, the person who met the person from Copenhagen, and a person who had visited the Wax Museum.
7. Leonardo isn't the teacher.
8. The Americans who sat at the Casiraghi, Grace Kelly, and Riviera tables are, in some order: a person who visited the Oceanographic Museum, a person who met a European woman, and a person who finished either fourth or fifth at his or her table.

9. The American who sat in seat B on the flight to Europe met a person from either Copenhagen or Madrid.

10. The au pair is from either Athens or Paris.

11. The six people are: the person who drank vodka martinis at the first night at the casino, the person who sat at the Grace Kelly table, the person who came in sixth place at his or her table, the person who met Jocelyn, the person who met the linguist, and the person who met the person from Copenhagen.

12. The table ranking of the person who was the last to leave the casino on the first night was either one place above or one place below that of the person who met Neil.

13. Mr. Renaldi didn't meet the person from Paris.

14. Either Jocelyn or Marco lives in Athens.

15. Bill's wife met a person from either Copenhagen or London.

16. The person who sat at the Riviera table is married to the person who met the writer.

17. The table ranking of the person who met Karl was either one place above or below that of the person who met the au pair.

18. The person who played craps on the first night at the casino didn't meet the linguist.

19. The person who met the historian ranked either second or third at his or her table.

20. The American who met the person from Athens had visited the Museum of Antique Autos.

21. The person who won the fifth hand of poker on the plane didn't sit at the Princess Caroline table.

22. The American who met Irena either finished fifth at his or her table or is the spouse of this person.

23. The person who met Marco had visited the National Museum.

Note: Solving grid appears on page 154.

table rank	first name	last name	person met	job	home city

See answer on pages 316–317.

Showdown

As their last hand of the night, one group plays a traditional hand of Showdown. Before the deal, all chips are turned in for cash. Then, everyone puts five dollars in the center of the square table (see below) for a final forty-dollar pot. Five cards are dealt face up, and the best hand takes the pot. See if you can piece together where everyone sat, each person's full name, how much money they won or lost (in whole-dollar amounts) and his or her final hand. Note on seat arrangement: Seat #1 is on the same side of the table as seat #2, directly facing seat #6, and between seats #2 and #8.

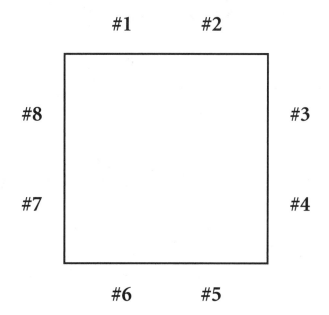

1. Mina was the dealer. The first eight cards she dealt were, in order: nine of clubs, four of hearts, nine of diamonds, king of diamonds, five of hearts, nine of hearts, five of spades, and ten of diamonds.
2. Either Beardsley or Hasagawa won $7.
3. The people who sat in seats #3, #6, and #8 are, in some order: Quentin, Abramson, and Thomas's sister.
4. The player who got the eight of hearts sat between two people whose hands both beat a pair of sevens.

Note: Information continues on page 156.

5. The person who got the king of hearts won exactly $20 more than DiSimone.
6. On the second card dealt, only two players—both men—paired up their first cards, but three other players—Nathan, Resnick, and a person who either won or lost $55—suited up in their first cards in three different suits.
7. The two people who sat next to the winner of the hand are Hasagawa's cousin and a person who held four clubs.
8. A person who either won or lost $67 received at least three cards that were higher than a six.
9. Either Patrick or Abramson got the ace of hearts.
10. The two people who sat next to Resnick both received spades as their third cards.
11. The queen of spades was dealt just after the five of diamonds.
12. DiSimone's last card was the three of hearts.
13. The players who got the six of hearts and the seven of clubs sat next to each other.
14. Olivia, who won money, got at least two pairs.
15. Beardsley and Kimmel sat directly facing each other, but neither of them is Quentin.
16. Thomas, who never met Abramson before the game, received hearts as his first four cards.
17. McGuirk and Ziller won and lost, in some order, the same amounts of money.
18. The person who got the six of spades lost money.
19. Patrick sat on the same side of the table as Olivia and directly facing Thomas's girlfriend.
20. Kimmel and Ziller either both had sixes or neither of them did.
21. On his or her last card, the person in seat #7 caught the card that Mina needed to complete four of a kind.
22. Neither Olivia nor Abramson won the showdown hand.
23. Robert's last card was a nine, which didn't improve his hand.
24. The player whose last two cards were the jack of hearts and the king of spades either won or lost no more than $10.

25. McGuirk sat in either seat #2 or seat #4.

26. Either Mina or Samantha received the queen of diamonds.

27. The only person who won more than $70 drew the ten of spades as his or her final card.

28. The man who had a pair of queens won either $37 or $73.

29. Samantha and her brother found that together they were up $18 for the evening.

30. Kimmel's last card was the ace of clubs.

31. The pair of players who sat in seats #5 and #7 are a husband and wife, in some order.

32. Hasagawa held the five of clubs.

33. Thomas's sister lost money in the game.

34. The person who won showdown had been losing money before winning this pot, but ended up in the black for the night.

35. The hand that took the showdown pot was lower than a full house.

seat #	first name	last name	won/lost	$	five cards in hand

See answer on pages 317–320.

PART III
False Logic Puzzles

Before You Begin

There are five different types of logic puzzles in this section. They have one particular thing in common—each contains at least one false statement, which must be identified in order to solve the puzzle. You may assume that all people who make statements in the puzzles have perfect knowledge, even about events that might happen in the future. You may also assume that each statement is either true or false and that there is always at least one consistent way of assigning true/false values to statements, even if there isn't enough information to determine which assignment is the case if multiple options are possible. (For example, a puzzle can say "This sentence is true" without it being a paradox.)

In solving puzzles, it is important to follow a sound method of analysis, including trial and error. After all the alternatives in a puzzle are clear to you, assume that each one in turn is correct, and test each against the puzzle's considerations. Eliminate those assumptions that reveal inconsistencies or contradictions, and what remains is the solution. For most puzzles, use diagrams to aid in your analysis and in organizing tentative conclusions. Suggested diagrams are presented in both the Hints and Solutions sections. Also, the Solutions section contains detailed methods for solving the puzzles. These will be helpful in solving other puzzles of the same type.

The puzzles are grouped by type, and you will find a wide range of difficulty within each type.

Socrates Lends a Hand

Socrates is credited with being the first known formal logic thinker. He devoted his life to expanding his knowledge, and helping others to do the same. His method was to employ a questioning technique using given propositions and arriving at answers by deductive reasoning. Since Socrates was known among his fellow Athenians as possessing great skill in analysis and deductive reasoning, he was frequently called upon to resolve disputes and to solve crimes.

Each of the puzzles in this section involves problems or crimes, and contains statements by individuals, some of which are true and some of which are false. To find the solutions it is necessary to determine which statements are false and which are not. You may assume that all information given in each problem's introduction is true (and sometimes you will need that information to solve the puzzle).

Who Owns the Mule?

Three farmers who have shared the use of a mule for some time disagree as to who owns the animal. It is not certain, however, that the responsibility of ownership is desired. They have asked Socrates to settle the issue. The three make the following statements. Each makes one true and one false statement.

- A. 1. It is C's mule.
  2. I can make no claim to it.
- B. 1. C has no right to it.
  2. It is A's mule.
- C. 1. It is my mule.
  2. B's second statement is false.

Socrates hesitates for scarcely an instant and determines the owner. To which farmer does the mule belong?

(Hints on page 253)
See answer on page 321.

Theft of Homer's Writings

Valuable writings of Homer are missing. They have been stolen from the library in Athens by one of three suspects. The three are questioned by Socrates, and each makes one true and two false statements, as follows:

A. 1. I did not even know that Homer's books were in the library.
    2. C is innocent.
    3. B must be the thief.
B. 1. I did not do it.
    2. A is innocent.
    3. A's first statement is true.
C. 1. Homer's writings are not worth taking.
    2. A did it, or else it was B.
    3. I would never consider such a dishonest thing.

Which one is guilty?

(Hints on page 253)
See answer on page 321.

Who Left the Cell Door Open?

When Socrates was imprisoned for being a disturbing influence, he was held in high esteem by his guards. All four of them hoped that something would occur that would facilitate his escape. One evening, the guard who was on duty intentionally left the cell door open so that Socrates could leave for distant parts.

Socrates did not attempt to escape, as it was his philosophy that if you accept society's rules, you must also accept its punishments. However, the open door was considered by the authorities to be a serious matter. It is not clear which guard was on duty that evening. The four guards make the following statements in their defense:

A. 1. I did not leave the door open.
   2. C was the one who did it.
B. 1. I was not the one who was on duty that evening.
   2. A was on duty.
C. 1. B was the one who was on duty that evening.
   2. I hoped Socrates would escape.
D. 1. I did not leave the door open.
   2. I am not surprised that Socrates did not attempt to escape.

Considering that, in total, three statements are true, and five statements are false, which guard is guilty?

(Hints on page 253)
See answer on page 322.

A Secret Observer

As Socrates' reputation grew, there were those who were jealous of his fame, and who had been embarrassed by his method of cross-examining to gain the truth. There was a movement to indict Socrates as a negative and disturbing influence. A citizen was chosen to secretly pose as a student of Socrates, to observe his teaching and gain evidence against him. Socrates was informed that one of four followers was, in reality, such an observer. Socrates questioned the four. Their statements follow. All statements are true except any mentioning the secret observer.

A. 1. C is definitely a student, here to learn.
   2. D is a stranger to me.
B. 1. A and D are not acquainted.
   2. C is not the observer.
C. 1. B's first statement is false.
   2. A's second statement is true.
D. 1. C's first statement is false.
   2. A's first statement is true.

Which of the four speakers is the observer?

(Hints on page 253)
See answer on pages 322–323.

Theft From the Statue of Athena

A piece from the gold-and-ivory statue of Athena was stolen. There was evidence that the thief, acting alone, entered the temple in the dead of night and used a large hammer to dislodge a piece of the statue. Socrates agreed to cross-examine four suspects, all of whom were in Athens when the crime occurred. Exactly one of them is guilty. One suspect makes three true statements; one suspect makes three false statements. As to the truthfulness of the statements by the other two suspects, little is known. Their statements follow:

A. 1. I did not do it.
   2. I was in Philius when the crime occurred.
   3. B is guilty.
B. 1. I am innocent.
   2. C owns a large hammer.
   3. C was seen at the Acropolis late that night.
C. 1. I do not own a large hammer.
   2. A and B are both guilty.
   3. I went to bed early that night.
D. 1. Only one of my statements is false.
   2. C was out late that night.
   3. I am innocent.

Which one is the thief?

(Hints on page 254)
See answer on page 323.

Who Should Lead the Victory Parade?

At the successful end of the war with Persia, it was decided that there should be a parade through the main streets of Athens. At the front of the procession should be the soldier who had led the charge during the last battle, but the identity of this soldier was unclear. Socrates was asked to decide who should lead the parade, and he questioned three candidates. One of them makes one false statement, one makes two false statements, and one makes three false statements, as follows:

   A. 1. I led the charge in the last battle.
        2. I am the logical choice to lead the parade.
        3. C was in the reserve ranks during the battle.
   B. 1. C did not lead the charge during the last battle.
        2. I am the logical choice to lead the parade.
        3. I could keep in time with the parade music very well.
   C. 1. I should be selected.
        2. B would not be able to keep in time with the parade music.
        3. I was not in the reserve ranks during the last battle.

Which soldier should lead the parade?

(Hints on page 254)
See answer on page 324.

Socrates Plans a Trip

Socrates wanted to take a trip to Philius, and decided that one of his young followers should accompany him. Three of them expressed keen interest, and Socrates questioned them to determine which one of the three should be selected.

The disciple selected makes three true or three false statements. Of the other two, one makes two true statements and one false statement, and one makes one true statement and two false statements. Their statements follow:

A. 1. C is the oldest.
   2. B is unwilling to carry the baggage.
   3. I am the one with three true statements.
B. 1. I am willing to carry the baggage.
   2. C will be chosen.
   3. A's first statement is false.
C. 1. I am the oldest.
   2. B will be selected.
   3. B's third statement is true.

Which follower did Socrates select to accompany him?

(Hints on page 254)
See answer on page 325.

Who Should Repair the Statue?

After the damage to the statue of Athena, Socrates was requested to select the most qualified craftsman to undertake the necessary repairs (the most qualified craftsman would need to own all the necessary tools and have worked with ivory before). He interviewed four recommended craftsmen. Their statements were not all truthful. However, each of the four makes the same number of true statements and the same number of false statements.

- A. 1. I do not have all the necessary tools.
  2. D is the most qualified.
  3. C is experienced in this type of work.
- B. 1. A is the most qualified.
  2. D has never worked with ivory.
  3. A's first statement is false.
- C. 1. I am experienced in this type of work.
  2. B is the most qualified.
  3. A does not have all the necessary tools.
- D. 1. C is the most qualified.
  2. A does not have all the necessary tools.
  3. I have never worked with ivory.

Which craftsman should Socrates select?

(Hints on page 254)
See answer on page 326.

Who Won the Discus Throw?

The Athenian Games involved several athletic events. Following the games one season, there was a dispute as to who had won the discus throw. Socrates agreed to question the competitors and determine the winner. The statements of four of the athletes are below. No two make the same number of false statements. Note that if two athletes train together, then they do not train with anyone else, and there were no ties in the event.

A. 1. C did not win the discus throw.
    2. I was second.
    3. C and I trained together.
B. 1. A was the winner.
    2. I placed a close second.
    3. C and I trained together.
C. 1. B was the winner.
    2. I did not train with anyone.
    3. A was second.
D. 1. A was not the winner.
    2. B was second.
    3. C and I trained together.

Who won the discus event?

(Hints on page 254)
See answer on page 327.

The Food Produce Thief

Five citizens were asked to deliver food to the Acropolis to provide a meal for city dignitaries who were meeting there. One delivered bread; one delivered goats' cheese; one delivered honey; one delivered milk; and one delivered nuts. Shortly after the produce was left, significant amounts of the food were found to be missing, illegally acquired, it was determined, by one of the five citizens.

Socrates agreed to cross-examine the suspects. Their statements are below. The one who delivered the milk makes three true statements; the one who delivered the cheese makes two true statements and one false statement; the one who delivered the honey makes one true statement and two false statements; and the one who delivered the bread and the one who delivered the nuts each make three false statements.

- A. 1. I did not deliver the bread.
  - 2. D is the one who stole the food.
  - 3. B delivered the honey.
- B. 1. I did not deliver the cheese.
  - 2. I am certainly not guilty.
  - 3. C delivered the honey.
- C. 1. I did not deliver the honey.
  - 2. B's second statement is false.
  - 3. D is not the thief.
- D. 1. I did not deliver the nuts.
  - 2. A is the thief.
  - 3. E delivered the bread.
- E. 1. I did not deliver the milk.
  - 2. C stole the food.
  - 3. A delivered the bread.

Which one delivered which food product, and who is guilty?

(Hints on page 254)
See answer on pages 328–329.

Theft at the Open Market

A theft has occurred at the Athenian open market. A variety of goods has been stolen including a large quantity that would require a cart to transport.

Four suspects are questioned by Socrates and one of them is the culprit. The statements of the four are below. None of the suspects is completely truthful, and no two make the same number of true statements.

A. 1. D has been to the open market on several occasions.
   2. None of us is guilty.
   3. B, who is a visitor, has been observed at the open market.
   4. All of my statements are false.
B. 1. A is not the guilty one.
   2. D owns a cart.
   3. I have never been to the open market.
   4. D is a visitor to Athens, but has been here several times.
C. 1. A's first and third statements are false.
   2. D does not own a cart.
   3. D has only been to the open market once.
   4. B's statements are all true.
D. 1. I do not own a cart.
   2. B is the guilty one.
   3. I have only been to the open market once.
   4. B's third statement is true.

Which of the four is guilty?

(Hints on page 254)
See answer on pages 329–330.

Mordin's Maze

A knight, far from home and seeking shelter in a storm, happened upon what appeared to be an abandoned castle. In reality it was the abode of Mordin the Sorcerer. The knight was received and provided with food and drink containing a potion that rendered him senseless.

When his head cleared, the knight found that he was in a room in the depths of the castle. His gaze fell on a stone tablet leaning against the nearby wall, with this message:

You are about to encounter Mordin's Maze. If you wish to be freed, you must make correct judgments as you travel through eight rooms. At each decision point you will find a choice of doors to pass through. You will be guided by a sign on each door. Select the correct one (there will be exactly one correct door in each room) and you will continue on your way through the maze. All other doors lead to dead ends from which there is no escape or return. Be warned: Signs may be true or false.

Since no other option presented itself, the knight was determined to successfully negotiate the maze.

(You may assume that everything written on the stone tablet is true. When reading the signs on the doors, interpret direct commands such as "Go through this door" as meaning "Going through this door is the correct thing to do.")

The First Choice

The knight approached two doors at the end of the room and read these signs:

A

Only one of these signs is false.

B

This is the door you should go through.

Which door should be opened?

(Hints on page 255)
See answer on page 330.

The Second Choice

Having selected the right door, the knight passed into a second room and found two doors from which to choose. Each contained a sign, as follows:

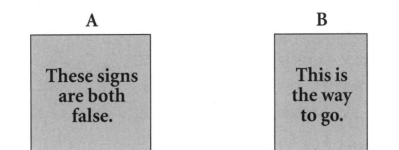

Which door is the correct one?

(Hints on page 255)
See answer on page 331.

The Third Choice

Again the knight went through the correct door and entered another room, this time containing a choice of three doors, with these signs:

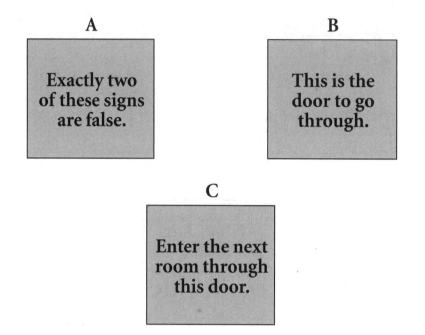

A

Exactly two of these signs are false.

B

This is the door to go through.

C

Enter the next room through this door.

Which door should be chosen?

(Hints on page 255)
See answer on page 331.

The Fourth Choice

Having made the right selection, the knight continued through the maze, and encountered a choice of three doors, with these signs:

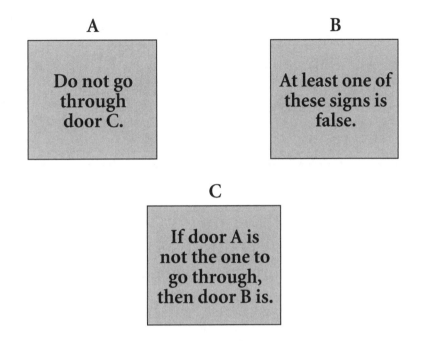

A

Do not go through door C.

B

At least one of these signs is false.

C

If door A is not the one to go through, then door B is.

Which is the right choice?

(Hints on page 255)
See answer on page 332.

The Fifth Choice

Proceeding correctly into the fifth room, the knight perceived three doors. He read their signs, as follows:

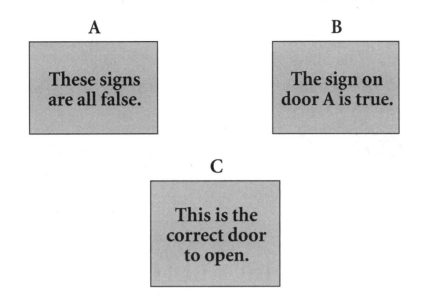

Which door leads to the next choice?

(Hints on page 255)
See answer on page 332.

The Sixth Choice

Once again, the knight selected the correct door and entered the sixth room, which contained three doors, with these signs:

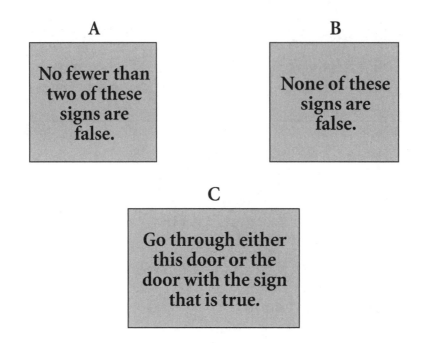

A

No fewer than two of these signs are false.

B

None of these signs are false.

C

Go through either this door or the door with the sign that is true.

Which door is the one to go through?

(Hints on page 255)
See answer on page 333.

The Seventh Choice

After taking a deep breath, the knight chose one of the doors and entered the seventh room. He observed four doors, as follows:

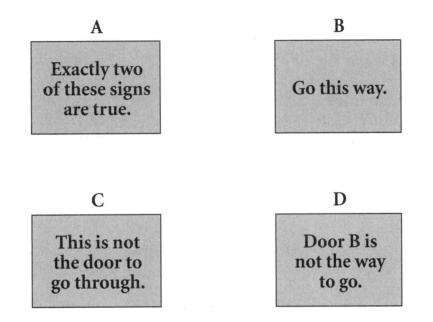

A

Exactly two of these signs are true.

B

Go this way.

C

This is not the door to go through.

D

Door B is not the way to go.

Which door should the knight select?

(Hints on page 255)
See answer on page 333.

The Eighth Choice

Having successfully passed the first seven decisions, the knight entered the eighth and final room of the maze. He found three doors, with these signs:

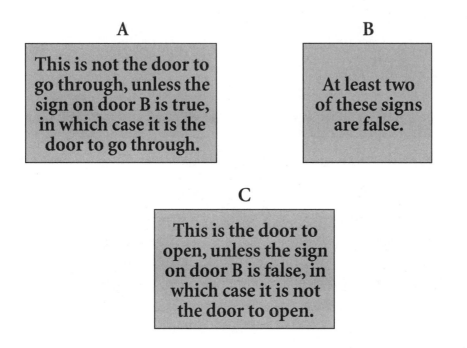

A

This is not the door to go through, unless the sign on door B is true, in which case it is the door to go through.

B

At least two of these signs are false.

C

This is the door to open, unless the sign on door B is false, in which case it is not the door to open.

The knight entered the correct door, which opened into a wooded area near the entrance to the castle, where he found his faithful horse awaiting him.

What door was opened?

(Hints on page 255)
See answer on page 334.

The Isle of Ave

Somewhere in the far and forlorn reaches of the North Sea is the small island of Ave, on which strange things happen. That the island is watched over by Neptune, and that some say it is enchanted, are only part of its uniqueness.

The Isle of Ave is inhabited by an unusual people. Avians have their own standards of veracity.

Neptune Establishes Communication

The inhabitants of the Isle of Ave belong to three groups: Soravians, who always speak truthfully; Noravians, who always speak falsely; and Midravians, who make statements that are alternately true and false—in which order is unknown.

Since the Isle of Ave is under his watchful eye, Neptune would like to establish communication with the Avians. To do so, it is necessary to know who has what standard of veracity. He approaches three inhabitants, A, B, and C, known to be a Soravian, a Noravian, and a Midravian, not necessarily in that order. He asks one of them two questions:

Neptune: Are you the Soravian?	A: No.
Neptune: Is B the Soravian?	A: No.

Neptune now knows which of the three is the Soravian, which is the Noravian, and which is the Midravian. Do you?

(Hints on page 256)
See answer on page 335.

Two Avians

Avians belong to three different groups: Soravians, who always speak truthfully; Noravians, who always speak falsely; and Midravians, who make statements that are alternately true and false, but not necessarily in that order. The two speakers below are known to belong to different groups.

A. B is a Noravian.
B. A's statement is truthful.

To what groups do A and B belong?

(Hints on page 256)
See answer on page 335.

Umbrellas to Sell

Since it rains continually on the Isle of Ave, you would think that an umbrella purveyor would find it an ideal place to ply his trade. The problem in dealing with Avians, however, is communication. A visiting seller of umbrellas approaches three Avians and asks which group each represents.

The three are known to be a Soravian, who always speaks truthfully; a Noravian, who always speaks falsely; and a Midravian, who makes statements that are alternately true and false, but the order is uncertain. The three make the following statements:

A. C will answer falsely to all questions.
B. A's statement is false.
C. B's statement is false.

Frustrated by his inability to interpret the Avians' statements, the visitor leaves, deciding that it would be best to sell his umbrellas in some other place.

Which one is the Soravian, which one is the Midravian, and which one is the Noravian?

(Hints on page 256)
See answer on page 336.

Visit From a Hippogriff

The Isle of Ave seems to be a stopping place for all manner of strange beasts. There is, however, considerable excitement among the inhabitants today, as a hippogriff has visited the island, and no hippogriff has ever visited the island before. This monster has the body of a horse and the wings, head, and talons of an eagle. Three inhabitants are discussing the visitor.

The three are known to be a Soravian, who always speaks truthfully; a Noravian, who always speaks falsely; and a Midravian, who makes statements that are alternately true and false, or false and true. Their statements follow:

A. 1. I have seen hippogriffs on the island several times.
   2. You cannot believe anything that B says.
B. A has never seen a hippogriff before.
C. A is a Soravian.

Who is the Soravian, who is the Noravian, and who is the Midravian?

(Hints on pages 256)
See answer on page 336.

To Catch an Aspidochelon

The aspidochelon is a sea monster so huge that it resembles an island. However, it is rumored to be a gastronomical delicacy. Three Avian fishermen are contemplating an aspidochelon hunt.

Avians belong to three different groups: Soravians, who always speak truthfully; Noravians, who always speak falsely; and Midravians, who make statements that are alternately true and false, although not necessarily in that order. As to the three fishermen, little is known as to their group or groups. Their statements follow:

A. 1. C and I have caught an Aspidochelon before.
    2. I am a Soravian.
B. 1. I am not a Midravian.
    2. We do not know for sure if aspidochelon is good to eat.
    3. A's first statement is false.
C. 1. None of us has ever seen an aspidochelon.
    2. I am a Noravian.

What group or groups do the three fishermen represent?

(Hints on page 256)
See answer on page 337.

Is D Neptune Visiting in Disguise?

The Avians are watched over by Neptune, who occasionally visits them in disguise (but does not live on the island himself). Three Avians are discussing a fourth individual, who may be Neptune in disguise, although there seems to be a difference of opinion.

Inhabitants of Ave are known to be Soravians, who always speak truthfully; Noravians, who always speak falsely; or Midravians who make statements that are alternately true and false, or false and true. The group or groups of the three speakers below are unknown:

A. 1. I saw D suddenly appear from behind a tree.
   2. None of us is a Soravian.
   3. B is a Noravian.
B. 1. D is Neptune visiting us in disguise.
   2. Only one of us is a Soravian.
   3. I am not a Midravian.
C. 1. D is my next-door neighbor.
   2. A is a Soravian, as is D.

What group or groups are represented by the three speakers?

(Hints on page 256)
See answer on pages 337–338.

A's Statement Is Truthful

Neptune is finding that establishing meaningful dialogue with the Avians is not as easy as he thought it would be. Perhaps he needs to be a little more direct. Neptune steps up to four inhabitants and insists on a truthful statement.

Among the four, at least one is known to be a Soravian, who always speaks truthfully; at least one is known to be a Noravian, who always speaks falsely; and at least one is known to be a Midravian, who makes statements that are alternately true and false, but in unknown order. Each makes one statement, as follows:

A. I am either a Soravian, a Noravian, or a Midravian.
B. I am either a Soravian or a Midravian.
C. I am either a Noravian or a Midravian.
D. I am either a Soravian or a Noravian.

Considering that two of the four statements are truthful and two are false, what does Neptune now know about each of the four?

(Hints on page 256)
See answer on page 338.

A Problem With a Sea Monster

Three Avian fishermen are known to be a Soravian, who always speaks truthfully; a Noravian, who always speaks falsely; and a Midravian, who makes statements that are alternately true and false. A sea monster has been caught in their nets and the three are discussing the problem, as follows:

A. 1. This is not the first time the sea monster has gotten caught in our nets.
   2. I am allergic to sea monsters.
   3. C speaks truthfully only part of the time.
B. 1. This is the first time a sea monster has gotten caught in our nets.
   2. C was so frightened that he fell overboard.
   3. The sea monster took more fish than we did.
C. 1. A is not allergic to sea monsters.
   2. I did not fall overboard.
   3. The sea monster did not take more fish than we did.

Neptune resolved the problem by advising the sea monster to leave the area. Which is the Soravian, the Noravian, and the Midravian?

(Hints on pages 256)
See answer on page 339.

There Are Outliers

> The Avians' unusual standards of veracity are important to the island's traditions. There are a few, however, who do not accept the value of tradition, and who do not observe the conventional island standards of veracity. These are Outliers. How truthful they are is not known, except that their responses are different from those of the Soravians, Noravians, and Midravians.

Visitors From the Sea

Once a year, the Isle of Ave is visited by the Sea People for their special feast day, to which Avians are invited. Four inhabitants are discussing the festivities.

As to the four who make the statements below, one is a Soravian, who always speaks truthfully; one is a Noravian, who always speaks falsely; and one is a Midravian, who makes statements that are alternately true and false. The fourth does not follow the customary Avian standards of veracity and must be considered an Outlier.

- A. 1. My statements are not all truthful.
     2. We are lucky to be part of the festivities.
     3. I find it difficult to relate to these people, with their fins, tails, and scales.
     4. I am the Midravian.
- B. 1. A's third statement is true.
     2. I am doing more than my share helping to get ready for the big feast.
     3. My statements are all truthful.

C. 1. My statements are all truthful.
  2. With all these people crowded onto the island it will surely sink.
  3. I am to be the guest of honor at the feast.
  4. We are all overworked.
D. 1. A's first statement is true.
  2. C's first statement is truthful.
  3. I am the Midravian.

Which one is the Soravian, which one is the Noravian, which one is the Midravian, and which one is the Outlier?

(Hints on page 257)
See answer on pages 339–340.

Recreational Activities on Ave

There are four principal recreational activities enjoyed by the inhabitants of Ave: giant sea horse racing, boating, fishing, and swimming. Five Avians are discussing these activities and who enjoys each.

Avians are divided into three groups according to their standards of veracity: Soravians always speak truthfully, Noravians always speak falsely, and Midravians make statements that are alternately true and false. There are also those few inhabitants who insist on being different. Their standards of veracity are unlike those of the three traditional groups. They are Ave's Outliers. As to the five who make the statements below, their groups are unknown except that one and only one of them is an Outlier.

A. 1. D enjoys boating.
  2. E enjoys both swimming and fishing.
  3. B is a Soravian.
  4. E is not a Noravian or a Midravian.

B. 1. C enjoys all four recreational activities.
   2. A is not a Midravian.
   3. D's third statement is true.
   4. I am a Soravian.
C. 1. B enjoys all four recreational activities.
   2. D has no interest in fishing.
   3. I do not enjoy boating.
   4. E is not a Soravian.
D. 1. I enjoy three recreational activities.
   2. I enjoy boating.
   3. C's recreational interest is limited to fishing.
   4. A's third statement is false.
E. 1. C enjoys giant sea horse racing and swimming.
   2. Two of my recreational activities are giant sea horse racing and boating.
   3. A's recreational activities are limited to giant sea horse racing and boating.
   4. D only enjoys one of the four recreational activities.

What is the standard of veracity of each of the five Avians, and, considering that no two of them enjoy the same number of the four activities, what recreational activities are enjoyed by each?

(Hints on pages 257)
See answer on pages 340–341.

The Villagers of Farmwell

These puzzles involve the activities of the people who inhabited a shire within the kingdom of Lidd.

The puzzles contain statements that provide limited amounts of pertinent information. They afford just enough information for you to arrive at the correct solutions. However, you will find that there is one false statement in each puzzle. To find the correct solution, first determine which statement should be discarded.

The Village Fair

The annual village fair is a much-anticipated event, and the livestock showings and awards are an important part of the festivities. This year it was necessary to have four separate showings to accommodate the large number of entries: daybreak to midmorning, midmorning to midday, midday to midafternoon, and midafternoon to sundown. One showing was for cows, one for goats, one for pigs, and one for sheep—not necessarily in that order. The animals winning the four categories were owned by Dor, Edvo, Frer, and Har, and one of their entries won the blue ribbon for best animal in the fair.

Of the six statements that follow, five are valid and one is false. Based on these statements, who owned which animal, what was the showing time for each, and which animal was awarded the blue ribbon?

1. The sheep escaped from its owner shortly after midmorning and was not recaptured until the next day.
2. Edvo owns the goat.
3. Dor stopped showing her entry at midday and left the fair.
4. The blue ribbon winner was entered in the midday to midafternoon showing, immediately following the goat's showing.
5. Frer's animal was entered in a later showing than that in which the pig was entered.
6. Edvo's animal was entered in the first showing of the day.

(Hints on page 258)
See answer on page 342.

Encounter With the Dragon Meduso

A comely village lass had been captured by the dreaded dragon Meduso. This dragon was not only large and fierce, with fiery breath, but had the power to turn anyone to stone who looked directly into his eye. The village leaders appealed to the King for knightly assistance to free the lass. Sir Hector, who had the duty that day, set out on his steed.

Sir Hector made four attempts to rescue the village lass. In one attempt, he used his peripheral vision to fight the dragon. However, the smoke and fire from Meduso's breath caused irritation to his eyes and the resulting tears restricted his vision. In another attempt, he used his highly polished shield as a mirror in which to see the dragon, but clouds of smoke from the dragon's breath obscured the reflection. In one attempt, he slipped into the cave at night while the dragon was sleeping. However, the dragon, who was a very light sleeper, awoke and chased Sir Hector from the cave. In another attempt, he blindfolded himself and located the dragon by his sound. However, his lance struck a sturdy oak tree, jolting him from his mount.

As Sir Hector was preparing for a fifth attempt, his squire arrived with the news that the fair damsel had returned, having escaped while the dragon was out foraging for food.

From the following statements, what was the sequence of Sir Hector's four attempts to rescue the village lass? Of the six statements, five are valid and one is false.

1. At least one other attempt followed Sir Hector's attempt to use his peripheral vision.
2. Sir Hector's attempt to use a blindfold was not immediately before or immediately after the attempt to slip into the cave.
3. The attempt by Sir Hector to slip into the dragon's cave was not his fourth attempt.
4. Sir Hector's attempt to use his polished shield was immediately before his attempt to slip into the dragon's cave.
5. Sir Hector's attempt to use a blindfold was not after his attempt to use his polished shield.
6. Sir Hector's attempt to use his peripheral vision was not immediately before or immediately after his attempt to use a blindfold.

(Hints on page 258)
See answer on page 343.

The Dragon Watch

Because of the ever-present danger of dragons, the villagers took turns keeping watch. During one particular period, five people were assigned watch duty, each on one of five shifts. Their ages varied, with no two being the same age. From the statements below, determine the order in which the watches were held and the relative age of each of the five villagers. One statement below is false; the others are valid.

1. Har was not the oldest, the youngest, nor did he have the first or fifth watch.
2. The youngest of the five, who was neither Edvo nor Tolo, did not have the fifth watch.
3. Winn was younger and had a later watch than Edvo, who stood a later watch and was younger than Frer.
4. Tolo, who was not the second oldest or fourth oldest, was older than Har, and had an earlier watch than Frer.
5. Edvo's relative position in the order of the watches was the same as his relative position in age when ordered from youngest to oldest.
6. Har was next to Tolo in age and next to Edvo in the order of watches held.
7. The fourth oldest held a later watch than Tolo, but an earlier watch than Edvo, who had a later watch and was younger than Frer.
8. The one who held the second watch was the oldest of the five villagers.

(Hints on page 259)
See answer on pages 344–345.

New Ponies

Ponies were used for labor and were the primary means of transportation in Farmwell. Four villagers, who were neighbors, each recently acquired a pony. One was black, one was palomino, one was gray, and one was white. They varied in height from nine to twelve hands, no two being the same height. The four neighbors were Boro, Jes, Kover, and Tolo. Their second names were Son of Alfo, Son of Dirk, Son of Evel, and Son of Fergy, not necessarily in that order.

From the statements below, determine the first name and second name of each of the four neighbors, and the color and height of the pony each acquired. One of the six statements is false; the rest are valid.

1. Tolo, who lived next to Son of Fergy and across from Son of Evel, did not acquire a pony that was ten hands high, nor was his new pony's color palomino or black; his pony was acquired immediately after Kover's pony.

2. Boro, whose new pony was white, was the second to acquire a pony, followed by Son of Evel, whose pony was not eleven hands high.

3. Son of Dirk's new pony was the second one to be acquired; it was neither nine hands high nor eleven hands high.

4. Neither the first nor the last of the four to acquire a pony owned the one that was eleven hands high.

5. Son of Alfo, who lived next to Kover, acquired a black pony.

6. The neighbor whose new pony was twelve hands high was the first of the four to acquire a pony.

(Hints on page 259)
See answer on pages 345–346.

Work and Recreation

The villagers were industrious, each working hard at a particular trade. Among five of them, one was a weaver, one was a carpenter, one was a blacksmith, one was a cobbler, and one was a miller.

A happy people, they enjoyed singing, dancing, instrumental music, telling stories, and sharing puzzles. Each had a favorite and a second-favorite activity, different from each other, both of which they enjoyed. Based on the statements below, what was the vocation of each and what was the favorite and second-favorite activity of each? No two had the same favorite and no two had the same second-favorite. One statement below is false; the rest are true.

1. The one whose favorite activity was singing was much in demand because of the simplicity and high quality of the furniture he built.
2. Dancing was the favorite activity of the cobbler, whereas he didn't care for puzzles at all.
3. Fram's second-favorite was the same as Dok's favorite; Zett's second-favorite was the same as Winn's favorite.
4. Neither the blacksmith nor the miller enjoyed telling stories.
5. Winn, who was not the miller or the cobbler, enjoyed storytelling most; his second-favorite activity was dancing.
6. The weaver enjoyed instrumental music most; his second-favorite activity was singing.
7. The cobbler, Hober, and the miller were good friends.
8. The second-favorite activity of the carpenter was storytelling.

(Hints on page 260)
See answer on pages 346–348.

A Giant in the Shire

The villagers were fortunate that relatively few monsters or other adversaries invaded their shire. When a giant looking for an easy meal began stealing livestock, a group of the people united and, presenting a formidable presence, were successful in driving the giant away. Among those in the group were Alf, Bord, Dek, Fober, and Hon. Their second names were Son of Edno, Son of Lor, Son of Quin, Son of Rup, and Son of Tas. Their occupations were as follows: two raised sheep, one raised cattle, one raised goats, and one raised pigs. In chasing the giant away, two wielded pitchforks, one wielded an ax, one wielded a club, and one wielded a spade.

From the statements that follow, what was the first name and second name of each of the five, what was the occupation of each, and what weapon was wielded by each? Of the seven statements, one is false; the rest are valid.

1. Neither Son of Rup nor Son of Tas, both of whom wielded pitchforks, raised sheep or goats.
2. Dek, Hon (who raised cattle), Alf (who was not Son of Rup), and Son of Tas were among the leaders in organizing the group to attack the giant.
3. Son of Edno and Son of Quin raised sheep.
4. Dek, who was not Son of Tas, and Fober, who wielded a spade, had adjacent farms.
5. Although Son of Quin was reluctant, at the last minute he was persuaded by Son of Edno and Alf to join the group.
6. Son of Lor did not raise goats or pigs.
7. Alf, who did not raise sheep, wielded an ax.

(Hints on page 261)
See answer on pages 348–349.

Pony Races

The most important sporting events in the shire were pony races. In one series of four races, six riders competed. No rider won more than one race, and no rider finished last in more than one race. From the statements below, what was the ranking of each rider in each race? ("Before" means in a higher-ranking position, not necessarily immediately before; "after" means lower-ranked, not necessarily immediately after.) Of the sixteen statements, fifteen are valid and one is false.

1st race

1. Pro finished before Pen, who finished before Ismo.
2. Lak finished before Pro.
3. Pir finished after Ismo.
4. Adus finished in third place.

2nd race

5. Lak finished before Ismo, who finished before Adus.
6. Pro finished somewhere between his places in the 1st and 3rd races.
7. Pir finished in fifth place.
8. Pen finished before Lak.

3rd race

9. Pro finished before Pen, who finished before Pir.
10. Pir finished after Lak and before Ismo.
11. Lak finished before Pro, who finished before Ismo.
12. Pir did not finish in the same place as he did in either of the first two races.

4th race

13. Pir finished two positions better than his best position in any of the other three races.
14. Pro finished before Adus and after Lak.
15. Pen finished in fifth place.
16. Lak finished after Pir.

(Hints on page 261)
See answer on pages 350–351.

The Valley Liars

Among strange lands, the Land of Liars is unparalleled. The inhabitants all make false statements. However, they adhere to definite patterns according to the time of day. There are those who speak the truth in the morning and lie in the afternoon. The inhabitants in this group are known as Amtrus. There are also those who speak the truth in the afternoon and lie in the morning. The inhabitants in this group are known as Pemtrus.

There is a valley in the Land of Liars, in which the inhabitants have their own patterns of veracity: The Amtrus are like others in the Land except that in any statements specifically mentioning other Amtrus they lie in the morning and tell the truth in the afternoon. The Pemtrus are like other Pemtrus in the Land except that in any statements specifically mentioning other Pemtrus they lie in the afternoon and tell the truth in the morning.

To solve each puzzle, you must determine which speakers are Amtrus and which are Pemtrus, and whether it is morning or afternoon. (You may assume that all puzzles take place either in the morning or the afternoon.)

A Visitor to the Land of Liars

A traveler enters the Land of Liars intending to visit the Valley of Liars. He is aware that Amtrus speak the truth in the morning and lie in the afternoon, and that Pemtrus speak the truth in the afternoon and lie in the morning. The visitor encounters two inhabitants. He inquires as to the time of day and as to the group or groups to which the two belong. They reply as follows:

A.   B and I are Pemtrus.

B. 1. A is not a Pemtru.

     2. It is either morning or afternoon.

Is it morning or afternoon, and to what group or groups do the two inhabitants of the Land of Liars belong?

(Hints on page 262)
See answer on page 351.

En Route to the Valley of Liars

Still heading toward the Valley of Liars, the visitor approaches a fork in the road. One road leads north and the other east. Two inhabitants are asked for directions. The two reply as follows:

A. 1. Take the road leading east.

     2. It is morning.

B. 1. Take the road leading north.

     2. I am an Amtru.

Which road should the visitor take?

(Hints on page 262)
See answer on page 352.

Two Valley Liars

The visitor reaches the Valley of Liars. He has been advised that they have their own patterns of veracity. They are like others in the Land of Liars except that when Amtrus specifically mention other Amtrus they lie in the morning and speak the truth in the afternoon; and when Pemtrus specifically mention other Pemtrus they lie in the afternoon and speak the truth in the morning.

Two Valley inhabitants are asked the time of day and to what group or groups they belong. They respond as below:

A. B and I are Pemtrus.
B. A is not a Pemtru.

Is it morning or afternoon, and to what group or groups do the two Valley inhabitants belong?

(Hints on page 262)
See answer on pages 352–353.

Two More Valley Liars

Two Valley inhabitants, A and B, are asked to what group or groups they belong. They respond as follows:

A. 1. B is a Pemtru.
   2. B and I belong to the same group.
B.   A's statements are false.

Is it morning or afternoon, and to what group or groups do A and B belong?

(Hints on page 262)
See answer on page 353.

Three Valley Liars

The statements below are made by three Valley inhabitants, whose group or groups are unknown.

A. B and I do not belong to the same group.
B. If asked now, C will say it is morning.
C. B and I are both Pemtrus.

Is it morning or afternoon, and to which group does each of the three speakers belong?

(Hints on page 262)
See answer on page 354.

Three Valley Liars Again

Three Valley inhabitants make statements. As to their group or groups, little is known.

A. C and I are not both Pemtrus.
B. C and I belong to the same group.
C. A and I do not belong to the same group.

Is it morning or afternoon, and to which group does each belong?

(Hints on page 262)
See answer on pages 354–355.

Four Valley Liars

Four Valley inhabitants make the following statements. Of these four, little is known as to their group or groups.

A. If you were to ask D, he would say that I am a Pemtru.
B. I am the only one from my group.
C. If asked, B would claim that he and I belong to the same group.
D. B and I are Amtrus.

Is it morning or afternoon, and to which group or groups do the four Valley inhabitants belong?

(Hints on page 262)
See answer on pages 355–356.

Who Is the Impostor?

Of the five individuals who make the statements below, one is a visitor from another land and not subject to the Valley standards of veracity. He is an impostor, posing as an inhabitant. As to the four inhabitants, Amtrus and Pemtrus are equally represented.

A. C and I do not belong to the same group.
B. It is either afternoon, or else I am a Pemtru, but not both.
C. A is not a Pemtru.
D. Either A is an Amtru, or else I am an Amtru, but not both.
E. It is either afternoon, or else I am an Amtru, but not both.

Which speaker is the impostor, is it morning or afternoon, and what group is represented by each of the four inhabitants?

(Hints on page 262)
See answer on pages 356–357.

PART IV
Mystifying Logic Puzzles

Before You Begin

Solving logic puzzles is challenging and enjoyable, as well as worthwhile. They will not necessarily expand your knowledge, but if approached conscientiously, they can help to develop your mental power. The puzzles involve formal logic requiring deductive reasoning based on given statements or propositions—and they will stretch your ability to successfully exercise reasoned trial and error and analyze alternatives.

One key is to resist turning to the solution for a given puzzle—until you believe you have solved the puzzle, or until you are convinced you have given it your very best effort. Finally, if you do need to turn to the answer, review the considerations leading to the solution so that you will become familiar with the approach and can use it to solve other puzzles of the same type.

Within this section are six puzzle sections. Each contains a different type of logic puzzle, and in each section the puzzles are organized by level of difficulty beginning with the least difficult and progressing to the most difficult.

For most puzzles, diagrams will be helpful in testing alternatives and forming conclusions. You will find suggested diagrams in both the Hints and Solutions sections of the book.

In all the logic puzzles in this book, characters with male-sounding names are male, and those with female-sounding names are female. You'll never encounter a female Lancelot or a male Mary.

Prince Tal's Adventures

The adventures of Prince Tal take place in a faraway kingdom at a distant time. Prince Tal encounters the ferocious beasts, giants, and enchantresses that abound in that land.

The puzzles in this section contain assumptions, only some of which will lead you to the correct solutions. The challenge is to determine which assumptions are valid and which are invalid.

Educational Accomplishments

Even though noblemen of the kingdom spent considerable time seeking adventures, education was not neglected. Prince Tal excelled in one area of his education and did especially well in another. From the following statements, determine in which subject Prince Tal excelled and in which second subject he did especially well.

1. If Prince Tal excelled in chivalry, he did especially well in horsemanship.
2. If Prince Tal excelled in horsemanship, he did especially well in fencing.
3. If Prince Tal did especially well in horsemanship, he excelled in fencing.
4. If Prince Tal excelled in fencing, he did especially well in chivalry.
5. If Prince Tal did especially well in chivalry, he excelled in horsemanship.

(Hints on page 263)
See answer on page 358.

Battles With Dragons

For noblemen to do battle with dragons was considered the ultimate adventure. Sir Aard, Sir Bolbo, and Sir Delfo have each had a successful encounter with one or two dragons. Among the three noblemen, they encountered a total of five dragons: Biter, Black Heart, Dante, Flame Thrower, and Old Smoky. No dragon was encountered by more than one nobleman. Consider the following statements:

1. If Sir Aard encountered Dante, then Sir Delfo did not encounter Flame Thrower.
2. If Sir Aard did not encounter both Biter and Black Heart, then Sir Bolbo encountered Flame Thrower and Sir Delfo encountered Old Smoky.
3. If Sir Delfo encountered Black Heart, then Sir Aard encountered Dante.
4. If Sir Bolbo did not encounter both Dante and Biter, then Sir Delfo encountered Flame Thrower and Sir Aard encountered Black Heart.
5. Flame Thrower and Dante were not encountered by the same nobleman.
6. If Sir Delfo did not encounter both Black Heart and Flame Thrower, then Sir Aard encountered Biter and Sir Bolbo encountered Old Smoky.

Which noblemen encountered which dragons?

(Hints on page 263)
See answer on pages 358–359.

Who Tilted With Whom?

It was the custom for noblemen to practice tilting when there were no pressing adventures. One afternoon, Sir Aard, Sir Bolbo, Sir Delfo, Sir Gath, Sir Keln, and Prince Tal paired off for this exercise into three matches. Consider the following statements:

1. If either Prince Tal or Sir Aard tilted with Sir Keln, then Sir Bolbo tilted with Sir Gath.
2. If Sir Gath tilted with Prince Tal, then Sir Keln tilted with Sir Delfo.
3. If Prince Tal tilted with Sir Delfo, Sir Keln tilted with Sir Gath.
4. If Sir Gath tilted with Sir Bolbo, Sir Delfo tilted with Prince Tal.
5. If Prince Tal tilted with Sir Aard, then Sir Bolbo tilted with Sir Gath.
6. If Sir Gath tilted with Sir Keln, then Prince Tal tilted with Sir Aard.
7. If Prince Tal tilted with Sir Bolbo, then Sir Keln tilted with Sir Aard.

Who tilted with whom?

(Hints on pages 263–264)
See answer on pages 359–360.

Encounter With the Fearsome Beast

The Fearsome Beast, whose head was like that of a lion and whose hair was black and shaggy, was said to be as big as an elephant and faster than a deer. Few had ever seen it, but the beast reportedly had been observed in a remote area of the kingdom. Prince Tal and his three comrades, Sir Aard, Sir Bolbo, and Sir Delfo, were determined to confront the elusive monster. To this end, they set out in the search.

They encountered the monster, but at the first sight of the beast, their horses reared, threw two of the riders, and bolted for distant parts. One of the two thrown noblemen quickly climbed a tree, while the other was left prostrate on the ground, momentarily stunned. The Fearsome Beast jumped over the fallen nobleman and quickly departed.

From the following statements determine which nobleman was prostrate on the ground, which one climbed a tree, and which two were not unhorsed.

1. If Sir Bolbo climbed a tree, then Sir Delfo and Prince Tal were not thrown.
2. If Sir Delfo climbed a tree, then Sir Aard and Prince Tal were not thrown.
3. If Sir Aard was prostrate on the ground, then Prince Tal and Sir Bolbo were not thrown.
4. If Sir Aard was not thrown, then Sir Bolbo was not thrown, and Sir Delfo was prostrate on the ground.
5. If Prince Tal did not climb a tree, then either Sir Bolbo or Sir Delfo climbed a tree.
6. If Sir Bolbo was prostrate on the ground, then Prince Tal and Sir Delfo were not thrown.

(Hints on page 264)
See answer on pages 360–361.

Strange Creatures

Strange creatures are occasionally seen in the kingdom and different kinds have been seen by different inhabitants. Given the following statements, can you determine which of Prince Tal and his four fellow noblemen saw which kind of creature? (No two saw the same kind of creature.)

1. If Sir Bolbo saw a monoceros, then Sir Delfo saw a satyr.
2. If Sir Bolbo saw a bonnacon, then Prince Tal saw a monoceros.
3. If Sir Keln did not see a leucrota, then Sir Aard saw a satyr.
4. If either Sir Bolbo or Sir Aard saw a basilisk, then Sir Delfo did not see a monoceros.
5. If Prince Tal saw a bonnacon, then Sir Aard saw a basilisk.
6. If Prince Tal saw a monoceros, then Sir Delfo saw a leucrota.
7. If Sir Delfo did not see a basilisk, then he saw a monoceros.
8. If Sir Delfo did not see a satyr, then Sir Bolbo did not see a leucrota.

(Hints on page 264)
See answer on pages 361–362.

Prince Tal and the Enchantress

As a knight-errant, Prince Tal traveled the kingdom in search of adventure. He frequently relied on hospitality in the castles, abbeys, and hermitages along his way. One evening he was invited into a strange castle that, unknown to Prince Tal, was inhabited by an enchantress who cast a sleeping spell on him. When Prince Tal awoke, he found himself in the castle dungeon, where he was held for ransom.

After he was ultimately released, Prince Tal, still suffering some aftereffects of the sleep-inducing spell, had difficulty recalling how long he had been imprisoned, or how he had been freed. He could not remember whether his fellow noblemen had stormed the castle and released him, whether he had broken the dungeon door and escaped, whether the dungeon keeper (who was a loyal subject of the king) had left the dungeon door open for him, or whether the ransom had been paid.

Based on the following statements, can you clarify the outcome of Prince Tal's misadventure?

1. If the noblemen stormed the castle or the dungeon keeper left the door open, then Prince Tal was imprisoned for one day or three days.

2. If Prince Tal's imprisonment was for one day or one week, then he broke the dungeon door or the noblemen stormed the castle.

3. If Prince Tal's imprisonment was neither for three days nor for one week, then the dungeon keeper didn't leave the door open nor was the ransom paid.

4. If he broke the dungeon door or the ransom was paid, then Prince Tal was imprisoned for one week or two weeks.

5. If he did not break the door and the ransom was not paid, then Prince Tal was imprisoned for three days or the dungeon keeper left the door open.

6. If Prince Tal's imprisonment was not for one day nor two weeks, then he didn't break the dungeon door and the castle wasn't stormed.

7. If Prince Tal's imprisonment was for three days or two weeks, then the dungeon keeper left the door open or the ransom was paid.

(Hints on pages 264–265)
See answer on pages 362–363.

To the Rescue

Rescuing fair damsels in distress was an important responsibility of Prince Tal and his fellow noblemen. A total of six maidens were rescued by five noblemen. Based on the following statements, determine which damsels were rescued by which noblemen.

1. If Sir Keln rescued either Maid Marion or Maid Mary, then Sir Aard rescued either Maid Muriel or Maid Marie.

2. If Prince Tal rescued either Maid Matilda or Maid Marie, then Sir Bolbo rescued either Maid Mary or Maid Marion.

3. If Prince Tal rescued either Maid Mary or Maid Morgana, then Sir Bolbo rescued either Maid Matilda or Maid Marion.

4. If Sir Bolbo rescued either Maid Mary or Maid Marie, then Sir Keln rescued either Maid Matilda or Maid Morgana.

5. If Sir Aard rescued either Maid Muriel or Maid Marie, then Prince Tal rescued either Maid Mary or Maid Morgana.

6. If Sir Keln did not rescue either Maid Marion or Maid Mary, then Sir Aard rescued Maid Marion, unless he rescued Maid Muriel.

7. If Sir Bolbo rescued either Maid Marion or Maid Matilda, then Sir Delfo rescued both Maid Muriel and Maid Marie.

8. If Sir Aard did not rescue Maid Marie, then Prince Tal rescued Maid Marion, unless he rescued both Maid Matilda and Maid Muriel.

(Hints on page 265)
See answer on pages 363–364.

Prince Tal's Encounters With Four Dragons

Among the dragons that Prince Tal has encountered, four were especially ferocious and challenging: Dante breathed plumes of flame 50 feet long (or so it seemed), Quicksilver could fly as fast as sound (or so it seemed), Vesuvius was as large as a mountain (or so it appeared), and Meduso was capable of turning to stone anyone who looked him directly in the eye (Prince Tal fought this dragon using his peripheral vision).

None of the confrontations with these four dragons was conclusive. In one case, Prince Tal's fellow noblemen arrived in time to save him. In another case, just before being overwhelmed, Prince Tal feigned death until the dragon departed. At another time, the dragon quit after developing an uncontrollable coughing fit from inhaling too much smoke (a common affliction among dragons). In another case, Prince Tal forgot his shield and had to leave without actually fighting.

From the following statements, determine the order in which Prince Tal encountered the four dragons, and what the outcome was in each case.

1. If Vesuvius was not the second or third dragon encountered, then Prince Tal's fellow noblemen arrived in time to save him during this confrontation.

2. If the first encounter was with the dragon Dante, then the fourth encounter was with the dragon Meduso.

3. If Prince Tal did not feign death during the fourth encounter, then the fourth confrontation was not with the dragon Dante.

4. If Prince Tal's fellow noblemen arrived in time to save him during the first encounter, then the first encounter was with the dragon Quicksilver.

5. If the second encounter was with the dragon Dante, then Prince Tal's fellow noblemen arrived in time to save him.

6. If Prince Tal feigned death in his confrontation with the dragon Meduso, then it happened during the third encounter.

7. If Prince Tal's second confrontation was with Quicksilver or Vesuvius, then the dragon suffered a coughing fit during this encounter.

8. Prince Tal did not forget his shield during the first and third encounters, unless he feigned death during the second encounter.

(Hints on page 265)
See answer on pages 364–365.

Dragons of Lidd and Wonk

There are few dragons in the kingdom of Lidd, and they have been put on the endangered species list.

Dragons are of two types. Some have reasoned that devouring domestic animals and their owners is, in the long run, not healthy for dragons. They are known as rationals. Some dragons, on the other hand, are reluctant to give up their traditional ways, nor do they fear humans. They are known as predators. The King has decreed that rational dragons shall be protected. Knights caught slaying a rational dragon are dealt with severely.

In addition to being rationals or predators, dragons in Lidd are of two different colors related to their veracity. Gray rational dragons always tell the truth; red rationals always lie. Red predators always tell the truth; gray predators always lie.

There is something appealing to a dragon about being in a land in which knights are not constantly trying to build their reputations by slaying them. It was not surprising, therefore, that the blue dragons from the adjacent land of Wonk began appearing in the kingdom of Lidd. Blue dragons are rationals or predators, but they all lie.

To tell if a dragon is protected, it would help to know its color. However, there is an affliction endemic to humans in Lidd: they are colorblind. To them, all dragons look gray.

One Dragon

A dragon is approached by a knight looking for adventure. The dragon, asked his color and type, responds as follows:

Dragon: I am either blue or gray.

What type is the dragon?

(Hints on page 266)
See answer on page 365.

Two Dragons

Two armed knights confront two dragons, each of which is asked his color and type. Their answers follow:

A. 1. I am from Wonk.
   2. B and I are both predators.
B 1. A is not from Wonk, but I am.
   2. I am a rational.

What color and type are each dragon?

(Hints on page 266)
See answer on page 366.

Three Dragons

A knight in armor cautiously approaches three dragons, who offer the following information:

    A. 1. C is from Wonk.

          2. I am not a red predator.

    B. 1. A is from Wonk.

          2. A and C are both rationals.

    C. 1. B is from Wonk.

          2. B is a predator.

What are the color and type of each dragon?

(Hints on page 266)
See answer on page 366.

Two Are From Wonk

A knight confronts three dragons, exactly two of which are known to be blue dragons from Wonk, and asks each his color and type. Their answers follow:

    A. 1. B is from Wonk.

          2. I am a rational.

    B. 1. C is from Wonk.

          2. I am a rational.

    C.   I am a rational.

What color and type are each dragon?

(Hints on page 266)
See answer on page 367.

One Dragon From Wonk

Three dragons, exactly one of which is blue, give the following information:

A. 1. C is a gray rational.
   2. I am a gray rational.
B. 1. A is a predator.
   2. A is blue.
   3. I am a rational.
C. 1. A is not gray.
   2. B is from Wonk.

What color and type are each dragon?

(Hints on page 266)
See answer on page 367.

At Least One From Wonk

The knights of Lidd are seeing more blue dragons than usual. Four knights encounter four dragons, at least one of which is blue, and ask about their colors and types. The dragons' statements follow:

A. 1. I am either a gray predator or a red rational.
   2. B is red.
B. 1. A and I are both rationals.
   2. C is a red predator.
   3. I am gray.
C. 1. I am not gray.
   2. I am a rational.
   3. B is a predator.
D: 1. C and I are both predators.
   2. I am red.
   3. A and B are both blue.

What are the color and type of each dragon?

(Hints on page 266)
See answer on page 368.

Three Dragons Again

A lone knight nervously approaches three dragons, at least one of which is from Wonk. They volunteer the following information:

A. 1. I am either red or gray.
   2. C and I are the same color.
B. 1. A is not red.
   2. C is blue.
C. 1. A's statements are false.
   2. B is not a rational.

What color and type are each dragon?

(Hints on page 266)
See answer on pages 368–369.

How Many Are Protected?

A knight looking for a dragon to slay confronts three. He asks each about his color and type. Their answers follow:

A. 1. I am gray.
   2. We three are protected by the King's decree.
   3. C is red.
B. 1. I am not protected by the King's decree.
   2. C is gray.
C. 1. A and I are not the same type.
   2. A is red.
   3. B is a rational.

What color and type are each dragon?

(Hints on page 266)
See answer on page 369.

Who Speaks for Whom?

Three dragons respond to a very wary knight as follows:

A. 1. If asked, B would claim that C is a predator.
   2. I am gray.
   3. B is a rational.
B. 1. If asked, C would claim that A is a rational.
   2. C is red.
C. 1. If asked, A would claim that B is red.
   2. A is gray.

What color and type are each dragon?

(Hints on page 267)
See answer on page 370.

The Trials of Xanthius

Among the ancient Greeks, the people of Athens led all others in their mental acuity. The gods created a series of trials to test the Athenians' reasoning ability, as well as their courage (and perhaps to amuse themselves). As an incentive, they provided a fabulous treasure to be won by whoever was successful in passing every trial.

The trials involved following a path through a dense forest, across a large savanna, and up a tall mountain, with choices to be made at seven points. There was to be no turning back once the challenge was accepted, and no retracing steps at any time. Dire consequences awaited any challenger who made an incorrect judgment.

No citizen of Athens desired to accept the risk until Xanthius, a young student of Socrates, accepted the challenge.

The First Trial

Hardly had Xanthius entered the forest on the designated path, when it branched into two. He was told that this was the first trial and that one way led to the second trial, while the other led near the domain of a giant serpent, for which he would undoubtedly become a meal. A sign at each path gave instruction.

However, Xanthius was informed that at least one of the signs was false. The signs read as follows:

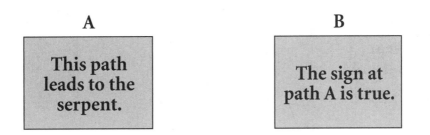

A

This path leads to the serpent.

B

The sign at path A is true.

Which path is the one Xanthius should follow?

(Hints on page 267)
See answer on page 371.

The Second Trial

Xanthius chose the correct path and, after proceeding into the forest for some time, he came to a branching of the path into three paths. He was informed that one path led to the third trial, while the other two led deep into the forest and eventually in large circles, to which there was no end. Xanthius was told that of the signs at the three paths, two were true and one was false. The signs read as follows:

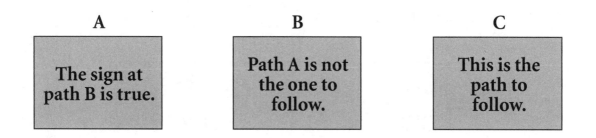

A

The sign at path B is true.

B

Path A is not the one to follow.

C

This is the path to follow.

Which path is the one to follow?

(Hints on page 267)
See answer on page 371.

The Third Trial

Again, Xanthius chose correctly and proceeded further into the forest before the path branched into three more paths. His information this time was that one path led to the fourth trial. The other two led over large hidden pits that could not be avoided, and from which escape would be impossible. Xanthius was told that one of the signs at the three paths was false, and two were true. They read as follows:

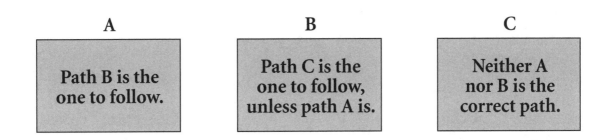

A	B	C
Path B is the one to follow.	Path C is the one to follow, unless path A is.	Neither A nor B is the correct path.

Which path is the one to follow?

(Hints on page 267)
See answer on page 372.

The Fourth Trial

Xanthius, having made the correct judgment, followed the path until he came to a deep ravine over which were three bridges. He was told that only one of these could carry him over the ravine. The other two would crumble when he was halfway across, dropping him on the jagged rocks far below. He was informed that two of the three signs at the three bridges were false, and one was true. The three signs follow:

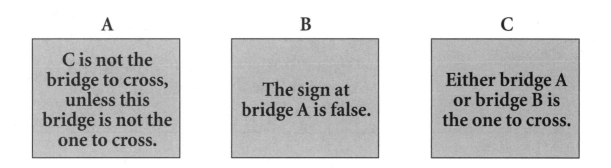

A	B	C
C is not the bridge to cross, unless this bridge is not the one to cross.	The sign at bridge A is false.	Either bridge A or bridge B is the one to cross.

Which is the correct bridge to cross?

(Hints on page 267)
See answer on pages 372–373.

The Fifth Trial

A large open savanna greeted Xanthius as he left the forest after selecting the correct bridge. At this point, the path Xanthius was following branched into four paths. He was informed that a pride of fierce lions lived and hunted in the immediate area. They napped in the afternoon, and the only chance was to proceed very quietly, so as not to awaken them. One of the four paths would provide that opportunity. The other three were liberally strewn with twigs and dry leaves, to the extent that exiting the area without alerting the lions would be impossible. Of the four signs at the four paths, he was told that at least two were false. The signs follow:

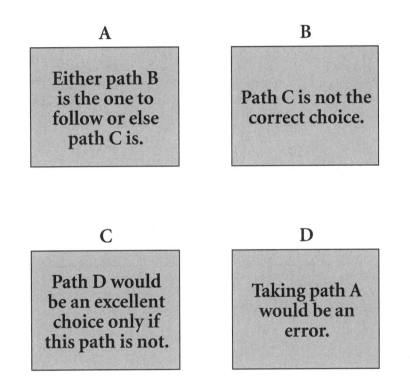

A

Either path B is the one to follow or else path C is.

B

Path C is not the correct choice.

C

Path D would be an excellent choice only if this path is not.

D

Taking path A would be an error.

Which path should be followed?

(Hints on page 268)
See answer on page 373.

The Sixth Trial

After successfully selecting the path and exiting the area, Xanthius came upon a wide area with a profusion of many kinds of fragrant flowers, and a branching of his path into five paths. He was informed that one variety of flower that was prevalent in the area caused anyone who chanced to breathe its perfume to fall immediately into a permanent sleep. Only one of the five paths would circumvent these flowers. Xanthius was informed that of the instructional signs at the five paths, at least three were false. The signs follow:

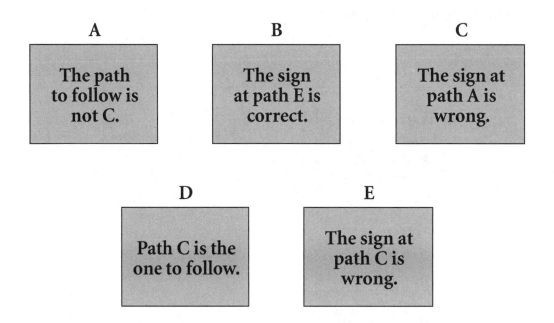

A

The path to follow is not C.

B

The sign at path E is correct.

C

The sign at path A is wrong.

D

Path C is the one to follow.

E

The sign at path C is wrong.

Only one path is correct. Which one is it?

(Hints on page 268)
See answer on page 374.

The Final Trial

As a true disciple of Socrates, Xanthius made correct evaluative judgments through the first six trials. He found the seventh trial at the foot of a high mountain. Seven paths led high up on the face of the mountain and disappeared in the clouds. Xanthius was told that one of the paths led to a cave containing the treasure, while the other six paths climbed ever more steeply until the climber could only struggle in place until overcome by exhaustion. Of the seven signs placed at the paths, he was informed that four were true and three were false. The signs follow:

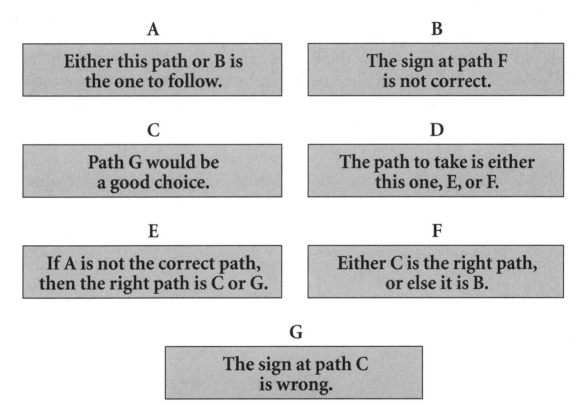

A

Either this path or B is the one to follow.

B

The sign at path F is not correct.

C

Path G would be a good choice.

D

The path to take is either this one, E, or F.

E

If A is not the correct path, then the right path is C or G.

F

Either C is the right path, or else it is B.

G

The sign at path C is wrong.

Xanthius, after lengthy deliberation, selected the correct path and followed it to a cave high on the mountain, where he found the fabulous treasure that he had earned. Which path did he take?

(Hints on page 268)
See answer on page 375.

Problems From the Addled Arithmetician

Letters and numbers—to the Addled Arithmetician they are much the same thing. At least it appears so, as he has them reversed.

In this section you will find addition, subtraction, and multiplication problems that he has prepared. Your challenge is to replace the letters with the correct digit. (A zero never appears as the leftmost digit of a number.)

As if mixing digits with letters was not confusing enough, the Addled Arithmetician has forgotten that each letter should represent the same digit wherever it occurs in a puzzle.

In these puzzles, each letter represents the same digit wherever it occurs in a given mathematical problem (above the line). Wherever a letter appears in the answer to the problem (below the line) it represents a digit that is one more than or one less than the digit represented by the same letter above the line. For example, if B equals 4 above the line, all B's below the line will be equal to 3 or all B's below the line will be equal to 5.

Addition, Six Digits

Each letter above the line represents a digit that has a difference of one from the digit represented by the same letter below the line.

The digits are 0, 1, 2, 3, 4, and 5.

```
    A   F   C   E
+   A   D   D   B
    B   F   B   F
```

What digit or digits does each letter represent?

(Hints on page 268)
See answer on page 376.

Subtraction, Six Digits

Each letter above the line represents a digit that has a difference of one from the digit represented by the same letter below the line.

The digits are 0, 1, 2, 3, 4, and 5.

```
    F   B   A   C   B
-   D   A   F   E   B
        C   F   D   E
```

What digit or digits does each letter represent?

(Hints on page 268)
See answer on page 377.

Addition, Seven Digits

Each letter above the line in this puzzle represents a digit that has a difference of one from the digit represented by the same letter below the line.

The digits are 0, 1, 2, 3, 4, 5, and 6.

```
      D   G   A   E   C
  +   E   F   B   A   C
  ─────────────────────
  C   F   G   D   G   F
```

What digit or digits does each letter represent?

(Hints on page 268)
See answer on page 378.

Addition, Seven Digits Again

Each letter above the line represents a digit that has a difference of one from the digit represented by the same letter below the line.

The digits are: 0, 1, 2, 3, 4, 8, and 9.

```
      E   D   B   D   D
      E   D   B   D   D
  +   E   D   B   D   D
  ─────────────────────
  C   F   A   B   D   E
```

What digit or digits does each letter represent?

(Hints on page 269)
See answer on page 379.

234

Multiplication, Six Digits

Each letter in the multiplication problem (above the top line) represents a digit that has a difference of one from the digit represented by the same letter in the answer to the problem (below the top line).

The digits are 0, 1, 2, 3, 4, and 5.

```
              C    A    E
      ×       E    C    E
              E    C    A
         D    F    B
    E    C    A
    E    B    B    B    A
```

What digit or digits does each letter represent?

(Hints on page 269)
See answer on page 380.

Subtraction, Seven Digits

Each letter above the line represents a digit that has a difference of one from the digit represented by the same letter below the line.

The digits are 0, 1, 2, 3, 4, 5, and 6.

```
    B    D    C    A    B    F    B
  − E    E    B    G    E    A    E
         G    E    E    F    C    F
```

What digit or digits does each letter represent?

(Hints on page 269)
See answer on page 381.

Addition, Seven Digits Once Again

Each letter above the line represents a digit that has a difference of one from the digit represented by the same letter below the line.

The digits are 0, 1, 2, 3, 4, 5, and 6.

```
            F   C   C
        F   A   C   C
    B   A   E   C   A
+ A D   C   F   A   A
  A C   B   A   C   A
```

What digit or digits does each letter represent?

(Hints on page 269)
See answer on page 382.

Multiplication, Seven Digits

Each letter in the problem (above the top line) represents a digit that has a difference of one from the digit represented by the same letter in the answer (below the top line).

The digits are 0, 2, 3, 5, 6, 8, and 9.

```
        D   E   B
    ×       D   G
        E   E   E
    B   F   G
    A   E   C   E
```

What digit or digits does each letter represent?

(Hints on page 269)
See answer on page 383.

What's in a Name?

A rose by any other name would smell as sweet. In these puzzles, the name's the thing: characters in a play, man's best friends, author's pseudonyms, steeds, or other kinds of names. Your challenge is to correctly connect the names of individuals with other names.

Four Horses

Alice, Danielle, Harriet, and Mary each own a horse and enjoy riding together. One day they decided to trade horses for the afternoon. Each woman rode a horse owned by one of the others, and no two women traded horses. From the statements below, what is the name of each friend's horse (one is Champ), and what is the name of the horse each rode?

1. Harriet rode the horse owned by Danielle.
2. Mary's horse was ridden by the owner of the horse named Charger.
3. The horse named El Cid was ridden by the owner of the horse ridden by Alice.
4. The horse named Charger was ridden by the owner of the horse ridden by Harriet.
5. The horse named Silver was ridden by the owner of the horse named El Cid.

(Hints on page 270)
See answer on page 384.

Five Thespians

Five local actors presented a murder mystery play in the Midville theater. The five actors were Raymond, Rodney, Roland, Ronald, and Rupert. The five characters in the play were, interestingly enough, all namesakes of the actors, although no actor performed the role of his namesake. The parts in the play were magistrate, murderer, sheriff, victim, and witness. Based on the following, what was each actor's part and what was the name of the character he played?

1. The character played by Raymond was the namesake of the actor who played the murderer.
2. The namesake of the actor who played the magistrate was the character that was the murderer.
3. The character that was the sheriff was played by the actor whose namesake was the character played by Rupert.
4. The character played by Roland was the namesake of the actor who played the witness.
5. Roland did not play the victim, murderer, or sheriff.
6. The character played by Ronald was the namesake of the actor who played the magistrate.
7. The character that was the victim was played by the actor whose namesake was the character played by Rodney.
8. The namesake of the actor who played the murderer was the character that was the victim.

(Hints on page 270)
See answer on pages 384–385.

Five Authors

Authors James Blackledge, Sarah Hastings, John Montague, Milton Quincy, and Florence Williams met at a convention. In a casual conversation, they were surprised to discover that each writes using a pseudonym that is the surname of one of the others. Further, no two writers use the same pseudonym. Based on the following statements, what pseudonym does each use and what is the category of book that each author writes?

1. The one who writes historical novels, who is not Sarah, uses as a pseudonym the surname of the author of mystery novels.
2. John's surname is used as the pseudonym of the author of mystery novels.
3. The one who writes mystery novels had one of his books on a bestseller list.
4. Milton, who writes general fiction, uses the surname of the author of biographies as his pseudonym.
5. Blackledge is the pseudonym of the writer whose surname is used as the pseudonym of the author of travel books.
6. The surname of the author of historical novels is used as the pseudonym of the author of travel books, who considers that the research involved is his favorite recreation.

(Hints on page 270)
See answer on pages 385–386.

St. Bernards and Dalmatians

Four friends, Sam, Sidney, Simon, and Smitty, enjoy dogs, and each has a St. Bernard and a Dalmatian. Each friend has named his two dogs after two of the other three friends. There are no duplicate names among the four St. Bernards and no duplicate names among the four Dalmatians. Based on the following statements, what are the names of each owner's dogs?

1. Simon's St. Bernard is the namesake of the owner of the Dalmatian named Sidney.
2. Smitty's Dalmatian is the namesake of the owner of which Sam's St. Bernard is the namesake.
3. The Dalmatian named Sam is owned by the owner of which Smitty's St. Bernard is the namesake.
4. Sam's Dalmatian is the namesake of the owner of the St. Bernard named Simon.
5. Sidney's Dalmatian is the namesake of the owner of the St. Bernard named Smitty.

(Hints on page 271)
See answer on pages 386–387.

Islanders' Boats

Of four friends, O'Boyle, O'Brien, O'Bradovich, and O'Byrne, each has one daughter, spends considerable time on the water, and has both a sailboat and a fishing boat. Each friend has named his two boats after two different daughters of the other three friends. There are no duplicate names among the four sailboats and no duplicate names among the four fishing boats. Based on the following statements, who is the daughter of each of the four friends (one daughter is named Odette), and what are the names of each owner's boats?

1. O'Byrne's fishing boat is named after the owner's daughter after which O'Boyle's sailboat is named.
2. Neither Olivia O'Boyle nor Ophelia O'Byrne enjoy boating.
3. O'Byrne's sailboat is named for the daughter of the owner of the fishing boat named *Olivia*.
4. O'Brien's fishing boat, which is not named *Olga*, is named after the daughter of the owner of the sailboat named *Ophelia*.
5. O'Bradovich's fishing boat is not named *Ophelia*, nor is his sailboat named *Olivia*.

(Hints on page 271)
See answer on pages 387–388.

Writers of Classic Books

Six couples, the Brontës, the Conrads, the Dickenses, the Forsters, the Kafkas, and the Tolstoys, belong to a classics book club. Recently, they exchanged gifts of books. Each couple gave a book to one of the other couples. Each couple is the namesake of the author of one of the books given; no two couples gave a book by the same author; and no couple gave or received a book by an author of which they were the namesakes. The following statements apply:

1. The Conrads did not give or receive a book by Brontë, Forster, or Tolstoy.
2. The namesakes of the author of the book given by the Dickenses gave a book by Dickens to the Tolstoys.
3. The book by Forster was received by the namesakes of the author of the book that was given to the couple who gave the book by Dickens to the namesakes of the author of the book received by the Forsters.
4. The Brontës received a book by Conrad from the namesakes of the author of the book given by the Conrads.
5. The namesakes of the author of the book received by the Dickenses gave a book by Forster to the namesakes of the author of the book given by the namesakes of the author of the book given by the Kafkas.

Which couples gave books by which authors, and who received them?

(Hints on page 271)
See answer on pages 388–389.

Land, Valley, and Hill Liars

Remember that strange land you were told all about on page 201, the Land of Liars? Just in case: In the Land of Liars, there are those who speak the truth only in the morning and lie in the afternoon. They are called Amtrus. There are also those who speak the truth only in the afternoon and lie in the morning. They are known as Pemtrus.

If it were only that simple. You will also find some do not fit the traditional Land of Liars veracity patterns. More on them later.

Two Inhabitants

Two inhabitants make the statements below. One is an Amtru and one is a Pemtru.

A. It is afternoon.
B. I am a Pemtru.

Is it morning or afternoon, which is the Amtru, and which is the Pemtru?

(Hints on page 272)
See answer on pages 389–390.

Is A's Statement True?

Of the three who make the following statements, two are Pemtrus and one is an Amtru.

A. B is a Pemtru.
B. A's statement is true.
C. A's statement is false.

Is it morning or afternoon, and to which group does each inhabitant belong?

(Hints on page 272)
See answer on page 390.

Three Inhabitants

Two Pemtrus and an Amtru make the statements below:

A. B is a Pemtru.
B. C is a Pemtru.
C. A is the Amtru.

Is it morning or afternoon, which is the Amtru, and which are the Pemtrus?

(Hints on page 272)
See answer on pages 390–391.

Four Inhabitants

Four inhabitants make the following statements. They are two Amtrus and two Pemtrus.

A. B is an Amtru.
B. C is a Pemtru.
C. A and D are from different groups.
D. A and B are from the same group.

Is it morning or afternoon, and to which group does each of the four inhabitants belong?

(Hints on page 272)
See answer on page 391.

Five Inhabitants

Five inhabitants are asked to which group each belongs. They are three Amtrus and two Pemtrus. They respond:

A. I am a Pemtru or it is morning.
B. I am an Amtru or it is afternoon.
C. D and E belong to the same group.
D. A is an Amtru.
E. B is a Pemtru.

Is it morning or afternoon, which ones are Amtrus, and which ones are Pemtrus?

(Hints on page 273)
See answer on page 392.

Valley Liars

In the Land of Liars, there is a *valley* in which the inhabitants have their own lying patterns. The Amtrus speak the truth in the morning and lie in the afternoon, except in statements in which they directly refer to another individual in the same group by name (letter designation), they lie in the morning and speak the truth in the afternoon. The Pemtrus speak the truth in the afternoon and lie in the morning, except that in statements in which they directly refer to another in the same group by name, they lie in the afternoon and speak the truth in the morning.

Four Valley Inhabitants

Four valley inhabitants, who are represented equally by both groups, are asked to which group each belongs. They make the statements below, although the fourth valley inhabitant, D, chooses to remain silent.

- A. D and I belong to the same group.
- B. A and I belong to the same group.
- C. B is a Pemtru.

Is it morning or afternoon, and what group is represented by each of the four inhabitants?

(Hints on page 273)
See answer on pages 392–393.

Three Valley Inhabitants

Three valley inhabitants asked their groups respond as follows:

A. C and I are both Pemtrus.
B. C and I are not both Amtrus.
C. If you were to ask A about this guy [pointing to B] and A used this guy's name, A would say that this guy is an Amtru.

Is it morning or afternoon, and what group is represented by each of the three speakers?

(Hints on page 273)
See answer on pages 393–394.

Liars on the Hill

On a small isolated *hill* in the Land of Liars live a few who are obstinate and who pride themselves on being different. They are neither Amtrus or Pemtrus. In making statements when in the company of other inhabitants of the Land of Liars, a hill inhabitant will speak the truth only if none of the others speak the truth, and will lie if any of the others speak the truth.

Does C Live on the Hill?

It is afternoon. Of the four speakers, exactly one is a hill inhabitant. C claims he is the one. Their statements follow:

A. B is an Amtru.
B. C is a Pemtru.
C. I live on the hill.
D. A is a Pemtru.

Which speaker is the hill inhabitant and what are the other three?

(Hints on page 273)
See answer on page 394.

One From the Hill

Four from the Land of Liars, including exactly one hill inhabitant, make the following statements:

A. Either D is an Amtru or he lives on the hill.
B. C is either an Amtru or a Pemtru.
C. I live on the hill or B lives on the hill.
D. C's statement is true or C is a Pemtru.

Is it morning or afternoon, which one is the hill inhabitant, and what are the other three speakers?

(Hints on page 273)
See answer on page 395.

HINTS

PART III–False Logic Puzzles

SOCRATES LENDS A HAND

Diagrams will be helpful in solving these puzzles. List the speakers on one axis and the statement numbers on the other, as below.

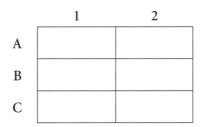

Assume that each speaker in turn affords the correct solution, and mark T or F as you form conclusions.

Who Owns the Mule?   Consider that each farmer made one true and one false statement. Review A's statements. Could A be the owner?

Theft of Homer's Writings   Consider that each suspect made one true and two false statements. Review A's statements assuming that B is guilty. Could B be guilty?

Who Left the Cell Door Open?   Consider that among the four guards, three of their statements are true, and five of their statements are false. If A is guilty, how many true statements are there?

A Secret Observer   Consider that all statements are true except any mentioning the secret observer. Consider A's and B's statements. Could A be the observer?

Theft From the Statue of Athena   Consider that one suspect made three true statements, and one suspect made three false statements. Which one of the four suspects made three true statements?

Who Should Lead the Victory Parade?   Consider that one soldier made one false statement, one made two false statements, and one made three false statements. Assume that A should lead the parade. If so, is this consistent with the statements made by the three speakers?

Socrates Plans a Trip   Consider that the disciple selected made either three true or three false statements. Of the other two, one made two true statements and one false statement, and one made one true statement and two false statements. Consider C's statements. Could C be the disciple selected?

Who Should Repair the Statue?   Consider that each of the craftsmen made the same number of true statements. Assume that A is the most qualified. If so, do all four have the same number of true statements?

Who Won the Discus Throw?   Consider that no two made the same number of true statements. Can you determine which one made three true statements?

The Food Produce Thief   Consider that the one who delivered the milk made three true statements; the one who delivered the cheese made two true statements; the one who delivered the honey made one true statement; and the one who delivered the bread and the one who delivered the nuts each made no true statements. What can you determine from A's and D's first statements?

Theft at the Open Market   Consider that since none of the suspects is completely truthful, one made three true statements, one made two true statements, one made one true statement, and one made no true statements. What can you conclude from A's fourth statement? How about A's second statement?

MORDIN'S MAZE

For each of these puzzles, one of the signs makes a statement about the truthfulness or falseness of the group of signs. In each case, consider the possibility of the sign being true or false. In determining the solution, be sure that the answer is conclusive.

For choices 1 and 2, the following diagram is suggested:

	sign A	sign B
if door A is correct		
if door B is correct		

For choices 3, 4, 5, 6, and 8, add door and sign C to your diagram.

The First Choice   Could sign B be true?

The Second Choice   Could sign A be true?

The Third Choice   Could sign A be false?

The Fourth Choice   Could sign B be false?

The Fifth Choice   Could sign A be true?

The Sixth Choice   Could sign B be true?

The Seventh Choice   The diagram below is suggested:

Consider the implication of sign A being true.

	sign A	sign B	sign C	sign D
if sign A is true				
if sign A is false				

The Eighth Choice   Consider that the sign on door B is true. How about if it is false?

THE ISLE OF AVE

Prepare a diagram such as the following and enter "+" or "−" as you formulate conclusions regarding the group of each speaker:

	Soravian	Noravian	Midravian
A			
B			
C			

Neptune Establishes Communication   Could A be a Soravian? How about a Noravian?

Two Avians   Consider that the two speakers belong to two different groups. Could B's statement be truthful? If not, why not?

Umbrellas to Sell   Consider C's response to A's statement. What does it tell you?

Visit From a Hippogriff   What is wrong with A's first statement? What does it tell you about C's statement?

To Catch an Aspidochelon   Consider that the group or groups represented are unknown. Could C's statement be truthful? What are the possibilities for B?

Is D Neptune Visiting in Disguise?   Again the group or groups represented are unknown. Consider C's second statement and A's second statement. What can we say about C?

A's Statement Is Truthful   A key to this puzzle is that two of the four statements are truthful and two are false. Consider C's statement; is it truthful or false?

A Problem With a Sea Monster   Consider A's third statement. If it is truthful, what does that say about the standards of veracity of the three Avians? Are their statements consistent?

Visitors From the Sea and **Recreational Activities on Ave** contain the additional complication of an Outlier. To be different, an Outlier must make at least two consecutive statements that are both truthful or both false and at least one statement that is false or truthful, not necessarily in that order.

Visitors From the Sea   Prepare a diagram, as below:

	Soravian	Noravian	Midravian	Outlier
A				
B				
C				
D				

We can conclude that A's first statement is truthful. What does that say about A's other three statements?

Recreational Activities on Ave   The following diagram will be helpful:

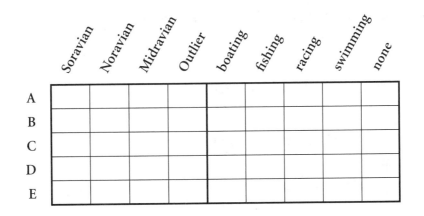

No two of the five Avians have the same number of the four principal activities. Therefore, we can conclude that one enjoys four activities, one enjoys three, one enjoys two, one enjoys one, and one enjoys none of the four activities.

Compare A's first statement and D's second statement. Also compare A's third statement and D's fourth statement. What do these comparisons tell you?

THE VILLAGERS OF FARMWELL

For these puzzles, it is suggested that the reader analyze the statements in each, considering that they are valid until a contradiction appears. Careful review at this point will identify possible invalid statements, and provide a basis for determining the false one.

The Village Fair Construct a diagram, such as below. Mark a plus or minus sign as you confirm or reject a conclusion:

	cow	goat	pig	sheep	daybreak to midmorning	midmorning to midday	midday to midafternoon	midafternoon to sundown
Dor								
Edvo								
Frer								
Har								

Consider statement 1. What showing for the sheep is indicated?

Encounter With the Dragon Meduso Prepare a diagram, such as below:

	blindfold	vision	shield	cave
first				
second				
third				
fourth				

Consider statements 1, 3, 4, and 5. Can you determine which encounter was fourth?

The Dragon Watch   Prepare a diagram, as below:

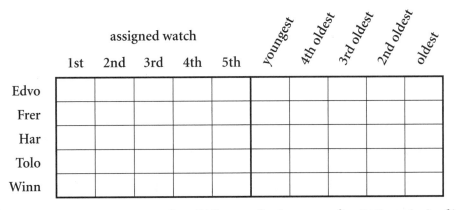

Consider statements 1, 3, and 4. What relative age for Winn is indicated? Is this consistent with statement 2?

New Ponies   Prepare a diagram, such as the following. Enter the requested information as you determine it.

first name	second name	size	color	order of acquisition
Boro				
Jes				
Kover				
Tolo				

Although the order of acquisition is not requested in the solution, it is helpful in analyzing the required information.

From statements 1 and 5, if true, what was Tolo's second name?

Work and Recreation   Two diagrams, such as those following, will be helpful:

	trade	favorite recreation	second-favorite recreation
Dok			
Fram			
Hober			
Winn			
Zett			

trade	favorite recreation
blacksmith	
carpenter	
cobbler	
miller	
weaver	

Consider statements 1, 2, and 6; if true, what are the two possibilities as to the villager who enjoyed storytelling most?

A Giant in the Shire   A composite diagram, such as the one shown here, will be helpful.

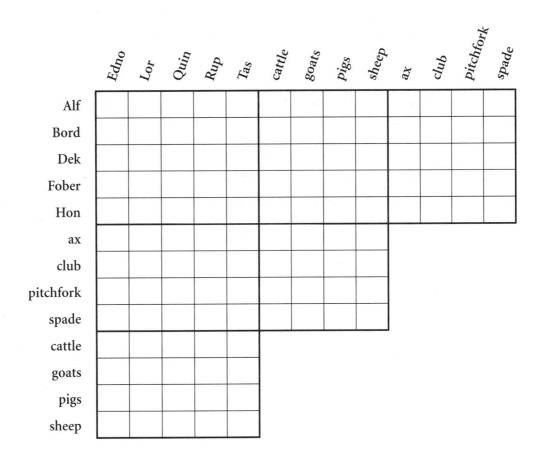

From statement 1, if true, what were the occupations of the two villagers who wielded pitchforks?

Pony Races   For this puzzle, list the riders in each race generally in the order in which they finished and readjust the rankings until there is no conflict.

THE VALLEY LIARS

For each puzzle, prepare a diagram indicating Amtru and Pemtru on one axis and listing each speaker on the other axis. Assume either morning or afternoon and test the consistency of the statements against your assumption. As you test your assumptions, look for contradictions.

A Visitor to the Land of Liars   What does B's second statement tell us about B? How about A?

En Route to the Valley of Liars   What can we conclude from A's second statement? What about B's second statement?

Two Valley Liars   If it is morning, could A's statement be true? What about B's statement?

Two More Valley Liars   Is this puzzle essentially the same as the previous one? If not, why not? Test A's first statement against the possibility of it being afternoon.

Three Valley Liars   Consider B's statement. Could he make such a statement in the morning?

Three Valley Liars Again   Consider A's statement. What are the possibilities for A?

Four Valley Liars   What do we know from B's statement? Consider the possibilities and compare them to D's statement and its possibilities.

Who Is the Impostor?   Consider B's statement. What are the possibilities? Also consider that there are two Amtrus and two Pemtrus.

PART IV–Mystifying Logic Puzzles

Prince Tal's Adventures

Educational Accomplishments   Construct a diagram such as the following:

	chivalry	fencing	horsemanship
excelled			
did well			

Indicate + or − on it as you draw your conclusions. What can you conclude from statements 1 and 3?

Battles with Dragons   A diagram like this is helpful:

	Biter	Black Heart	Dante	Flame Thrower	Ol' Smoky
Sir Aard					
Sir Bolbo					
Sir Delfo					

Consider statements 2 and 4. What do they tell you about which nobleman encountered Flame Thrower?

Who Tilted With Whom?   Prepare a diagram such as the one below:

	Sir Aard	Sir Bolbo	Sir Delfo	Sir Gath	Sir Keln	Prince Tal
Sir Aard						
Sir Bolbo						
Sir Delfo						
Sir Gath						
Sir Keln						
Prince Tal						

Consider statements 1, 3, and 4. What do they tell you about Sir Aard and Sir Keln?

Encounter With the Fearsome Beast   Use a diagram:

	climbed a tree	prostrate on the ground	was not thrown
Sir Aard			
Sir Bolbo			
Sir Delfo			
Prince Tal			

Consider statement 3. If the assumption is valid, what happened to Sir Delfo?

Strange Creatures   Construct a diagram like this:

	basilisk	bonnacon	leucrota	monoceros	satyr
Sir Aard					
Sir Bolbo					
Sir Delfo					
Sir Keln					
Prince Tal					

Start with statement 7. Compare it to 1 and 6.

Prince Tal and the Enchantress   Prepare a diagram such as the following:

	door open	stormed castle	ransom paid	broke door
one day				
three days				
one week				
two weeks				

Start by comparing statements 1 and 2. Attempt to correlate potential lengths of time of imprisonment with different ways of release as you review all seven statements in this puzzle.

To the Rescue   Construct a diagram like this one:

	Marie	Marion	Mary	Matilda	Morgana	Muriel
Sir Aard						
Sir Bolbo						
Sir Delfo						
Sir Keln						
Prince Tal						

This puzzle requires that you group more than two statements to determine whether or not an assumption is valid. Start with statement 1. Follow a pattern by relating to other statements.

Prince Tal's Encounters With Four Dragons   Prepare a diagram such as the following:

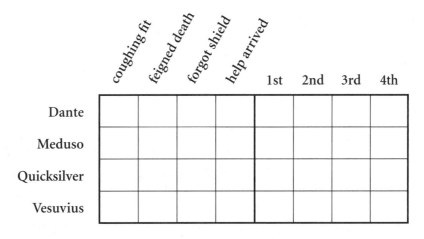

Start with statement 8 and compare it with statements 5, 6, and 7. What can you conclude at this point?

Dragons of Lidd and Wonk

One Dragon   Is the statement true or false? In either case, what type is the dragon?

For these puzzles construct diagrams in this fashion:

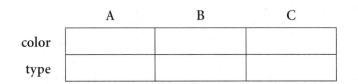

Indicate red, gray, or blue, and rational or predator in the coordinates provided.

Two Dragons   Could A be from Wonk?

Three Dragons   Could A's second statement be false?

Two Are From Wonk   Consider that two of the three dragons are blue. Could A's and B's first statements both be false?

One Dragon From Wonk   Consider that one dragon is blue. Consider A's first and second statements and C's first statement. What can you conclude?

At Least One From Wonk   Consider that at least one dragon is blue. What can be concluded from A's first statement?

Three Dragons Again   If A's first statement is true, what can be concluded about A? What about if A's first statement is false?

How Many Are Protected?   Compare A's second statement, B's first statement, and C's first statement. If A's statement is true, what can you conclude? How about if A's statement is false?

Who Speaks for Whom?   A's second statement and C's second statement are in agreement. If true, A is a gray rational and C is either a gray rational or a red predator. Is this consistent with their statements regarding B and B's statements?

The Trials of Xanthius

The First Trial

Consider that at least one of the signs was false. Since they are in agreement, what can you conclude?

Considering the following puzzles, prepare a diagram, similar to the following, and indicate T or F, considering each path in turn to be the correct one:

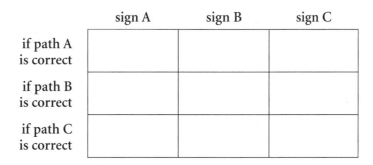

	sign A	sign B	sign C
if path A is correct			
if path B is correct			
if path C is correct			

The Second Trial   Consider that two signs were true and one was false. Could sign C be the path to follow? If not, why?

The Third Trial   Consider that one of the three signs is false and two were true. Could path A be the one to follow? If not, why?

The Fourth Trial   Consider that, in this trial, two of the three signs were false and one was true. Could bridge B be the one to cross over? If it is not, why not?

The Fifth Trial   Consider that at least two of the signs were false. Could path D be the one to follow? If not, why?

The Sixth Trial   Consider that at least three signs were false. Could path A be the one to follow? If not, why?

The Final Trial   Consider that, of the seven signs, four were true and three were false. Could path F be the one to follow? If not, why?

Problems From the Addled Arithmetician

Note that, for these puzzles, each letter represents the same digit wherever it occurs in a given mathematical problem (above the line). Wherever a letter appears in the answer to the problem (below the line) it represents a number that has a difference of one from the digit represented by the same letter above the line. If a given letter represents 4 above the line, it must equal 3 or 5 below the line.

Make a list of the letters then match the digits above and below the line as they become known to you by carefully considering known mathematical facts.

Addition, Six Digits   The digits are 0, 1, 2, 3, 4, and 5. Since the largest available digit is 5, what are the possible digits for A? How about B, in the left-hand column?

Subtraction, Six Digits   The digits are 0, 1, 2, 3, 4, and 5. What is the only possibility for E below the line?

Addition, Seven Digits   The digits are 0, 1, 2, 3, 4, 5, and 6. What is the only possibility for C below the line? What are the possibilities for C above the line? How about F below the line?

Addition, Seven Digits Again   The digits are 0, 1, 2, 3, 4, 8, and 9. There are only two possibilities for D above the line (second column from the right). In examining this consider the possibilities for D below the line.

Multiplication, Six Digits   The digits are 0, 1, 2, 3, 4, and 5. What are the possibilities for E above the line? In considering this think about E times a three-digit number.

Subtraction, Seven Digits   The digits are 0, 1, 2, 3, 4, 5, and 6. In the leftmost column in the problem, what can you say about the relationship between B and E? Consider the same letters in the rightmost column.

Addition, Seven Digits Once Again   The digits are 0, 1, 2, 3, 4, 5, and 6. Consider that in the leftmost column A is found both above and below the line. What does that tell you about the addition of B and D in the adjacent column? What are the two possibilities for C below the line?

Multiplication, Seven Digits   The digits are 0, 2, 3, 5, 6, 8, and 9. There is no digit 1 in the puzzle. Therefore, what can you conclude about 0 above and below the line?

What's in a Name?

Characters and their namesakes can create confusion and require careful attention to each statement to reach correct solutions.

These puzzles are different from the others in the book in that correct interpretation of the statements themselves can be challenging. Careful attention must be paid to all of the possibilities within each statement. Set out the pertinent data, including possibilities, in tabular form. Incorrect considerations can then be eliminated when they are revealed as such.

Four Horses Set up a diagram like this. As you form conclusions, insert the names of the horses.

	Alice	Danielle	Harriet	Mary
horse owned				
horse rode				

Consider statements 1, 2, and 4. Who owned Charger?

Five Thespians Construct a diagram. Indicate plus or minus as you form each conclusion. Insert the names of the characters in the right-hand column.

Consider statements 4 and 5. What role did Roland play?

	magistrate	murderer	sheriff	victim	witness	character name
Raymond						
Rodney						
Roland						
Ronald						
Rupert						

Five Authors A diagram like this one will be helpful. As you draw conclusions, indicate pluses and minuses. As you determine each author's pseudonym, indicate it in the right-hand column.

From statements 2, 3, and 4, who writes mystery novels?

	biography	general	historical	mysteries	travel	pseudonym
Florence						
James						
John						
Milton						
Sarah						

St. Bernards and Dalmatians   A diagram like this will be helpful. Indicate each dog's name as you determine it.

	Sam	Sidney	Simon	Smitty
St. Bernard				
Dalmatian				

From statement 1, what are the possible names for Simon's St. Bernard?

Islanders' Boats   A diagram such as this will be helpful. As you determine the correct daughters' names, insert them in their proper places.

	O'Boyle	O'Bradovich	O'Brien	O'Byrne
daughter				
sailboat				
fishing boat				

From 2, 4, and 5, whose fishing boat is named *Ophelia*?

Writers of Classic Books   On this such diagram, indicate G (given) or R (received) in the proper places.

	Brontë	Conrad	Dickens	Forster	Kafka	Tolstoy
Brontës						
Conrads						
Dickenses						
Forsters						
Kafkas						
Tolstoys						

From statement 1, what are the possible writers' books given and received by the Conrads?

Land, Valley, and Hill Liars

Prepare a diagram for each puzzle depicting Amtru and Pemtru on one axis and the letter representing each speaker on the other axis. Assume either morning or afternoon and test the consistency of the speakers' statements against your assumption.

The first 5 puzzles represent traditional Land of Liars standards of veracity. The Amtrus speak the truth in the morning and lie in the afternoon. The Pemtrus speak the truth in the afternoon and lie in the morning.

Valley Liars represent inhabitants of a valley whose patterns of veracity are traditional except that in statements in which Amtrus refer directly to other Amtrus, they speak the truth in the afternoon and lie in the morning. In statements in which Pemtrus refer directly to other Pemtrus, they speak the truth in the morning and lie in the afternoon.

Liar on the Hill represent inhabitants of an isolated hill whose patterns are different. When in the company of other inhabitants of the Land of Liars, they will speak the truth only if none of the others speak the truth; they will lie if any of the others speak the truth.

Two Inhabitants   One speaker is an Amtru, the other is a Pemtru. What can you say about A's statement?

Is A's Statement True?   Two of the speakers are Pemtrus, and one is an Amtru. A states that B is a Pemtru. What are the possibilities for A?

Three Inhabitants   Two of the speakers are Pemtrus, and one is an Amtru. C claims that A is the Amtru. Test this considering both morning and afternoon.

Four Inhabitants   Two speakers are Amtrus, and two are Pemtrus. Test A's statement against the other speakers considering both morning and afternoon.

Five Inhabitants   Three of the speakers are Amtrus, and two are Pemtrus. Consider that if either part of A's or B's statement is true, the statement is true. D says that A is an Amtru. Consider the possibilities for A.

Four Valley Inhabitants   Two of the speakers are Amtrus, and two are Pemtrus. Assume it is afternoon. Consider the possibilities for C.

Three Valley Inhabitants   The number in each group is unknown. Start by analyzing A's statement. If it is afternoon, what can you conclude from B's and C's statements?

Does C Live on the Hill?   One of the speakers is a hill inhabitant. Consider C's statement. Could it be true?

One from the Hill   One of the speakers is a hill inhabitant. Assume C is the hill inhabitant. Test this against the statements by the other speakers.

SOLUTIONS

PART I
Brainbender Puzzles

At the Shoulder

Paulo Alpaca   36″   Sofia Llama   52″
Max Antelope   68″   Milly Moose   60″
José Argali   42″   Lars Reindeer   41″
Louie Elk   54″   Viola Vicuna   39″
Paco Guanaco   49″

At the Zoo

The emu is 10.   The leopard is 13.
The lion is 11.   The otter is 14.
The hippo is 12.

Babysitting

Amelia Gray was paid $4.75 per hour, and earned $166.25 for a
    bicycle.
Barry Wills was paid $4.50 per hour, and earned $189.00 for clothes.
Carson Jones was paid $5.25 per hour, and earned $99.75 for a
    computer.
Dylan Sands was paid $4.00 per hour, and earned $264.00 for a trip.
Elvis Ellison was paid $5.00 per hour, and earned $190.00 for college.

Berry Streets Bus

Danny lives on Cherry Street and leaves the bus first.
Justin lives on Huckleberry Avenue and leaves the bus second.
Diana lives on Elderberry Road and leaves the bus third.
Bruce lives on Mulberry Street and leaves the bus fourth.
Tracy lives on Blueberry Street and leaves the bus last.

Beverly's Yard Sale

	Earned	Left over
	$6.60	6
	$8.64	3
	$3.72	2.5
Totals	$18.96	11.5

Bobcats

Name	Height	Average
Aaron Ross	6'3"	14.6
Ben Katz	5'9"	8.0
Dan Blum	6'9"	19.0
Jon Delg	6'7"	8.8
Sid Lien	6'0"	4.5

Bogmen

Billy's Berries	1,200	Bog by the Bay	2,100
Cranberries, Inc.	900	Grand Cranberries Ltd.	1,800
Miles o' Bogs	1,500	Tiny's Bog Co.	600

Bone Hunters

Dolly, the Labrador, found 0.
Blue, the boxer, found 1.
Baggy, the Dalmatian, found 2.
Muffin, the shepherd, found 3.

B-r-r-r-r-r

Average median temp	−1.2 degrees
Coldest median	1.3 degrees below average
Warmest median	2.2 degrees above average
Closest to average	Sunday
Biggest change	3.5 degrees
Same three-day temp	−2 degrees
Weekend	colder by 0.8 degrees

Catapult

Kurt gets Hallie, who weighs 13 oz.
Martha gets Codi, who weighs 14 oz.
Ted gets Catapult, who weighs 17 oz.
Pam gets Bandit, who weighs 20 oz.

Check!

Al has 46.25 points. Bob has 48.5 points, winning the match.

Corn Dogs

Corn dogs	75
Hot dogs	160
Peanuts	120
Popcorn	40
Pretzels	30

Cornivores

Body Grabbers	32
Lagoon Slimeballs	44
Lizard Lair	9
Trout School	19
Wombat Willies	11

Dale's Trip

Total gallons bought	51
Total spent	$98.87
Total mileage	864
Average $ per gallon	$1.94
Miles per gallon	23.4

Note that you don't count the final 11 gallons (or the 3 left in the 14-gallon tank) when calculating the average mpg, as it wasn't used for the driving.

The Dalton Express

City	Arrive	Depart
Dalton	—	7:15 a.m.
Farmington	7:30 a.m.	7:36 a.m.
Newton	7:51 a.m.	7:57 a.m.
Carroll	9:27 a.m.	9:33 a.m.
Portsmouth	10:48 a.m.	10:54 a.m.
Reedville	11:09 a.m.	11:15 a.m.
Dalton	2:15 p.m.	—

Do the Math

Graph C

Sum	19
Difference	7
Product	20
Quotient	4

Double Bogey

Par	4	5	3	4	4	3	5	4	4	36
Hole	1	2	3	4	5	6	7	8	9	Total
Dyment	3	5	5	4	6	3	6	4	3	39
Horn	4	6	4	4	2	5	4	4	6	39
Munro	6	4	3	3	4	4	5	3	4	36
Smith	2	5	2	4	3	2	3	4	5	30

Farmer Bob's Barn

Cats	6
Chickens	10
Cows	4
Goats	8
Horses	2

Five Boxes

A	B	C	D	E
48	4	6	24	10

Flapdoodle

Tony Shrike is 15 inches and slides 1st.
Milly Merganser is 20 inches and slides 2nd.
Jake Oystercatcher is 25 inches and slides 3rd.
Sal Egret is 30 inches and slides 4th.
Willy Spoonbill is 45 inches and slides last.

Flying Wool Ranch

Clark's Flying Wool Ranch, 384 sheep, 32-pound Skip, 2,400 acres.
Hunter's B-Baa-B Ranch, 320 sheep, 40-pound Joey, 1,800 acres.
Medici's Black Sheep Ranch, 480 sheep, 48-pound Blue, 1,200 acres.
Sullivan's Merino Ranch, 240 sheep, 21-pound Dingo, 1,500 acres.

Four Football Fans and Four Pizzas

Bob ate one of each.
Hank ate one of each.
Jason ate one pepperoni slice, two sausage, and one vegetarian.
Peter ate three slices of cheese and one slice of vegetarian.

Fraction Match

G	$3/5$	E	$2/6$
A	$1/4$	——	$3/8$ (circled)
I	$2/7$	C	$4/6$
F	$3/4$	A	$2/8$
H	$7/8$	D	$5/8$
C	$2/3$	B	$2/5$
E	$1/3$	F	$6/8$

Grandpa Willard's Applesauce

Rod Cooper uses:
 2.5 lbs. of Delicious apples and 2 c. of brown sugar.
Ted Frandsen uses:
 1 lb. of Granny Smith apples and 1 oz. of almond extract.
Neil McGee uses:
 3 lbs. of Northern Spy apples and 3 tsp. of horseradish.
Dick Smith uses:
 2 lbs. of Gravenstein apples and 4 oz. of cinnamon.
John Willard uses:
 1.5 lbs. of Yellow Transparent apples and 2 tbsp. of lemon extract.

Half-Off Dale's Deli

Beverly had soup, a cinnamon roll, and an espresso for $7.25.
C.J. had 1/2 a cinnamon roll for $1.20.
Geri had 1/2 sandwich, 1/2 chili, a cinnamon roll, and an espresso for $9.35.
Ginger had 1/2 a cinnamon roll for $1.20.
Kelsey had 1/2 sandwich, 1/2 soup, 1/2 a cinnamon roll, and a soft drink for $7.85.
Ted had a sandwich, 1/2 soup, and a soft drink for $9.05.
Tristan had a tuna sandwich, chili, a cinnamon roll, and a soft drink for $11.25.
Total (paid by Tristan): $47.15

Halloween Party

Dina won the pumpkin-carving contest and drank 1 glass of cider.
Erin got sick and drank 2 glasses.
Sam broke the dish and drank 3 glasses.
Katie helped clean up and drank 4 glasses.
Donny won the apple-bobbing contest and drank 5 glasses.
Emily wore the witch's costume and drank 6 glasses.

Hogs in a Fog

Chevrolet	24
Dodge	96
Ford	40
GMC	64
Mack	112

How Far?

The man in the green coat drove a red motorcycle 48 kilometers (30 miles).

The woman with the gold earrings drove a blue sportscar 57.6 kilometers (36 miles).

The teen in ski boots drove his dad's green station wagon 43.2 kilometers (27 miles).

The old woman in tennis shoes drove a black pickup 55.2 kilometers (34.5 miles).

The basketball referee in the fleece jacket drove an orange SUV 36 kilometers (22.5 miles).

Jessica

The oldest, Angela, is 16 years, 4 months.

Ryan is 15 years, 4 months, 3 weeks.

Jessica is 14 years, 11 months, 3 weeks.

Doug is 14 years, 9 months, 3 weeks.

The youngest, Lida is 14 years, 7 months, 1 week.

Kids and Cars

Chevy	2	Dodge	6	Ford	4
Jeep	3	Toyota	5	VW	2

Kookaburra Stew

Augustus, from Wagga Wagga, prefers half a gallon (1.88 liters) of scampi.

Caesar, from Kangaroo Island, prefers half a pint (.235 liters) of angleworm.

Plato, from Gympie, prefers 3 pints (1.41 liters) of perch.

Pluto, from Wollongong, prefers 3 quarts (2.82 liters) of sardines.

Kurt's Bicycle Ride

Km	Miles	MpD
838.4	524	74.9
528.0	330	82.5
713.6	446	63.7
811.2	507	84.5
217.6	136	68
764.8	478	79.7
939.2	587	73.4
Totals	3,008	75.2

Lily Claire and the Pirates

Julia made 1 basket, 0 free throws, played on the varsity team, and scored 2 points.

Lily Claire made 8 baskets, 4 free throws, played on the varsity team, and scored 20 points.

Rachel made 6 baskets, 6 free throws, played on the junior varsity team, and scored 18 points.

Teresa made 4 baskets, 2 free throws, played on the varsity team, and scored 10 points.

Tina made 5 baskets, 1 free throw, played on the junior varsity team, and scored 11 points.

Magazine Drive

1. 142, 302
2. 62
3. December, 147
4. 142, 131
5. 204, 302
6. December
7. 142, October
8. December, 302, 204
9. 302
10. 204, 26, November, 73, December

Martha's Books

A	48		A	60
B	12		B	24
C	36	or	C	12
D	24		D	48
E	60		E	36

Misplaced Numbers

Box A 16, 20, 26, 38
Box B 1, 13, 19
Box C 45, 99, 117, 135
Box D 49, 91, 105
Box E 2, 8, 10, 57, 59, 73, 83, 87, 95

Mr. Clark's PE Storage Room

- 12 basketballs
- 4 footballs
- 8 soccer balls
- 16 softballs
- 10 tetherballs

Mr. Lockety's New Carpet

Mrs. Ebuley in Room 194 needs 506 sq. ft. of mauve carpet.

Mrs. Eddy in Room 193 needs 552 sq. ft. of taupe carpet.

Mr. Lockety in Room 186 needs 594 sq. ft. of sage carpet.

Ms. Stalk in Room 168 needs 625 sq. ft. of navy carpet.

Mrs. Wilcox's Challenge

Mrs. Lindly teaches algebra in Room 101 and collected 900 pounds.

Ms. St. John teaches biology in Room 110 and collected 800 pounds.

Mrs. Williams teaches English in Room 201 and collected 1,000 pounds.

Mrs. Wilcox teaches French in Room 210 and collected 1,200 pounds.

Mustardville

Hiram drove the red cucumber truck 32 miles at 16 mph.

Townes drove the blue onion truck 4 miles at 20 mph.

Vance drove the green dill truck 4.5 miles at 18 mph.

My Favorite Class

Art	10
Biology	8
English	12
Math	5
PE	25
Social Studies	20

N & G

V.M.	24 books	Room 101
B.T.	12 books	Room 102
G.P.	22 books	Room 103
S.L.	16 books	Room 104
N.R.	20 books	Room 105

Nico's Algebra Test

	Sum	Average
Liz	59	6.6
Max	73	9.1
Moss	131	16.4
Nico	50	7.1
Rob	47	15.7
Ruby	46	7.7
Shaw	149	24.8
Tyne	120	10.9
Zane	114	22.8

Odometer

Danny Delphino drove a black car 186.3 miles.

Roberta Fisher drove a red car 181.9 miles.

Curley Lester drove a green car 187.7 miles.

Rudy Shepard drove a white car 179.4 miles.

Willy Swank drove a tan car 188.5 miles.

Paper Clips

Boxes	A	B	C	D	E	F
	19	16	13	40	55	4

	G	H	I	J	K	L
	22	20	39	26	38	11

Paul's Guppies

Full bowl	15
Heather	4
Michele	1
Nancy	2
Rod	8

Really Exotic Aliens

Name	Lines read	Words	Average
Alex	12	84	7
Dennis	14	126	9
Derrick	19	114	6
Leah	11	110	10
Noah	10	130	13
Ryan	16	128	8
Stacie	9	108	12

Saturday Jobs

Jered Blue weeded 15 and earned $2.50.

Kim Gray raked 45, mowed 60, and earned $17.50.

Joey Green washed 15, trimmed 45, mowed 30, and earned $15.00.

Sarah White raked 30, trimmed 30, and earned $10.00.

Sit-ups

Andy 40   Axel 45   Chan 15   Dale 120
Leo 60   Logan 30   Nicky 10   Zack 5

Slapjack

Sam Brown won the 3rd game and lost the 4th.
Lisa Green won the 4th game and lost the 2nd.
Mary Jones won the 1st game and lost the 3rd.
John Moore won the 2nd game and lost the 1st.

Soccer Schedule

Team	1st	2nd	3rd	4th	5th
Bobcats	Rockets	Panthers	Cyclones	Buffaloes	Spartans
Buffaloes	Spartans	Rockets	Panthers	Bobcats	Cyclones
Cyclones	Panthers	Spartans	Bobcats	Rockets	Buffaloes
Panthers	Cyclones	Bobcats	Buffaloes	Spartans	Rockets
Rockets	Bobcats	Buffaloes	Spartans	Cyclones	Panthers
Spartans	Buffaloes	Cyclones	Rockets	Panthers	Bobcats

Stephanie's Water Bottle

20 ounces

Summer Birthdays

Eli Avery, age 14, was born on July 3rd.
Ken Elliott, age 12, was born on August 6th.
Iris Scott, age 11, was born on June 30th.
Amy Turner, age 12, was born on July 16th.
Ada Wyatt, age 13, was born on August 19th.

Sweaty Cities

Bakersfield	202
El Paso	194
Las Vegas	216
Phoenix	214
Sacramento	193
Tucson	198

Ten-Pin Alley

Frame	Jeremy	Wynona	Jill	
1	20	9	19	
2	40	29	28	
3	59	49	48	
4	68	66	77	
5	88	75	96	
6	107	95	105	
7	116	111	123	
8	136	120	143	
9	155	139	162	
10	164	148	171	= **Totals**

Traffic Flow

	Southbound	Northbound	Total	Average
Monday	1,242	1,364	2,606	1,303
Tuesday	1,035	1,299	2,334	1,167
Wednesday	1,224	1,280	2,504	1,252
Thursday	935	1,229	2,164	1,082
Friday	1,229	1,363	2,592	1,296
Total	5,665	6,535		
Average	1,133	1,307		

Vanilla Swirl

Caleb ate 6 scoops of chocolate.
Dakota ate 4 scoops of vanilla swirl.
Joey ate 2 scoops of strawberry.
Loren ate 7 scoops of peach.
Sara ate 3 scoops of raspberry.
Sydney ate 5 scoops of rocky road.

Walking for Wilma

Ada walked 7 miles and earned $17.50.
Eve walked 2 miles and earned $5.00.
Fay walked 7 miles and earned $17.50.
Ian walked 2.5 miles and earned $6.25.
Ira walked 4 miles and earned $10.00.
Joy walked 6.5 miles and earned $16.25.
Kim walked 5.5 miles and earned $13.75.
Liv walked 3 miles and earned $7.50.
Luc walked 5 miles and earned $12.50.
Von walked 6 miles and earned $15.00.
The total earned was $121.25.

Warm-ups

Penni earned 97 points.
Sam earned 91 points.
Willy earned 104 points.
Jo earned 88 points.

WES Favorites

		favorite lunch			favorite game			favorite holiday		
		chicken	corn dog	pizza	4-square	soccer	tetherball	Halloween	Thanksgiving	Christmas
Mr. Bodle	room 196	1	10	14	21	3	1	4	2	19
Mrs. Clark	room 191	1	3	8	7	4	1	1	2	9
Mrs. Olson	room 190	5	4	7	19	5	2	1	2	23

Wholesome Decimals

$$
\begin{array}{ccccccc}
& & & & & .878 & \\
6.09 & 5.47 & 7.997 & 4.78 & 3.96 & .121 & 9.25 \\
+.91 & +.53 & +.003 & +.22 & +.04 & +.001 & -.25 \\
\hline
7.00 & 6.00 & 8.000 & 5.00 & 4.00 & 1.000 & 9.00
\end{array}
$$

Wildcats

Atkins was catcher, averaged .278, and stole 2 bases.
Billsly was at shortstop, averaged .240, and stole 9 bases.
Downey was pitcher, averaged .198, and stole 3 bases.
Johnston was in center field, averaged .309, and stole 8 bases.
Lewis was at second base, averaged .260, and stole 7 bases.

Woody's Tires

Right front tire: add 12.84 kPa's.
Left front tire: subtract 5.84 kPa's.
Right rear tire: subtract 6.40 kPa's.
Left rear tire: add 45.06 kPa's.
Spare tire: subtract 6.74 kPa's.

PART II
Poker Logic Puzzles

Dreams and Nightmares

Adam's nightmare is that his wife won't give him money for the final bet (1). Geoff's nightmare isn't betting four kings in Lowball (2), so this is Pete's nightmare. By elimination, Geoff's nightmare is that he can't remember what beats what, so his dream is winning the World Series of Poker (3). Pete doesn't dream of playing poker with the Rat Pack (4), so Adam does. By elimination, Pete dreams of owning his own casino resort.

Adam	Rat Pack	wife won't give money
Geoff	winning WSOP	can't remember hands
Pete	owning casino	four kings in Lowball

Poker Blogs

Maureen started 1eyedjill.com (1). Terence didn't start aloneinreno.com or queen-of-spades.com, so he started floptoriver.com. Alexander didn't start aloneinreno.com (5), so Lizzie did. By elimination, Alexander started queen-of-spades.com, which features poker celebrity gossip (3). aloneinreno.com doesn't specialize in poker variations or tournament schedules (5), so it features advice on betting. This is Lizzie's site (see above), so Terence's site has tournament schedules (4). By elimination, Maureen's site features poker variations.

Alexander	queen-of-spades.com	celebrity gossip
Lizzie	aloneinreno.com	advice on betting
Maureen	1eyedjill.com	poker variations
Terence	floptoriver.com	tournament schedules

Don't Quit Your Day Job

Biff lost on Sunday to the garden club (5). He lost to the Elks on Saturday and lost $31 on Wednesday (2). He lost $24 on Friday (4). He lost $82 to his fraternity brothers (1), so this was on Thursday. He lost to the Marines on Friday and lost $57 on Saturday (3). By elimination, he lost to the firefighters on Wednesday and lost $177 on Sunday.

Wed.	firefighters	$31
Thu.	fraternity	$82
Fri.	Marines	$24
Sat.	Elks	$57
Sun.	garden club	$177

The Road to Monte Carlo, Part 1: Planning the Trip

Diana and her husband arranged for all transportation (3). Fawn and her husband didn't research activities (5), so Alice and her husband did. By elimination, Fawn and her husband arranged for accommodations, so they're the Tanners (4). Alice isn't Mrs. Stormgren (2), so Diana is. By elimination, Alice is Renaldi. Bill isn't married to Fawn Tanner or Alice Renaldi (5), so he's married to Diana Stormgren. Chip isn't Mr. Renaldi (1), so he's Mr. Tanner. By elimination, Evan is Renaldi.

Alice and Evan Renaldi	activities
Diana and Bill Stormgren	transportation
Fawn and Chip Tanner	accommodations

Lionus Interruptus and Other Stories

Marjanne told a story about a wife who won the deed to the house in a game of poker with her husband (4). Neither Cyrus nor Kathleen told the story about a game between Churchill and De Gaulle (6), so Dirk did. Kathleen didn't tell the story about the bluffer who tore up his cards (3), so Cyrus did. By elimination, Kathleen told the story about the lion, which was the first story (1). Marjanne told the second story (2). Dirk didn't tell the third story (5), so Cyrus did. By elimination, Dirk told the fourth story.

1st	Kathleen	lion interrupted game
2nd	Marjanne	wife won deed
3rd	Cyrus	bluffer tore up cards
4th	Dirk	Churchill and De Gaulle

Poker Widows

The five women are: Annie, Paulette, Marvin's wife, and the women whose hobbies are karaoke and Scrabble (5). Edna's hobby is either aikido or horseback riding (6), so her husband is Marvin. Paulette hasn't taken up photography (3), so Annie has. She isn't married to George (2), or Drew or Tiger (3), so she's married to Kenny. Susan is married to Tiger (7). She doesn't play Scrabble (4), so she does karaoke. By elimination, Laverne plays Scrabble. Laverne isn't married to Drew (1), so she's married to George. By elimination, Paulette is married to Drew. Her hobby isn't aikido (1), so it's horseback riding. By elimination, Edna's hobby is aikido.

Annie	Kenny	photography
Edna	Marvin	aikido
Laverne	George	Scrabble
Paulette	Drew	horseback riding
Susan	Tiger	karaoke

King Arthur and the Round Table

Havermeyer held a pair of jacks (3). Arthur held a king and a six (4). James isn't Havermeyer (5) or the man who held the lowest pair (7), which was a pair of nines (1), so James held a pair of queens (2). Freddy folded (6), so he held the pair of nines (see above). By elimination, Roy is Havermeyer. The only person he had beaten was Freddy, so Freddy is Lipkin (8). Arthur isn't Washington (9), so James is Washington. By elimination, Arthur is Forrest.

Arthur Forrest	king and six
Freddy Lipkin	pair of nines
James Washington	pair of queens
Roy Havermeyer	pair of jacks

There Oughtta Be a Law

The first person who spoke complained about post mortems (1). Either Norm or Trisha spoke third (9). Jill spoke fourth, Larry spoke fifth, and Kevin spoke sixth (3). Doris mentioned either misdealing or splashing the pot (4), so she spoke second. The third speaker talked about peeking at discards (7). A woman spoke about betting out of turn (5), so she's Jill. By elimination, either Kevin or Larry talked about taking too long to bet, so a woman spoke about splashing the pot (2), so she's Doris. Thus, Trisha spoke first (6). By elimination, Norm spoke third. Larry didn't talk about misdealing (8), so Kevin did. By elimination, Larry spoke about taking too long to bet.

1st	Trisha	post mortems
2nd	Doris	splashing the pot
3rd	Norm	peeking at discards
4th	Jill	betting out of turn
5th	Larry	taking too long to bet
6th	Kevin	misdealing

Tidy Profits

Eloise's earnings of $1800 allowed her to take a trip to either Australia or Denmark (7). She earned $1200 the year she went to Japan and $800 in 2000 (2). She traveled to Greece in 1999 (8). This accounts for four of the six years. She traveled to Spain in either 2001 or 2004 (1), so this was during a fifth year. She went to Brazil the year she earned either $1100 or $1400 (9), so this accounts for the remaining year. She didn't win $1700 in 1999 (4), so she won this amount the year she went to Spain. This wasn't in 2004 (4), so it was in 2001. Thus, she went to Australia in 2000 (4). She went to Denmark the year she won $1800 (7). She didn't win $1400 in 1999 (4), so she earned $1100 that year. By elimination, she won $1400 the year she went to Brazil. We know that her $1800 took her to Denmark (see above), so this wasn't in 2004 (3) or 2002 (5), so it was in 2003. She went to Japan in 2002 and to Brazil in 2004 (6).

1999	$1100	Greece
2000	$800	Australia
2001	$1700	Spain
2002	$1200	Japan
2003	$1800	Denmark
2004	$1400	Brazil

Sidling up to Seidel

Rita met either Doyle Brunson or Phil Hellmuth (4). A woman met Eric Seidel (1), but not Jasmine (9), so Lottie. Wally met Stu Ungar (3). Jasmine met Johnny Chan (6). Chuck didn't meet Johnny Moss or Phil Hellmuth (10), so he met Doyle Brunson. Rita met Phil Hellmuth (4). By elimination, Harry met Johnny Moss. Rita didn't meet Phil Hellmuth in a toy store (4), so she met him in a supermarket (2). Jasmine met Johnny Chan in a flower shop (9). Chuck saw Doyle Brunson at a wedding chapel (8). Harry saw Johnny Moss at a plumbing supply store (5). Wally met Stu Ungar at an ice cream parlor (7). By elimination, Lottie met Eric Seidel at a toy store.

Chuck	Doyle Brunson	wedding chapel
Harry	Johnny Moss	plumbing supply store
Jasmine	Johnny Chan	flower shop
Lottie	Eric Seidel	toy store
Rita	Phil Hellmuth	supermarket
Wally	Stu Ungar	ice cream parlor

The Road to Monte Carlo, Part 2: The Flight

Alice is married to Evan, Diana is married to Bill, and Fawn is married to Chip (part 1). One couple sat in seats A and B, another in C and D, and the remaining couple in E and F (1). Nobody sat in a seat with the same letter as his or her initial (2). If Chip had sat in seat E, then his wife, Fawn, would have sat in seat F (1), which is impossible (2). Thus, Chip sat in seat D (7), so Fawn sat in seat C (1). Bill didn't sit in seat B (2), or seats A or F (4), so he sat in seat E. His wife, Diana, sat in seat F (1). Alice didn't sit in seat A (2), so she sat in B. By elimination, Evan sat in A. Diana won the third hand (8). Bill and Diana are the Stormgrens (part 1), so he won the fifth hand (9). Fawn won the sixth hand (5). Chip won the first hand (3). Alice and Evan are the Renaldis (part 1), so Alice won the second hand and Evan won the fourth (6).

A	Evan Renaldi	2nd
B	Alice Renaldi	4th
C	Fawn Tanner	6th
D	Chip Tanner	1st
E	Bill Stormgren	5th
F	Diana Stormgren	3rd

You Wear It Well

The necklace bears an image of the Binion's horseshoe (3). Either Maura or Sophy wears the poker bracelet (5). Amelia's jewelry either has the Bicycle logo or the words "lady luck" (6). Veronica wears either the pendant or the ring (8). The earrings depict a royal flush in spades (9). Laney's jewelry has one of the two red queens on it (11). This accounts for all six women. Amelia doesn't wear the anklet (7), so Laney does. It doesn't have the queen of diamonds on it (1), so it has the queen of hearts. Sophy's jewelry depicts the Bicycle logo (2), so this is the bracelet. Amelia's has the words "lady luck" (6). By elimination, Veronica's jewelry has the queen of diamonds. It isn't the ring (1), so it's the pendant. By elimination, Amelia has the ring. Amelia is Talese's sister (4), so Talese doesn't wear the necklace (10), so she wears the earrings. By elimination, Maura wears the necklace.

Amelia	ring	"lady luck"
Laney	anklet	queen of hearts
Maura	necklace	Binion's horseshoe
Sophy	bracelet	Bicycle logo
Talese	earrings	royal flush
Veronica	pendant	queen of diamonds

Don't Try This at Home

Anton held his breath for three minutes (5). Neither Jason nor Philip walked on his hands (2), so Matthew did. Philip didn't eat two dozen eggs in five minutes (6), so Jason did. By elimination, Philip bought beer wearing a hand towel, so he completed a full house (3). The person who completed a straight flush didn't hold his breath or walk on his hands (7), so he isn't Anton or Matthew (see above), so he's Jason. Matthew didn't fill in a flush (4), so Anton did. By elimination, Matthew completed four of a kind and won $91 (1). Anton, who completed a flush (see above), won $129. Jason won $88 and Philip won $45 (2).

Anton	held breath	flush	$129
Jason	ate eggs	straight flush	$88
Matthew	walked on hands	four of a kind	$91
Philip	wore hand towel	full house	$45

Family Circle

Audrey didn't sit in #2 (3), or #1 or #4 (4), so she sat in seat #3. Travis sat in #2 or #4 (4). Randall also sat in one of these two seats (7). By elimination, Wendy sat in #1. The child in #2 thought that Dennis had two pairs (2). The child in #4 thought he had made a flush (4). He isn't Travis (4), so he's Randall (see above). By elimination, Travis sat in #2. Randall sat next to the child who believed that Dennis had three of a kind (3), so this was Audrey. By elimination, Wendy thought their father had made a straight, so she's 14 (5). Travis is 11 (6). Randall, who sat in #4 (see above), is 12 (7). Audrey is older than 11 and younger than 14 (4), so she's 13.

#1	Wendy	14	straight
#2	Travis	11	two pairs
#3	Audrey	13	three of a kind
#4	Randall	12	flush

Women of Poker

The second woman who spoke has the same first name as Jennifer's heroine (2), so she isn't Jennifer (1), or Kathy (4), so she's either Annie or Barbara. If she's Annie, then her favorite player isn't Annie Duke (1). On the other hand, if she's Barbara, then her favorite player also isn't Annie Duke (3). Thus, in either case, the Annie Duke fan didn't speak second, so she spoke first (4). Her name is Annie (1). Barbara spoke second (see above). She isn't the Barbara Enright fan (1), so the latter woman spoke third and Kathy spoke fourth. By elimination, Jennifer spoke third. Kathy's favorite player isn't Kathy Liebert (1), so she's Jennifer Harman. By elimination, Barbara's favorite is Kathy Liebert.

1st	Annie	Annie Duke
2nd	Barbara	Kathy Liebert
3rd	Jennifer	Barbara Enright
4th	Kathy	Jennifer Harman

Night of the Eagle

Eagle spotted Joey for either aggressive betting or counting chips when he was bluffing (1). Either Drew or Mel smiles uncontrollably when he's holding good cards (2). The man whose hands shake when he has a winner also chats nervously when he's bluffing (4). When Trevor clinches a straight or a flush, either a vein appears in his forehead or he rechecks his hole card (7). When Walt bluffs, either his nose twitches or he bets out of turn (8). This accounts for five of the six men. The man whose breathing increases when he connects isn't Joey or Walt (5), so he's the sixth man in our enumeration. The man who averts his eyes when he bluffs doesn't smile or breathe more heavily when he actually has the cards (10), so he's Trevor. Thus, Walt's nose twitches when he bluffs (3). Aaron bets out of turn when he bluffs (11), so his breathing increases when he has good cards. Drew's hands shake when he has good cards (6). By elimination, Mel smiles uncontrollably. He doesn't bet aggressively when he bluffs (12), so he counts his chips. By elimination, Joey bets aggressively when he bluffs. Neither he nor Walt rechecks his hole card when he has good cards (9), so Trevor does. Joey doesn't have a vein that pops out on his forehead when he bluffs (12), so Walt does. By elimination, Joey speaks in a high voice.

	good cards	bluff
Aaron	increased breathing	betting out of turn
Drew	shaking hands	nervous chatter
Joey	speaking in high voice	aggressive betting
Mel	uncontrollable smiling	counting chips
Trevor	rechecking hole card	averted eyes
Walt	popping vein	twitching nose

Reading, Writing, and Poker

A girl went to the board fourth (2). The student who went to the board third calculated the probability of either three of a kind or a flush (4). Lance was fifth and the second student calculated the probability of a full house (5). Jake was third and the fourth student showed the class how to calculate the probability of two pairs (1). He didn't calculate the probability of a flush (2), so he calculated the probability of three of a kind (4). Eliza calculated a hand with higher probability, and therefore lower value (intro), than the hand that Jake calculated (6), so Eliza calculated the probability of two pairs, so she went to the board fourth (see above). A girl went to the board sixth (2). Another girl calculated the probability of a flush (2), so she went to the board first. By elimination, Bart went to the board second, so he calculated the probability of a full house (see above). Alyssa calculated the probability of four of a kind (3), so she went to the board sixth. By elimination, Mary calculated the probability of a flush and Lance a straight.

1st	Mary	flush
2nd	Bart	full house
3rd	Jake	three of a kind
4th	Eliza	two pairs
5th	Lance	straight
6th	Alyssa	four of a kind

Stardust Memories

The person who learned at nine years old learned from either a babysitter or an uncle (8). The person who learned from his or her grandfather learned at eight years old and Claude learned at eleven (2). The person who learned from his or her scout leader was ten and the person who used matchsticks was twelve (7). The person who first played poker with an older sister used either buttons or cookies for chips (1), so this is Claude. Virgil was eight and the person who used checkers was ten (5). Either Renee or Willis used jellybeans to play (3), so this person was nine. Jasper was ten and Renee was twelve (9). By elimination, Willis was nine. He didn't learn from his uncle (6), so Renee did. By elimination, Willis learned from his babysitter. Virgil used buttons (4). By elimination, Claude used cookies.

age 8	Virgil	grandfather	buttons
age 9	Willis	babysitter	jellybeans
age 10	Jasper	scout leader	checkers
age 11	Claude	older sister	cookies
age 12	Renee	uncle	matchsticks

The Road to Monte Carlo, Part 3: First Night at the Casino

Alice is Mrs. Renaldi and Chip is Mr. Tanner (part 1), so the six people are: Alice, Chip, a person who played seven-card hi-lo, the woman who played chemin de fer, the person who drank Manhattans, and the person who left at 2:30 (9). Evan sat in seat A (part 2). He didn't drink Manhattans and didn't leave at 2:30 (1), so he played hi-lo. His wife is Alice (part 1), so she also played hi-lo (3). Bill helped plan the transportation aspect of the trip (part 1), so he left the casino at 1:30 (6); therefore, he drank Manhattans. Evan left the casino at 12:30 (1). Since he left first, he drank vodka martinis (2). The person who drank margaritas left at 1:00, Evan played trente et quarante, and Bill played hold'em (12). By elimination, the woman who played chemin de fer and the person who left at 2:30 both played seven-card stud. Bill left at 1:30 (see above), so the person who left at 2:00 played hold'em. Alice played hi-lo and didn't leave at 2:30 (see above), so by elimination she left at either 1:00 or 3:00. In either case, the person who left at 2:00 played craps, so this person is Chip. The person who left at 1:00 is either Alice or the woman who played chemin de fer (9), so in either case she is a woman. A man drank tequila sunrises (7), so by elimination he's Chip. The person who drank black Russians didn't play seven-card stud (10), so she's Alice and she left at 3:00. By elimination, the person who left at 2:30 drank gin and tonics, and the woman who played chemin de fer drank margaritas and left at 1:00. The person who played English roulette left at 2:30 and the person who played European roulette left at 3:00

(5). By elimination, Bill played blackjack. His wife is Diana (part 1). Bill left at 1:30 (see above), so Diana left at 1:00 (8). By elimination, Fawn left at 2:30.

Evan	hi-lo	trente et quarante	vodka martinis	12:30
Diana	stud	chemin de fer	margaritas	1:00
Bill	hold'em	blackjack	Manhattans	1:30
Chip	hold'em	craps	tequila sunrises	2:00
Fawn	stud	English roulette	gin and tonics	2:30
Alice	hi-lo	European roulette	black Russians	3:00

Wild Times

Either Chambers or Freeman dealt the third hand (3). The person who made either 6's or 10's wild dealt the fifth hand (5). Tanslye dealt first and the person who made 5's wild dealt fourth (1). Rachel made 3's wild (4). Hank made queens wild (10). Jimmy made 10's wild, Saunders made 9's wild, and the person who dealt sixth made 6's wild (9). The person who dealt fifth made 10's wild (5), so he's Jimmy (see above). Saunders, who made 9's wild (see above) didn't deal fourth, fifth, or sixth (see above), so he or she dealt second. By elimination, Hank and Rachel dealt first and third, in some order, so they are surnamed either Tanslye or Chambers or Freeman. They made 3's and 10's wild, in some order (see above). Richter didn't make 5's or 10's wild (7), so he or she made 6's wild; therefore, he or she dealt sixth. Betty isn't Richter or Saunders (11), so she dealt fourth and made 5's wild (see above). Alex didn't make 9's wild (2), so he made 6's wild, so he dealt sixth (see above). By elimination, Tina dealt second and made 9's wild. Freeman didn't make 3's or queens wild (9), so he or she didn't deal third (see above), so Chambers did (3). Thus, either Chambers or Tanslye made 3's wild (see above). Freeman made 5's wild (9), so Betty is Freeman. By elimination, Jimmy Laughlin dealt fifth and made 10's wild. A woman dealt first (6), so she's Rachel, who made 3's wild (see above). By elimination, Hank dealt third and made Q's wild.

1st	Rachel Tanslye	threes
2nd	Tina Saunders	nines
3rd	Hank Chambers	queens
4th	Betty Freeman	fives
5th	Jimmy Laughlin	tens
6th	Alex Richter	sixes

Someday the Moon

The five places Elmer played poker are: the Monorail at Disneyworld, the Taj Mahal, the place where he played with the Buddhist monk, the place he played the year after he played on the Great Wall of China, and the place he played two years before he played with the cub scout (5). He didn't play at the Great Wall of China with the Buddhist monk (3), so he played there two years before he played with the cub scout. Thus, he didn't play at the Great Wall in 2003 or 2004, or in 2000 or 2001 (3), so he played there in 2002. He played with the Buddhist monk in 2000 (3) and the cub scout in 2004 (see above). The year after he played at the Great Wall was 2003 (see above). He played at the Monorail and the Taj Mahal, in some order, in 2001 and 2004 (5). He played on top of the Eiffel Tower in 2000 and with the U.N. ambassador in 2001 (1). By elimination, he played in a submarine in 2003. This wasn't with the Nascar driver (4), so he played with the Nascar driver in 2002. By elimination, he played with the nun in 2003. He didn't play in the Taj Mahal in 2004 (2), so it was in 2001. By elimination, he played on the Monorail in 2004.

2000	Eiffel Tower	Buddhist monk
2001	Taj Mahal	U.N. ambassador
2002	Great Wall	Nascar driver
2003	submarine	nun
2004	Monorail	cub scout

Lowball

The fifth person in the betting rotation was either Benjamin or Lou (5). The third had the 7-6 (3), so he or she isn't Artie or Maxine (7). He bet and folded (5), so he isn't Ernie (9), so he's also either Benjamin or Lou. The second person in rotation folded (2), so he or she wasn't Ernie (9), so, by elimination, he or she was either Artie or Maxine. He or she wasn't holding a 4 (2), so he or she had either 7-5 or 6-5. In either case, his or her remaining cards were 3-2-A. This isn't Maxine (11), so this is Artie. Lopez was third (12). He had the 7-6 (see above), so the person with the 8-4 checked (6), so this person was first (1). Since his or her second-highest card was 4, this person also held 3-2-A. Maxine held either a 7-5 or a 6-5 (7), so she was fourth. By elimination, Ernie was first. Also by elimination, the fifth person in rotation had 7-4. He or she also held

3-2-A (see above). Maxine is Pollock (13). She didn't hold an ace (11), so her remaining cards were 4-3-2. We have accounted for all the threes and deuces (see above), so Lopez's remaining cards were 5-4-A. He isn't Lou (8), so he's Benjamin. Epstein isn't Lou (8) or Ernie (10), so he's Artie. He held an ace (see above), so he didn't hold a six (8). Thus, he held the 7-5. By elimination, Maxine held the 6-5. Ernie is Trager (10). By elimination, Lou is Signorelli.

1st	Ernie Trager	8-4-3-2-A	check and call
2nd	Artie Epstein	7-5-3-2-A	check and fold
3rd	Benjamin Lopez	7-6-5-4-A	bet and fold
4th	Maxine Pollock	6-5-4-3-2	raise and re-raise
5th	Lou Signorelli	7-4-3-2-A	raise and call

Lending Library

Dawson lent a book to Anthony (1). Anthony lent a book to a third person (intro) who owns *Sklansky on Poker* (1). The latter person didn't lend *Sklansky on Poker* to Dawson (3), so he or she lent it to a fourth person. If this fourth person had lent a book to Dawson, then the remaining two people in the group would have, by elimination, lent books to each other, which is impossible (intro). Thus, the person who borrowed *Sklansky on Poker* lent another book to a fifth person. This fifth person also didn't lend a book to Dawson, because then the one remaining person in the group would have, by elimination, lent a book to himself or herself, which is impossible (intro). Thus, the fifth person lent a book to the sixth person, who, by elimination, lent a book to Dawson. The woman who owns *Super System* isn't Dawson or the person who borrowed *Sklansky on Poker* (3), so she's either the fifth or the sixth person in our enumeration above. In either case, she lent a book to Gallagher (5), so she isn't the sixth person, who lent one to Dawson (see above), so she's the fifth. Thus, she lent *Super System* to Gallagher, who is the sixth person in our enumeration. The person who owns and borrowed, in some order, *Hold'Em Excellence* and *The Fundamentals of Poker* isn't Dawson (3), so he's Anthony. Thus, Dawson owns one of these two books and the person who owns *Sklansky on Poker* borrowed the other one (see above), so the latter person is Theo (3). Gallagher owns *Zen and the Art of Poker* (3), so he lent it to Dawson (see above). By elimination, the person who borrowed *Sklansky on Poker* owns *Poker for Dummies*, and lent it to the person who owns *Super System*. We know that a woman owns *Super System* (see above).

Since Theo owns *Sklansky on Poker* (see above), a second woman borrowed this book (5). A third woman lent a book to Anthony (5). By elimination, Jason is Gallagher. Marya owns *Poker for Dummies* and Gracie owns *Super System* (2). By elimination, Natasha is Dawson. She doesn't own *The Fundamentals of Poker* (6), so she owns *Hold'Em Excellence* (see above) and lent this book to Anthony (see above). By elimination, Anthony owns *The Fundamentals of Poker* and lent it to Theo. Anthony isn't Slattery or Crawford (4), or Zebatinsky (6), so he's Harmon. Theo is Slattery and Marya is Crawford (4). By elimination, Gracie is Zebatinsky.

	owns	borrowed
Marya Crawford	*Poker for Dummies*	*Sklansky on Poker*
Natasha Dawson	*Hold'Em Excellence*	*Zen and the Art of Poker*
Jason Gallagher	*Zen and the Art*	*Super System*
Anthony Harmon	*The Fundamentals*	*Hold'Em Excellence*
Theo Slattery	*Sklansky on Poker*	*The Fundamentals of Poker*
Gracie Zebatinsky	*Super System*	*Poker for Dummies*

Insomniac's Heaven

The show on channel 45 began at 2:30 (8). The show on channel 27 began at 2:00 and the show on Thursday began at 3:30 (3). The show that began at 3:00 was on Friday and the show on channel 67 was on Tuesday (5). The latter show wasn't at 2:00, 2:30, 3:00, or 3:30 (see above), so it was at 4:00. This was on Tuesday (see above), so *Ultimate Poker Challenge* was on Monday (1). This was on either channel 27 or channel 45 (see above), but it wasn't on channel 27 (6), so it was on channel 45. This began at 2:30 (see above). By elimination, the show on channel 27 was on Wednesday. This show was *Celebrity Poker Showdown* (6), and it began at 2:00 (see above). *World Poker Tour* was on Tuesday (4). It began at 4:00 (see above), so the show on channel 88 began at 3:30 (7). By elimination, the show on channel 64 began on Friday at 3:00. *Poker Superstars Invitational* wasn't on channel 64 (2), so it was on channel 88. By elimination, *2004 World Series of Poker* was on channel 64.

Mon.	2:30	*Ultimate Poker Challenge*	channel 45
Tue.	4:00	*World Poker Tour*	channel 67
Wed.	2:00	*Celebrity Poker Showdown*	channel 27
Thu.	3:30	*Poker Superstars Invitational*	channel 88
Fri.	3:00	*2004 World Series of Poker*	channel 64

Poker School

Angela's class has twice as many people as Hi-Lo Strategy (5), so Angela's class has ten, 12, or 14 people and Hi-Lo Strategy has five, six, or seven (1). Similarly, Brandon's class has ten, 12, or 14 people and the Friday night class has five, six, or seven (12). This accounts for four of the six classes. A fifth class has 15 students (1), and a sixth has eight (4). Tina's class has 15 students (2). Peter's class meets on Tuesdays (10) and isn't the class with eight students (4), so it's Hi-Lo Strategy. Victor's class meets on Mondays (11), so it has eight students. By elimination, Isaiah's class meets on Fridays. It doesn't have five people (9), so it has six or seven (see above). Thus, Brandon's class has 12 or 14 (12). Peter's class has five students (1), so Angela's class has 10 (5). Peter's class, which meets Tuesdays (see above), meets the day before Angela's class (9), so Angela's class meets on Wednesdays. This is Poker 101 (3). Tina teaches Reading Your Opponents (7). No-Limit Poker meets on Thursdays (8), so Brandon teaches it. By elimination, Tina teaches on Saturdays. Money Management meets on Fridays and Figuring the Odds on Mondays (6). Money Management has seven people (6), so No-Limit Poker has 14 (12).

Mon.	Victor	Figuring the Odds	8 students
Tue.	Peter	Hi-Lo Strategy	5 students
Wed	Angela	Poker 101	10 students
Thu.	Brandon	No-Limit Poker	14 students
Fri.	Isaiah	Money Management	7 students
Sat.	Tina	Reading Your Opponents	15 students

Dealers' Choice

The sixth dealer called a wild-card game (5). A man dealt fourth (8). Therefore, Jeannie dealt first, Anaconda was dealt second, Maggie dealt third, and Lowball was dealt fourth (2). Omaha was dealt eighth (10). Baseball was dealt sixth (10). Naomi dealt second (10). Williamson dealt fourth (10). The fifth dealer, who dealt just after Williamson, was a man (8). Regina dealt Pineapple (7), so she dealt seventh. By elimination, the sixth and eight dealers were men. The eighth dealer was Ostroff (8). The sixth dealer dealt sometime before McGraw (8), so Regina is McGraw. Adam dealt a wild card game but didn't deal sixth (5), so he dealt fifth. Jeannie is Coleridge (5). Maggie dealt sometime after Fiorentino (5), so Naomi is Fiorentino. Latham dealt fifth and Nielsen sixth (1). By elimination, Huang dealt third. She dealt Follow the Queen (6). Jeannie dealt Woolworth (3). By elimination, Adam dealt Low Hole. Samuel is Williamson and Karl is Nielsen (4).

1st	Jeannie Coleridge	Woolworth
2nd	Naomi Fiorentino	Anaconda
3rd	Maggie Huang	Follow the Queen
4th	Samuel Williamson	Lowball
5th	Adam Latham	Low Hole
6th	Karl Nielsen	Baseball
7th	Regina McGraw	Pineapple
8th	Gregg Ostroff	Omaha

The Deli Game

Two men's highest hands were straights, including the man who sat in seat #1 (1). The men whose best hands were all flushes are: Larry, the man who ate the turkey sandwich, and the man who ate a sandwich on a bagel (7). The man who got a full house sat directly across from Ira (10). This accounts for all six men. The man who got a full house didn't sit in #4 (4), so Ira didn't sit in #1. Ira also didn't eat the turkey sandwich (3) or the sandwich on a bagel (10), so, by elimination, his highest hand was a straight. The man directly across from Larry didn't have the turkey sandwich (3). If the man directly across from Larry had sat in #1, then Larry would have sat in #4, and the man who sat to Larry's immediate right would have sat in #3, which is impossible (3). Thus, the man who sat directly across from Larry had the sandwich made with a bagel. By elimination, the man in seat #1 sat directly across from the man who had the turkey sandwich, so the latter man sat in #4. The man in seat #1 ate the sandwich on rye bread (9). Thus, the man in seat #1 is mentioned in clue 3 as the man who sat to the immediate right of Larry. Therefore, Larry sat in #2 and the man opposite Larry, who had the bagel sandwich (see above), sat in #5. Ira didn't sit in #3 (3), so he sat in #6. By elimination, the man who got the full house sat in #3. Larry is mentioned in clue 3 as the man whose sandwich was on a Kaiser roll (3). The man who got the full house ate the sandwich on whole wheat bread (4). Ira ate a tuna sandwich on white bread (2). By elimination, the man in #4 ate a sandwich on pumpernickel. Miklos sat in #1 (6). Larry had a liverwurst sandwich (6). Donnie sat in #4 and

Miklos had the bologna sandwich (8). Ralph didn't sit in #5 (5), so Frank did. By elimination, Ralph sat in #3. He didn't have the corned beef sandwich (5), so he had the roast beef. By elimination, Frank had the corned beef.

#1	Miklos	straight	bologna	rye
#2	Larry	flush	liverwurst	Kaiser roll
#3	Ralph	full house	roast beef	whole wheat
#4	Donnie	flush	turkey	pumpernickel
#5	Frank	flush	corned beef	bagel
#6	Ira	straight	tuna	white

The Road to Monte Carlo, Part 4: Sightseeing Excursions

Alice is Mrs. Renaldi and her husband is Evan (part 1). Evan played trente et quarante the first night (part 3), while Fawn won the last game of poker on the plane (part 2). Alice attended the Wednesday afternoon outing (6), but Evan didn't (11) and neither did Fawn (13). Thus, this outing included Alice but excluded both her husband and at least one woman, so this outing was to the Wax Museum (1), so Alice and Diana were the only two people who went here (1). The outing on Wednesday morning was to the Princess Grace Rose Garden (11). Note that from clue 1, we can conclude that for any of the eleven trips other than the one to the Wax Museum, if any person didn't attend, then the group consisted either of the remaining two couples or three people of the opposite sex. Thus, if any person didn't attend, then the two people of the opposite sex who aren't this person's spouse did attend. By this reasoning, since Evan didn't go on trip to the Princess Grace Rose Garden, both Diana and Fawn went on this trip. Diana is Mrs. Stormgren (part 1), and she went on both outings on Wednesday (see above), so her husband Bill didn't join her (10). Thus, the three women went on this outing (1), so Alice went there. The three women also went as a group to the Exotic Garden and on the Friday afternoon excursion (2). Diana wasn't on the Friday morning outing (10), so this wasn't to the Exotic Garden (see above), so it was to the Oceanographic Museum (12). The trip to the Exotic Garden wasn't Friday morning (10), so it was on Tuesday afternoon (12). It included Diana (see above), so Diana wasn't part of the Tuesday morning excursion (10). Her husband Bill played blackjack the first night (part 3), so he also wasn't part of the Tuesday morning excursion (3). Therefore, the other two couples were on this excursion (1). We know that Diana wasn't on Friday morning's trip to the Oceanographic Museum (see above), so Chip and Evan went on this trip

308

(1). Chip won the first game of poker on the plane (part 2), so he didn't join for the Monday morning trip (4), so Alice and Diana did (1). Diana didn't go on the Monday afternoon trip (10), so Chip and Evan did (1). All six people went to the Fort Antoine Theater on Thursday afternoon and the Louis II Stadium on Saturday afternoon (14). On Monday morning, a group went to Church Saint-Nicolas, on Monday afternoon to the National Museum, and on Tuesday morning to the Zoological Terraces (8). Bill didn't join Chip and Evan at the National Museum (3), so Alice and Fawn did (1). Diana was with the group on Thursday afternoon and Saturday afternoon (see above), so she wasn't there on Thursday morning or Saturday morning (10), so Chip and Evan went on both of these excursions (1). Chip didn't go to Fontvielle Park (4), so this was on Friday afternoon. Fawn didn't go on the Saturday morning outing (13), so Bill did (1). At least one woman went to the Prince's Palace (9), so this was on Thursday morning and both Alice and Fawn went there (1). By elimination, the Saturday morning outing was to the Museum of Antique Automobiles. The three men went to the Oceanographic Museum (5). Bill drank Manhattans on the first night (part 3), so he visited Church Saint-Nicolas (7), and Evan also visited there (1).

Mon. morning	Church Saint-Nicolas	Alice, Bill, Diana, Evan
Mon. afternoon	National Museum	Alice, Chip, Evan, Fawn
Tue. morning	Zoological Terraces	Alice, Chip, Evan, Fawn
Tue. afternoon	Exotic Garden	Alice, Diana, Fawn
Wed. morning	Princess Grace Rose Garden	Alice, Diana, Fawn
Wed. afternoon	Wax Museum	Alice, Diana
Thu. morning	Prince's Palace	Alice, Chip, Evan, Fawn
Thu. afternoon	Fort Antoine Theater	Alice, Bill, Chip, Diana, Evan, and Fawn
Fri. morning	Oceanographic Museum.	Bill, Chip, Evan
Fri. afternoon	Fontvielle Park	Alice, Diana, Fawn
Sat. morning	Museum of Antique Autos	Bill, Chip, Evan
Sat. afternoon	Louis II Stadium	Alice, Bill, Chip, Diana, Evan, and Fawn

Luck Be a Lady

One man got a royal flush in 1999 (14). Ernie got his highest hand in 1999 and another man got four aces in 2001 (2). A man got the queen-high straight flush in 1996 and the man with the keychain got his highest hand in 1997 (7). The man who got a nine-high straight flush has either the gold coin or the ring (7), so he got this hand in 2002. The man with the rabbit's foot is either Howard or Matt, and didn't get his highest hand in 1996 (9), so he got four aces in 2001. By elimination, another man caught four kings in 1997, so he's the younger of the two brothers (8). His elder brother got his best hand in 1996 (8). The remaining three men are mentioned in clue 11. Thus, Louis got a 9-high straight flush in 2002, Ernie carries the money clip, and Cassie gave the remaining man his rabbit's foot (11). Gregg's best hand wasn't four kings (3), so it was the queen-high straight flush. He doesn't wear the ring (3), so Louis does. By elimination, Gregg carries the gold coin. He isn't related to Howard (13), so Howard got four aces in 2001. By elimination, Matt got four kings in 1997. He didn't receive his gold coin from Peggy or Yvonne (1), or Suzanne (10), so he received it from Julie. Gregg is older than his brother Matt (see above), so he didn't date Peggy (6) and neither did Suzanne (10), so Yvonne did. Suzanne dated Ernie and Peggy dated Louis (12).

1996	Gregg	Q-high straight flush	gold coin	Yvonne
1997	Matt	four kings	keychain	Julie
1999	Ernie	royal flush	money clip	Suzanne
2001	Howard	four aces	rabbit's foot	Cassie
2002	Louis	9-high straight flush	ring	Peggy

Eight Movies in Eight Nights

On Saturday, Jennifer ate either chicken wings or pizza (9). On Monday, she watched a movie with a man (11). She didn't watch *Five Card Stud* on the first Sunday, Monday, Saturday, or the last Sunday (12). She also didn't watch it on Tuesday (3). If she had watched *Five Card Stud* on Wednesday, she would have seen Pamela on Monday (12), which is impossible. If she had watched *Five Card Stud* on Thursday, she would have had pu pu platter on Saturday (12), which is a contradiction. Thus, she watched *Five Card Stud* on

Friday, saw Pamela on Wednesday, and ate pu pu platter on the last Sunday (12). Jennifer watched *The Cincinnati Kid* on Thursday (14). With Olivia, she watched either *Luckytown* or *Rounders* while munching on either sushi or beef potpies (10), and this wasn't on Tuesday, so it was on the first Sunday. She saw Zach on the last Sunday (1), so they watched *House of Games* (11). She saw Marianne on Saturday (2). She watched *The Odd Couple* with Rosie (5), so this was on Tuesday. By elimination, she watched movies with men on Thursday and Friday. She watched *Kaleidoscope* on Saturday (11). She ate tacos on Thursday (11). She watched *Loaded Pistols* on Monday and ate fish and chips on Tuesday (6). She ate falafel on Wednesday (7). She ate sushi on Monday and pizza on Friday (13). By elimination, she ate beef potpies on the first Sunday and chicken wings on Saturday. She saw Victor on Monday (8). She saw Tyrone on Thursday and watched *Rounders* on Wednesday (4). By elimination, she saw Stan on Friday and watched *Luckytown* on Sunday.

Sun.	Olivia	*Luckytown*	beef potpies
Mon.	Victor	*Loaded Pistols*	sushi
Tue.	Rosie	*The Odd Couple*	fish and chips
Wed.	Pamela	*Rounders*	falafel
Thu.	Tyrone	*The Cincinnati Kid*	tacos
Fri.	Stan	*Five Card Stud*	pizza
Sat.	Marianne	*Kaleidoscope*	chicken wings
Sun.	Zach	*House of Games*	pu pu platter

Friendly Game

James sat between the person who brought soft drinks and the person who brought beer (12), so he didn't bring potato chips or poker chips (5), so he brought either the cards or the table. Thus, he sat across from either Alison or Eddie's cousin (4 and 8). Eddie sat in seat #3 (3), so James didn't sit in #6 (see above), therefore Tara did (6). Let's enumerate what we've established: Eddie sat in #3, Tara in #6, James brought either the cards or the table, and he sat directly across from either Alison or Eddie's cousin. This accounts for four positions at the table. Neither James nor the person across from him brought beer or soft drinks (12). Furthermore, the people who brought beer and soft drinks didn't sit opposite each other (12), so they aren't both Eddie and Tara. Therefore, a fifth person in our enumeration brought either beer or soft drinks. Stephanie brought either the poker chips or the potato chips (5), and she isn't Eddie's cousin (11), so she's the sixth person in our enumeration. By elimination, she sat across from the person whom we've established as having brought either the beer or the soft drinks (see above), so he or she is the history professor (11). Raphael sat in either #2 or #4 (2). By elimination, Raphael is either the history professor or the person who sat across from James. Let's look at both possibilities: If Raphael were the history professor, then Stephanie, across from him, would have sat in either #5 or #1. Then, since Raphael sat in #2 or #4 and brought either the soft drinks or the beer (see above), James would have sat next to him, either in #1 or #5. And in that case, the person across from James would have sat in either #2 or #4. Now let's look at the other possibility: If Raphael had sat across from James, then James would have sat in either #1 or #5 (see above). In that case, the people who brought beer and soft drinks would have sat either in #2 and #6 or in #4 and #6, so the professor would have sat either in #2 or #4. By elimination, then, Stephanie would have sat in #5 or #1 and, again, the person who sat to her left would have sat in either #2 or #6. Note that our only two possible premises—that Raphael is the history professor and that he sat across from James—lead to the same conclusions. Therefore, James and Stephanie sat, in some order, in #1 and #5, while the remaining two people sat in #2 and #4. Since James sat either in #1 or #5, Tara in #6 brought either beer or soft drinks. Thus, Stephanie didn't sit in #5 (5), so she sat in #1. The person to Stephanie's left, who brought either poker chips or potato chips (1), sat in #2. This person isn't the professor, who brought either beer or soft drinks (see above), so this person sat across from James. Thus, James sat in #5 and, by elimination, the professor sat in #4. We know that Eddie sat across from Tara (see above), so he didn't bring the table (8), so he brought the cards. Thus, Tara is Eddie's cousin (12). James brought the table (see above), so Alison sat across from him (8). By elimination, Raphael is the history professor. Alison is the dog walker (10). The sculptor brought the poker chips (9), so she's Stephanie. By elimination, Alison brought the potato chips. James is the chiropractor (1). Tara, who is Eddie's cousin (see above), isn't the realtor (4), so Eddie is the realtor. By elimination, Tara is the surfing instructor. She didn't bring the soft drinks (7), so Raphael did. By elimination, Tara brought the beer.

#1	Stephanie	sculptor	poker chips
#2	Alison	dog walker	potato chips
#3	Eddie	realtor	cards
#4	Raphael	history professor	soft drinks
#5	James	chiropractor	table
#6	Tara (Eddie's cousin)	surfing instructor	beer

Hawaiian Holidays

Monica lives on Niihau (8), so she isn't mentioned in clue 4, and Nancy and Nat also aren't mentioned there. Thus, the three people mentioned in clue 4 are from among the following four people: Helene, Keith, Michael, and Oliver. Thus, Helene played at the Irish Open, and she's from Hawaii (4). She played at the Showdown at Sands (12). Nancy lives on Molokai (12). Monica played at the Vienna Spring Festival (12). Nat lives on Maui (1). Keith lives on Kauai and Oliver lives on Oahu (4). By elimination, Michael lives on Lanai. The person who played at the Orleans Open lives on either Maui or Molokai (5), so he or she is either Nancy or Nat. The person who played at the L.A. Poker classic is also either Nancy or Nat (7). Thus, Nancy and Nat played at, in some order, the Orleans Open and the L.A. Poker Classic. Keith and Oliver played at, in some order, the Five Diamond and the Helsinki Freezeout (4). The person who played at the British Open also played at the World Poker Finals or at Shooting Star (2), so this person is Michael. He didn't play at the World Poker Finals (14), so he played at Shooting Star. The person who played at the Grosvenor Open lives on either Maui or Molokai (13), so he or she is either Nat or Nancy. He or she didn't play at the L.A. Poker Classic (3), so he or she played at the Orleans Open (see above). The person who played at the Euro Finals of Poker didn't also play at the Five Diamond (10), so this person isn't Keith or Oliver (see above). Thus, he or she is either Nancy or Nat. In either case, he or she played at the L.A. Poker Classic (see above). By elimination, the person who played at the Five Diamond also played at Poker Million. He isn't Keith (6), so he's Oliver. By elimination, Keith played at the Helsinki Freezeout. He's from Kauai (see above), so he didn't play at the California State Poker Championship (11), so Monica did. By elimination, Keith played at the World Poker Finals. Nancy played at the Grosvenor Open (9) and the Orleans Open (see above). By elimination, Nat played at the L.A. Poker Classic.

Helene	Hawaii	Showdown at Sands	Irish Open
Keith	Kauai	World Poker Finals	Helsinki Freezeout
Michael	Lanai	Shooting Star	British Open
Monica	Niihau	Cal. State Poker Ch.	Vienna Spring Festival
Nancy	Molokai	Orleans Open	Grosvenor Open
Nat	Maui	L.A. Poker Classic	Euro Finals of Poker
Oliver	Oahu	Five Diamond	Poker Million

Atlantic City Express

The four women who played poker played at the Taj Mahal, and the four remaining women played poker slots at the other four casinos (intro). Five women who all live in different boroughs are: Patrice, Ms. Kandelman, the women who played hold'em and Omaha, and the woman who played at the Tropicana (8). The woman who played seven-card hi-lo is the only one from Staten Island (12), so she's mentioned in clue 8. If she were Ms. Kandelman, either she would have played at the Hilton or she would be from Brooklyn (2), either of which would be a contradiction. Thus, Patrice is from Staten Island and played seven-card hi-lo at the Taj Mahal. She's mentioned in clue 1, so she's Ms. Schaefer. Beverley is Ms. Kandelman (13). She didn't play at the Hilton (7), so she's from Brooklyn (2). The women who played Hold'Em and Omaha and the one who played at the Tropicana are, in some order, from the Bronx, Manhattan, and Queens. Anita played at the Hilton (2). She isn't from Brooklyn (7), Staten Island (12), or Manhattan (14), so she's from either the Bronx or Queens. She's Ms. Brody (4). Cathy is Ms. Woods (9). She didn't play seven-card stud (11), but she did play poker at the Taj Mahal (1), so, by elimination, she played either hold'em or Omaha. The woman who played the slots at Caesar's is from either the Bronx or Queens (4). Either Denise or Trudy played seven-card stud at the Taj Mahal (11). By elimination, Beverly Kandelman played the slots at Wild Wild West. Ms. Lawford is from Brooklyn (6), so she's either Denise or Trudy. Trudy is from Manhattan (14), so Denise is Lawford (see above). By elimination, Trudy is the only woman from Manhattan, so Cathy is from either the Bronx or Queens. The woman who played at Caesar's isn't Francie (4) or Trudy (see above), so she's Ilene. Denise Lawford is mentioned in clue 1 as the woman who lives in a borough whose initial is "B." The woman who lives in the same borough as Ms. Fordi is the woman other than Cathy who played either Hold'Em or Omaha. She isn't Trudy, who is the only woman from Manhattan (see above), so she's Francie. She lives in the same borough as Ms. Fordi (see above), and Ms. Fordi didn't play at the Tropicana (8), so Ilene is Ms. Fordi. By elimination, Trudy played at the Tropicana. She is from Manhattan (see above) and is surnamed Nussbaum (3). By elimination, Francie is Gardiner. She didn't play Omaha (10), so Cathy did. By elimination, Francie played Hold'Em. She isn't from Queens (5), so she's from the Bronx and so is Ilene (see above). Cathy Woods is from Queens (8). Anita Brody isn't from Queens (9), so she's from the Bronx (4).

Anita Brody	Bronx	slots	Hilton
Ilene Fordi	Bronx	slots	Caesar's
Francie Gardiner	Bronx	hold'em	Taj Mahal
Denise Lawford	Brooklyn	stud	Taj Mahal
Beverly Kandelman	Brooklyn	slots	Wild Wild West
Trudy Nussbaum	Manhattan	slots	Tropicana
Patrice Schaefer	Staten Island	hi-lo	Taj Mahal
Cathy Woods	Queens	Omaha	Taj Mahal

Queens of Las Vegas

Ms. Starks won exactly half as much as the woman who won on Friday (9), so Ms. Starks won $300, $400, $500, or $600 and the woman who won on Friday won $600, $800, $1000, or $1200. However, the woman who won on Friday didn't win $800 (16), so Ms. Starks didn't win $400 (9). The woman who won $400 is either Polly or Roberta (5). This accounts for three of the five women. Jillian isn't Ms. Starks (6) and didn't win on Friday (11), so she's the fourth woman in our enumeration. Ms. Reynolds isn't Jillian and didn't win on Friday (11). Ms. Reynolds won more than $400 (4), so she's the fifth woman in our enumeration. The woman who won $900 (6) isn't Jillian or Ms. Starks (6), so she's Ms. Reynolds. The woman who won $800 (16) is Jillian. She won either three days before or three days after Ms. Reynolds (11), so Ms. Reynolds is from Scarborough (3). Margie won more than the woman from Scarborough (12), so she won either $1000 or $1200 on Friday. Thus, Ms. Starks won either $500 or $600 (9). Alyssa is Starks and Jillian is from Brewer (4). Since Jillian and Ms. Reynolds won exactly three days apart, the same is true of Alyssa and the woman who won $400. The woman from Arundel won on Saturday (8), so she's either Alyssa or the woman who won $400. Thus, these two women won on Wednesday and Saturday, in some order. Ms. Trower won on Sunday (14), so she's Jillian. By elimination, Ms. Reynolds won on Thursday. She had the second-highest winnings (see above), so Polly won on Wednesday. She won $400 (see above) at the Bellagio (1). By elimination, Alyssa Starks won on Saturday, so she's from Arundel (8). Also by elimination, Roberta won on Thursday. Margie won at Circus Circus (7). Alyssa won at Binion's (15). Polly is Haritel and Roberta won at the Mirage (13). By elimination, Jillian won at the Stardust and Margie is Ms. Lowell. She didn't win $1000 (10), so she won $1200. She isn't from Presque Isle (3), so Polly is. By elimination, Margie is from Lewiston. Alyssa won $600 (9).

Wed.	Polly Haritel	Presque Isle	Bellagio	$400
Thu.	Roberta Reynolds	Scarborough	Mirage	$900
Fri.	Margie Lowell	Lewiston	Circus Circus	$1200
Sat.	Alyssa Starks	Arundel	Binion's	$600
Sun.	Jillian Trower	Brewer	Stardust	$800

The Road to Monte Carlo, Part 5: Mini Millions

Evan drank vodka martinis (part 3), so the six people are: Evan, the person who sat at the Grace Kelly table, the person who came in fifth at his or her table, the person who met Jocelyn, the person who met the linguist, and the person who met the person from Copenhagen (11). The three men and three women met four men and two women, and only one met a person of the opposite sex (4), so this was a woman who met a man. She finished at least one position ahead of the person who met the linguist (4), so she didn't meet the linguist and didn't finish in sixth place. If she had met the person from Copenhagen, then they would have sat at the Prince Rainier table (2), which is impossible (6). Thus, the American woman who met a European man sat at the Grace Kelly table. She didn't visit the Oceanographic Museum (part 4), so she finished either fourth or fifth at her table (8). If she had finished fifth, then the person who met the linguist would have finished sixth (4), which is impossible (11). Thus, she finished fourth and the person who met the linguist finished fifth. By elimination, Evan was among the top three finishers at his table. He didn't visit the Wax Museum (part 4), so he sat at the Prince Rainier table (6). He met a man (4), but since Evan is Renaldi (part 1), he didn't meet the person from Paris (13), so he met the person from Budapest (2). The person who met Jocelyn was also among the three top finishers, so this person visited the Wax Museum (6), so she's either Alice or Diana (part 4). If she's Alice, who sat in seat B on the flight over (part 2), then she met the person from Madrid (9). If she's Diana, who is Bill's wife (part 1), then she met the person from London (15). Thus, in either case, the person she met is from either London or Madrid. Marco lives in Athens (14), so an American man met him (20), so this was either Bill or Chip. Bill, however, didn't visit the National Museum (part 4), so he didn't meet Marco (23), so Chip met Marco. Chip played craps the first night at the casino (part 3), so he didn't meet the linguist (18), so he finished sixth at his table. The person from Paris is either a woman or met an American man (2). In either case, he or she is the linguist.

The au pair is from Athens (10), so he's Marco (see above). The person who met Karl ranked fifth (17), and he's a man (4), so he's Bill. By elimination, Irena is from Copenhagen. Bill's wife is Diana (part 1), so Diana met Irena (22). Alice met Jocelyn (see above), so Jocelyn is from Madrid (9). By elimination, Fawn sat at the Grace Kelly table and met the man from London. Jocelyn is either the historian or the teacher (5). The nurse sat at the Mediterranean table (3), so Diana met her. Alice sat at either the Casiraghi table or the Riviera table (8). Bill won the fifth hand of poker on the plane (part 2), so he didn't sit at the Princess Caroline table (21), so Chip did. Diana met the nurse (see above), so her husband, Bill, didn't sit at the Riviera table (16), so he sat at the Casiraghi table. By elimination, Alice sat at the Riviera table. Her husband is Evan (part 1), so he met the writer (16). Alice met the historian and ranked either second or third (19). By elimination, Fawn met the teacher. He isn't Leonardo (7), so Leonardo is the writer. By elimination, Neil is the teacher. Fawn, who met Neil, ranked fourth (see above). Alice was the last to leave the casino on the first night (part 3), so she ranked third at her table (12). Evan was among the sightseeing group on Monday afternoon (part 4), so he won the tournament (1), so he ranked first at his table (intro). By elimination, Diana ranked second at her table.

1st	Evan	Prince Rainier	Leonardo	writer	Budapest
2nd	Diana	Mediterranean	Irena	nurse	Copenhagen
3rd	Alice	Riviera	Jocelyn	historian	Madrid
4th	Fawn	Grace Kelly	Neil	teacher	London
5th	Bill	Casiraghi	Karl	linguist	Paris
6th	Chip	Pr. Caroline	Marco	au pair	Athens

Showdown

The three people mentioned in clue 3 are Quentin, Abramson, and Thomas's sister (3). Quentin isn't mentioned in clue 19. Abramson isn't Patrick (9), Thomas's girlfriend (16), or Olivia (22), so Abramson also isn't mentioned in clue 19. Thomas's sister lost money (33), so she isn't Olivia (14), so Thomas's sister also isn't mentioned in clue 3. Thus, the three people in clue 3 and the three people mentioned in clue 19 are all different, so Patrick, Olivia, and Thomas's girlfriend didn't sit in seats #3, #6, and #8. Patrick sat on the same side of the table as Olivia (19), so they sat in seats #1 and #2, in some order.

Patrick sat directly facing Thomas's girlfriend (19), who didn't sit in #6 (see above), so Patrick didn't sit in #1. Thus, Olivia sat in #1, Patrick in #2, and Thomas's girlfriend sat in #5. Thomas sat in #7 (35). His first four cards were hearts (16). Mina was the dealer, and only the second, fifth, and sixth cards she dealt were hearts (1), so she could only have sat in #1, #2, or #5. We know, however, that Olivia and Patrick sat in #1 and #2, so Mina sat in #5, therefore she's Thomas's girlfriend (see above). Thus, the person in #6 received the 9 of clubs, Thomas in #7 received the 4 of hearts, the person in #8 received the 9 of diamonds, Olivia in #1 received the king of diamonds, Patrick in #2 received the 5 of hearts, the person in #3 received the 9 of hearts, the person in #4 received the 5 of spades, and Mina received the ten of diamonds (1). Robert's last card was a 9 (23), so by elimination it was the 9 of spades. It didn't improve his hand (23), so he didn't already have a 9; therefore, he sat in #4. With the second card dealt, two men paired up their first cards (6). These men didn't include Thomas, whose first and second cards were both hearts (16). They also didn't include the people in #3, #6, or #8, because by elimination none of them could have paired up their 9's. Thus, the two men who paired up are Patrick and Robert, so they received the 5 of diamonds and the 5 of clubs, in some order. Thus, one of them is McGuirk (25) and the other is Hasagawa (32). Beardsley and Kimmel sat facing each other (15). If they were in #3 and #8, in either order, then one of them would be Quentin (3), which is impossible (15). Thus, they sat, in some order, in #1 and #6. Thus, the person in #6 isn't Quentin (15), so she's a woman who lost money (3), so she's Samantha. On his second card, Thomas suited up in hearts (16), so Nathan suited up in a different suit (6). Thus, Nathan's first card wasn't a heart, so he didn't sit in #3, so Quentin did. By elimination, Nathan sat in #8. He's Abramson (3) and his second card was a diamond (16). The remaining person who suited up did so in either spades or clubs (6), so she's Samantha and her second card was a club. Thus, Thomas is Resnick and Samantha lost $55 (6). Samantha's brother is Thomas (see above), and together they won $18 (29), so Thomas won $73. His last card was the 10 of spades (27), which busted his flush (see above). Among Mina's second, third, and fourth cards were, in some order, the 10 of hearts and the 10 of clubs (21). Samantha's third card and Nathan's third card were both spades (10). Thus, the only three people who suited up their first two cards ended up with busted flushes, so no one got a flush. No one got a full house or better (35). If someone had gotten a straight, then that person would have had either a 5 or a 10, since every possible straight includes one of these cards. But we have accounted for all the 5's and 10's, which were all held by Patrick, Robert, Mina, and Thomas. Patrick and Robert both held at least one pair, Mina held three of a kind, and Thomas had a 4 and a 10 (see above), so none of them had a straight. Thus, no one had a straight. We know that Mina had three 10s, so either she or someone with a higher three of a kind took the pot. So we can rule out Robert and Thomas as winners. We can also rule out Patrick, since if he had gotten three of a kind, he would have added these to his pair of fives to make a full house, which is impossible (33). We can also rule out Samantha, since she ended up losing money (see above) while the winner of Showdown won money (34). We can also rule out Nathan Abramson and Olivia (22). This means that either Mina or Quentin won the hand. In either case, Robert sat next to the winner, so he's Hasagawa's cousin (7), so he's McGuirk and Patrick is Hasagawa (see above). Patrick held the 5 of clubs (32), so Robert held the 5 of diamonds (see above). Mina's second card was the queen of spades (11). If she had received the queen of diamonds, she would have gotten a full house (see above), which is impossible (35). Thus, Samantha got the queen of diamonds (26), so she didn't receive four clubs, so Mina didn't win the hand (7). By elimination, Quentin won the hand, so he won from $1 to $39 (34). He beat Mina's hand with three jacks, three kings, or three aces (see above). Patrick got four clubs (7). Nathan Abramson got the ace of hearts (9). One man had a pair of queens (28), so by elimination he had the queen of hearts and the queen of clubs. This can only be Robert (see above). He didn't win $73 (27), so he won $37 (28). Ziller lost $37 (17), so Mina is Ziller. By elimination, Quentin is DiSimone. His last card was the 3 of hearts (12). Olivia's last two cards were the jack of hearts and king of spades (24). She won (14) less than $10 (24). Kimmel's last card was the ace of clubs (30), so she's Samantha. By elimination, Olivia is Beardsley. We know that Quentin DiSimone won the hand, beating Mina Ziller's three 10s with a higher three of a kind (see above). By elimination among the cards that other players received, we can deduce that Quentin received the jack of spades, jack of diamonds, and jack of clubs. The person who got the king of hearts won $20 more than Quentin DiSimone (5), so he or she won from $21 to $59 (see above). Olivia didn't get the king of hearts, because then she would have won the pot, which is a contradiction. Thus, Nathan got the king of hearts. The wins and losses must total the same amount, and currently we have accounted for five winners winning more than two losers, so Patrick lost money. Olivia Beardsley won $7 (2). Patrick lost $67 (8). Nathan won $20 more than Quentin (see above), so to balance out the wins and losses, we can conclude that Nathan won $31 and Quentin won $11. Patrick received at least three cards higher than a 6 (8), and these were all clubs (see above), so by elimination he received the 7 of clubs, 8 of clubs, and king of clubs. Olivia got the six of hearts (13). Thomas received three hearts besides the four of hearts (see above), so by elimination these were the deuce of hearts, seven of hearts, and eight of hearts. Samantha's second card was a club (see above), so by elimination it was six or lower. She got better than a pair of 7's (4), so she paired up her ace of clubs with an ace of spades. Nathan also got better than a pair of 7's (4), so by elimination he got the 8 of diamonds and 8 of spades. Mina got the 6 of spades (18). Samantha got the 6 of clubs (20). Olivia got the 6 of diamonds (14).

#1	Olivia Beardsley	won $7	KD, 6H, 6D, JH, KS
#2	Patrick Hasagawa	lost $67	5H, 5C, 7C, 8C, KC
#3	Quentin DiSimone	won $11	9H, JS, JD, JC, 3H
#4	Robert McGuirk	won $37	5S, 5D, QH, QC, 9S
#5	Mina Ziller	lost $37	10D, QS, 10H, 10C, 6S
#6	Samantha Kimmel	lost $55	9C, 6C, AS, QD, AC
#7	Thomas Resnick	won $73	4H, 2H, 7H, 8H, 10S
#8	Nathan Abramson	won $31	9D, 8D, 8S, AH, KH

Part III
False Logic Puzzles

Who Owns the Mule?

Consider that each farmer made one true and one false statement.

Assume A is the owner. If so, both of A's statements are false. Therefore, A is not the owner. Assume C is the owner. If so, both of C's statements are true. Therefore, C is not the owner. Therefore, B is the owner, and the statements are true and false as shown in the diagram below.

	1	2
A	F	T
B	T	F
C	F	T

SUMMARY: It is B's mule.

Theft of Homer's Writings

Assume B is guilty. If so, A's second and third statements are true. Therefore, B did not do it. Assume C is guilty. If so, B's first and second statements are true. Therefore, C did not do it. Therefore, A is guilty.

	1	2	3
A	F	T	F
B	T	F	F
C	F	T	F

SUMMARY: A is the thief.

Who Left the Cell Door Open?

Consider that three statements are true, and five are false.

Assume that A is guilty. If so, A's first and second statements are both false; B's statements are both true; C's first statement is false, and second is true; and D's first statement is true. Therefore, since, if A did it, there are four true statements, A is not guilty.

Assume that B is guilty. If so, A's first statement, C's first and second statement, and D's first statement are true. Therefore, B did not do it.

Assume that C is guilty. If so, A's first and second statement, B's first statement, C's second statement, and D's first statement are true. Therefore, C did not do it. By elimination, D is guilty.

	1	2
A	T	F
B	T	F
C	F	T
D	F	F

SUMMARY: D is guilty.

A Secret Observer

Assume A is the observer. If so, A's statements are true. C's second statement, which refers to A, confirms A's second statement. Therefore, A is not the observer. Also, in confirming A's second statement, C's second statement verifies that D is not the observer.

Assume C is guilty. If so, A's first statement, which refers to C, must be false. However, D's second statement confirms A's first statement. Therefore, C is not the observer. Therefore, D's first statement, which claims C's first statement is false, is true. B is the observer.

	1	2
A	T	T
B	T	T
C	F	T
D	T	T

SUMMARY: B is the observer.

Theft From the Statue of Athena

Consider that one suspect made three true statements.

A's second statement is false, as it was given that all four suspects were in Athens when the crime occurred. C's second statement is false, as there was evidence that the thief acted alone. From D's first statement, we know that at least one of D's statements is false. Therefore, B is the one with three true statements.

From B's third statement, C was seen at the Acropolis late that night. This agrees with D's second statement. Therefore, since we know that at least one of D's statements is false, D's third statement must be false. D did it.

	1	2	3
A	T	F	F
B	T	T	T
C	F	F	F
D	?	T	F

SUMMARY: D is the thief.

323

Who Should Lead the Victory Parade?

Consider that one made one false statement, one made two false statements, and one made three false statements.

Assume that A should lead the parade. If so, A's first two statements are true. Therefore, A's third statement must be false. If so, C's third statement must be true, and C must be the one with one true statement. Therefore, C's second statement must be false. Therefore, B's third statement must be true. Therefore, since each soldier would have at least one true statement, A is not the correct choice.

Assume that B should lead the parade. If so, B's first two statements are true and third statement must be false. Therefore C's second statement must be true. Therefore C's third statement must be false. This means that A's third statement must be true. Again, each soldier would have at least one true statement.

Therefore, C is the correct choice. A has made three false statements; B has made two false statements; and C has made one false statement.

	1	2	3
A	F	F	F
B	F	F	T
C	T	F	T

SUMMARY: C should lead the parade.

Socrates Plans a Trip

Consider that the disciple Socrates selects made three true or three false statements. One of the other two made two true statements and one false statement. The remaining one made one true statement and two false statements.

C's first and third statements are contradictory. One is true and one is false. Therefore, C is not the one who is selected.

Assume that B is selected. If so, C is the one with two true statements, and A has made one true statement, either his first or second one. However, A's first and second statements contradict B's third and first statements. One of A's two statements and one of B's statements must be true. Therefore, since B's other statement must be false, B is not the one with three true or three false statements. B was not selected.

A is the disciple selected. If A's three statements were all true, then B's statements would all be false, which is not allowed. So, A's three statements are all false.

	1	2	3
A	F	F	F
B	T	F	T
C	F	F	T

SUMMARY: Socrates selects A.

Who Should Repair the Statue?

Consider that each of the four craftsmen made the same number of true statements and the same number of false statements.

Assume that A is the most qualified. If so, B has at least two true statements; and each of the other three has at least two false statements. Therefore, A is not the most qualified.

Assume that B is the most qualified. If so, A's and C's first and third statements are consistent. However their second statements are not. Therefore, each of these two has a different number of true statements. Therefore, B is not the most qualified.

Assume that D is the most qualified. If so, D's first and third statements are false, D's second and A's first statements agree, and A's second statement is true. Therefore, A and D each has a different number of true statements. Therefore, D is not the most qualified.

Therefore, C is the most qualified, and the craftsmen's statements are true and false as shown below.

	1	2	3
A	F	F	T
B	F	F	T
C	T	F	F
D	T	F	F

SUMMARY: C is the most qualified.

Who Won the Discus Throw?

Since no two made the same number of true statements, it is apparent that one made three true statements, one made two true statements, one made one true statement, and one made no true statements.

Assume that A was the winner. If so, only A's first statement and B's first statement confirm this. B must be the one with all true statements, since, if A was the winner, his second statement is false. If so, B was second and B and C trained together; A's third statement is false; D's first and third statements are false, and second statement is true. Therefore, A and D would each have made only one true statement. Therefore, A was not the winner.

Assume that C was the winner. If so, D must be the one with all true statements. If so, B was second, and C and D trained together. If so, A's three statements and C's three statements are false. Therefore, C was not the winner.

Assume that D was the winner. If so, either A or D could be the one with three statements. Assume it is A. If so, A was second, and A and C trained together. If so, both C and D would each have made only one true statement. Therefore, if D was the winner, A was not the one with three true statements.

Assume D was the winner, and D was the one with three true statements. If so, B was second, and C and D trained together. If so, A and B have each made only one true statement. Therefore, D was not the winner.

Therefore, B was the winner, and A was second (but we cannot determine whether C trained with A or with no one).

	1	2	3
A	T	T	?
B	F	F	F
C	T	?	T
D	T	F	F

SUMMARY: B was the winner.

The Food Produce Thief

Consider that the one who delivered the milk made three true statements, the one who delivered the cheese made two true statements and one false statement, the one who delivered the honey made one true statement and two false statements, and both the one who delivered the nuts and the one who delivered the bread each made three false statements.

A is the one who delivered the bread and D is the one who delivered the nuts. We know this since the two who delivered these two food products made only false statements, and neither B, C, nor E could have delivered the bread or nuts, as the first statement or statements would be true. A and D, who each accuse the other, are both innocent. Also, based on their first statements being false, A delivered the bread and D delivered the nuts.

E's first statement must be true, since it would be false only if made by the citizen who delivered the milk, and that citizen made three true statements. Therefore E must be the one who delivered the goat's cheese or the one who delivered the honey. If E is the one who delivered the honey, his second and third statements must be false. However, since we know E's third statement to be true, E is the one who delivered the cheese. E's second statement must be false. Therefore, C is not the thief. Since we know that D is not the thief, C's third statement is true. C is either the one who delivered the milk or the one who delivered the honey.

Our conclusions at this point are:

	1	2	3	delivery
A	F	F	F	bread
B				
C			T	
D	F	F	F	nuts
E	T	F	T	cheese

From A's third statement, which we know to be false, B did not deliver the honey. Therefore, B delivered the milk and his statements are all true, and C

328

delivered the honey and his first two statements are false. Finally, based on A2, B2, D2, and E2, we can eliminate four suspects, revealing E as the thief.

SUMMARY:

A delivered bread.
B delivered milk.
C delivered honey.
D delivered nuts.
E delivered cheese, and is the thief.

Theft at the Open Market

Since none of the suspects is completely truthful, and no two suspects made the same number of true statements, we can conclude that one made three true statements, one made two true statements, one made one true statement, and one made no true statements.

A's fourth statement is false as, if it were true, it would be a contradiction. Therefore, A made at least one true statement. A's second statement is clearly false, as it was given that one of the four is guilty. Therefore, either or both of A's first and third statements must be true.

D's second and fourth statements are contradictory: either one is true and one is false, or both are false. If D's third statement is true, A's first statement is false and his third statement must be true. However, this makes D's fourth statement false. If A's first statement is true, D's third statement is false. Therefore, either D's third or fourth statements are false, or both are false.

C's first statement is false, as either or both of A's first and third statements must be true. Also, C's fourth statement is false, as none of the four suspects is completely truthful.

The suspect with no true statements must be B, C, or D. Assume that B is the suspect with no true statements. If so, B's first statement is false and A is guilty. If so, D's second statement claiming B is guilty must be false. Since we know that either or both of D's third and fourth statements are false, D has made at least two false statements. Since either B or D must be the suspect with three true statements (A and C each have made at least two false statements), we can eliminate B as the suspect with no true statements.

Therefore, the suspect with no true statements must be either C or D. Since C's second statement and D's first statement both agree, they must both be false. Since C's third statement and D's third statement agree, they must also be false. Therefore, C is the suspect with no true statements.

Our conclusions, so far:

	1	2	3	3
A		F		F
B				
C	F	F	F	F
D	F		F	

We know that D's first and third statements are false. Since we know that either D's second or fourth statements are false, D must be the suspect with one true statement, and B is the suspect with three true statements.

Therefore, A is the suspect with two true statements, the first and third ones. Therefore, since D's fourth statement disagrees with A's third statement, which is true, D's only true statement is the second one, that B is guilty.

SUMMARY: B is guilty.

The First Choice

Whether or not sign A is true or false, sign B must be false. (If it's true, B must be the one false sign; if false, then there must be a second false sign.) Therefore door A is the correct door.

	sign A	sign B
if door A is correct	T or F	F
if door B is correct	contradiction	T

SUMMARY: Door A is the correct choice.

The Second Choice

The sign on door A must be false. (Assuming that it is true leads to a contradiction.) Therefore, the sign on door B is true. Therefore, door B is the correct choice.

	sign A	sign B
if door A is correct	contradiction	F
if door B is correct	F	T

SUMMARY: Door B is the correct choice.

The Third Choice

If door B is the correct door, the sign on door B is true and the sign on door C is false. This creates a logical contradiction on door A; if it is true, then it claims there are two false signs when there is only one, and if it is false, then there really are two false signs, so its statement cannot be a lie. If door C is the correct door, the sign on door C is true and the sign on door B is false. Again, the sign on door A presents a contradiction. Door A is the correct choice.

	sign A	sign B	sign C
if door A is correct	T or F	F	F
if door B is correct	contradiction	T	F
if door C is correct	contradiction	F	T

SUMMARY: Door A is the correct choice.

The Fourth Choice

The sign on door B must be true. Therefore, either or both of the signs on doors A and C are false. If door A is the one to go through, the signs at both doors A and C are true. If door B is the one to go through, the signs on doors A and C are, again true. Therefore, Door C is the correct choice.

	sign A	sign B	sign C
if door A is correct	T	contradiction	T
if door B is correct	T	contradiction	T
if door C is correct	F	T	F

SUMMARY: Door C is the correct choice.

The Fifth Choice

The sign on door A must be false. If it were true, it would be a contradiction. Since the sign on door B agrees with the sign on door A, it is also false. Therefore, since at least one sign must be true for sign A to be false, the sign on door C is true, and door C is the way to go.

	sign A	sign B	sign C
if door A is correct	F (contradiction)	F	F
if door B is correct	F (contradiction)	F	F
if door C is correct	F	F	T

SUMMARY: Door C is the correct choice.

The Sixth Choice

The sign on door B must be false, since it disagrees with the sign on door A, and claims no false signs. The sign on door A must be true, since if it were false, it would represent the second false sign, and validate its statement. Therefore, the sign on door C is the second false sign. (Note: Door A cannot be the way to go as the sign on door C agrees with this, and sets up a contradiction which is not resolved by the sign on door A being determined to be false.) Therefore, from C's false statement, door B is the way to go.

	sign A	sign B	sign C
if door A is correct	T	F	F (contradiction)
if door B is correct	T	F	F
if door C is correct	T	F	F (contradiction)

SUMMARY: Door B is the correct choice.

The Seventh Choice

Assume the sign on door A is true. If so, since the signs on doors B and D disagree, one of them must be false, and the sign on door C must be the second false sign, in which case, the sign on door D is true. Assume the sign on door A is false. If so, again, since the signs on doors B and D disagree, one of them must be false. If the sign on door A is false, there must be an additional false sign, the sign on door C; and the sign on door D is true.

In either case, the sign on door C is false; door C is the correct choice.

	sign A	sign B	sign C	sign D
if sign A is true	T	F	F	T
if sign A is false	F	F	F	T

SUMMARY: Door C is the correct choice.

The Eighth Choice

The sign on door A is only true if A is not the door to go through or the adjacent door is true but not if both are true. Thus, if sign A is false, then both A is not the door to go through and B's sign is true or else both A is the door to go through and B's sign is false.

Assume that the sign on door B is true. If so, the sign on door A is false, and is the wrong choice. If so, the sign on door C is false, and it also is the wrong choice. In this case, B is the door to take.

If the sign on door B is false, the signs on doors A and C must both be true. (If one of A and C were true and the other false, along with the false sign on door B the sign on door B would be true—a contradiction.) In this case as well, door B is the correct choice.

Regardless of whether the sign on door B is true or false, door B is the way to go. Consider both alternatives:

	sign A	sign B	sign C
if door A is correct	F (contradiction)	T	F
if door B is correct	F	T	F
if door C is correct	F	T	F (contradiction)

	sign A	sign B	sign C
if door A is correct	T (contradiction)	F	T
if door B is correct	T	F	T
if door C is correct	T	F	T (contradiction)

SUMMARY: B is the correct choice.

Neptune Establishes Communication

A must be the Midravian. Only a Midravian could answer "no" to the question "Are you the Soravian?" A Soravian, who always speaks truthfully, would answer "yes"; a Noravian, who always speaks falsely, would also answer "yes."

Since A's first response was truthful, his second response is false; B is the Soravian and C is the Noravian.

	Soravian	Noravian	Midravian
A	−	−	+
B	+	−	−
C	−	+	−

SUMMARY:

A. Midravian
B. Soravian
C. Noravian

Two Avians

B's statement must be false, since if truthful, it would confirm that B is a Noravian. A false statement would not be possible for a Soravian. B is a Midravian. Since the two represent different groups, A, whose statement is false, is a Noravian.

	Soravian	Noravian	Midravian
A	−	+	−
B	−	−	+

SUMMARY:

A. Noravian
B. Midravian

Umbrellas to Sell

If C is the always-truthful Soravian, then A's statement is false, but C identifies B's statement as a lie, creating a contradiction. If C is the always-lying Soravian, A's statement is true, but C's false statement means that B's statement is true, creating another contradiction. Therefore, C is the Midravian. A, who has made a false statement, is the Noravian and B is the Soravian.

	Soravian	Noravian	Midravian
A	−	+	−
B	+	−	−
C	−	−	+

SUMMARY:

   A. Noravian
   B. Soravian
   C. Midravian

Visit From a Hippogriff

C's statement states that A is the Soravian. If true, C is the Midravian and B is the Noravian. However, it was given that this was the first visit from a hippogriff. Therefore, both C's statement and A's first statement are false. Therefore, B is the Soravian, and, from A's second statement, which is false, A is the Noravian and C is the Midravian.

	Soravian	Noravian	Midravian
A	−	+	−
B	+	−	−
C	−	−	+

SUMMARY:

   A. Noravian
   B. Soravian
   C. Midravian

To Catch an Aspidochelon

C's second statement is false, since it claims that C is a Noravian. If true, it would be impossible, as Noravians always speak falsely. Therefore, C must be a Midravian, and his first statement is true.

Therefore, A's first statement is false, since it is contradicted by C's first statement. Therefore, A's second statement is also false. A must be a Noravian.

Since we know A's first statement to be false, B's third statement, which confirms this, is true. Therefore, B's first statement must also be true. Therefore, since B is not a Midravian, he must be a Soravian.

	Soravian	Noravian	Midravian
A	−	+	−
B	+	−	−
C	−	−	+

SUMMARY:

    A. Noravian
    B. Soravian
    C. Midravian

Is D Neptune Visiting in Disguise?

C's second statement is false, since it claims A is a Soravian, which A's second statement denies. Therefore, neither A nor C is a Soravian.

If A's second statement is truthful, he is a Midravian and his third statement is false. If so, at least one of B's statements is truthful. If B's third statement is truthful, B must be a Soravian. If so, this refutes A's second statement. If B's second statement is truthful, B must be a Soravian, since we know that neither A nor C is a Soravian. Therefore, A's second statement is false. One of the three speakers is a Soravian, and, again, it must be B.

Since A's third statement is refuted, A is a Noravian. Since B's first statement refutes C's first statement, C is a Noravian.

	Soravian	Noravian	Midravian
A	−	+	−
B	+	−	−
C	−	+	−

SUMMARY:

  A. Noravian
  B. Soravian
  C. Noravian

A's Statement Is Truthful

A's statement is truthful, since each of the three possibilities is covered. A is either a Soravian or a Midravian, since a Noravian cannot speak truthfully. C's statement must be truthful, as it could be false only if C were a Soravian, and a Soravian cannot make a false statement. C must be a Midravian, as a Noravian cannot make a truthful statement.

Therefore, B and D are the two who have made false statements. B must be a Noravian, as the statement would be truthful for either a Soravian or a Midravian.

D must be a Midravian, as the statement would be true if made by a Soravian or a Noravian. Therefore, A must be the Soravian.

	Soravian	Noravian	Midravian
A	+	−	−
B	−	+	−
C	−	−	+
D	−	−	+

SUMMARY:

  A. Soravian
  B. Noravian
  C. Midravian
  D. Midravian

A Problem With a Sea Monster

If A's third statement is truthful, C is the Midravian, A must be the Soravian, and B must be the Noravian. If so, C's first statement must be false, since it contradicts A's second statement. If so, C's second statement is truthful and third statement is false. However, C's third statement contradicts B's third statement. This is inconsistent with B being a Noravian. Therefore, A's third statement must be false. Therefore, A's first statement is also false. The Soravian is either B or C. B's first statement contradicts A's first statement. Therefore, B's first statement is truthful. Conclusions at this point are:

	Soravian	Noravian	Midravian
A	−		
B		−	
C			

Since B's first statement is truthful, his third statement is also truthful, but this contradicts C's third statement. C is not the Soravian. Therefore, B is the Soravian; C, who has made three false statements, is the Noravian; A, whose first and third statements are false and second statement is truthful, is the Midravian.

SUMMARY:
  A. Midravian
  B. Soravian
  C. Noravian

Visitors From the Sea

A's first statement must be true. It would be true for anyone but a Soravian, and this would be impossible as Soravians always speak truthfully. A is not the Soravian or the Noravian. A could be a Midravian, but, if so, the fourth statement must be false, because if A were a Midravian, the first and third statements would be true, and the second and fourth statements would be false. Therefore, A is not the Midravian; A is the Outlier.

D's first statement, which correctly states that A's first statement is true, is truthful. Therefore, D's third statement is also truthful. D is the Midravian.

At this point our conclusions are:

	Soravian	Noravian	Midravian	Outlier
A	–	–	–	+
B			–	–
C			–	–
D	–	–	+	–

D's second statement must be false. C is not the Soravian; C must be the Noravian, and B is the Soravian.

SUMMARY:

A. Outlier
B. Soravian
C. Noravian
D. Midravian

Recreational Activities on Ave

Since no two of the five enjoy the same number of the four recreational activities, it is apparent that one enjoys four activities, one enjoys three activities, one enjoys two activities, one enjoys one activity, and one enjoys none of the four activities.

A's first statement and D's second statement agree. They are either both truthful or both false. A's third statement and D's fourth statement are contradictory. One is truthful and one is false. Thus, one of these two must be the Outlier.

B's first statement, indicating that C enjoys all four activities, is inconsistent with B's third statement, which claims that (per D's third statement) C's interest is limited to fishing. Therefore, since both statements cannot be truthful, they must both be false. Therefore B's fourth statement, claiming to be a Soravian, is also false. B is a Noravian. Therefore, B's second statement, indicating that A is not a Midravian, is false. A is a Midravian. Therefore, D is the Outlier. A's first and third statements are false, and second and fourth statements are truthful. D's second statement is false and fourth statement is truthful.

A's fourth statement, which is truthful, indicates that E is not a Noravian or a Midravian. Since D is the Outlier, E must be a Soravian. C's fourth statement, that E is not a Soravian, is false. Therefore, C's second statement is also false. A's second statement, which is truthful, indicates that E enjoys both swimming and fishing. E's second statement, which is also truthful, claims giant sea horse racing and boating. Therefore, E is the one with all four recreational activities. Therefore, C's first statement that B enjoys all four recreational activities is false. C is a Noravian. At this point our conclusions are:

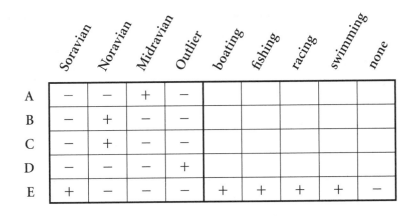

C's third statement falsely claims not to enjoy boating. E's first statement indicates that C enjoys giant sea horse racing and swimming. Therefore, C enjoys boating, giant sea horse racing, and swimming. C's second statement, which is false, indicates that D has no interest in fishing. E's truthful fourth statement indicates that D enjoys only one of the four principal recreational activities. Therefore, D's sole activity is fishing.

A's two recreational activities, as indicated by E's third statement, are sea horse racing and boating. Therefore, B must be the one with none of the four principal activities.

SUMMARY:

A. Midravian; boating, giant sea horse racing
B. Noravian; none
C. Noravian; boating, giant sea horse racing, and swimming
D. Outlier; fishing
E. Soravian; boating, fishing, giant sea horse racing, and swimming

The Village Fair

Statement 1 suggests that the sheep must have won in the daybreak to midmorning showing. From statement 6, Edvo's animal was entered in the daybreak to midmorning showing. From these two statements we would conclude that Edvo's animal was the sheep. However, statement 2 indicates that Edvo's animal was the goat. Therefore, the false statement is either 1, 2, or 6. From statement 4, the goat's showing must have been from midmorning to midday. Therefore, the false statement must be either 2 or 6.

From statements 1 and 3, Dor, who did not own the sheep, must have won the midmorning to midday showing.

From statement 4, Dor's animal is the goat. Therefore, the false statement is 2. From statement 6, Edvo's animal is the sheep.

Conclusions at this point are:

	cow	goat	pig	sheep	daybreak to midmorning	midmorning to midday	midday to midafternoon	midafternoon to sundown
Dor	−	+	−	−	−	+	−	−
Edvo	−	−	−	+	+	−	−	−
Frer		−		−	−	−		
Har		−		−	−	−		

From statements 4 and 5, Frer's animal, the cow, was entered in the midafternoon to sundown showing; Har's animal, the pig, was entered in the midday to mid-afternoon showing, and from statement 4, was the blue ribbon winner.

SUMMARY:

Dor   goat   midmorning to midday
Edvo   sheep   daybreak to midmorning
Frer   cow   midafternoon to sundown
Har   pig   midday to midafternoon (blue ribbon winner)

Encounter With the Dragon Meduso

From statement 1, Sir Hector's attempt to use his peripheral vision was not his fourth one. From statement 3, the attempt by Sir Hector to slip into the dragon's cave was not his fourth one. From statements 4 and 5, we can conclude that neither the attempt to use his polished shield nor the attempt to use a blindfold was the fourth one. Since one of these four attempts had to be the fourth one, it is apparent that one of statements 1, 3, 4, and 5 must be the false one.

This means that statements 2 and 6 are both true. Therefore, the attempt to use a blindfold is not immediately before or after two of the three other attempts, which means it can only be immediately before or after the attempt to use a shield. This means that the attempt to use a blindfold must be first or fourth.

Assume the attempt to use a blindfold is fourth. The attempt to use a shield must be third, which makes both statements 4 and 5 false.

Therefore, the attempt to use a blindfold must be first. The attempt to use a shield must be second, and statement 5 is true. This also means that one of the other two attempts must be fourth, so the false statement is either 1 or 3.

Therefore, statement 4 is true, which means that the attempt to slip into the cave was third and the attempt to use peripheral vision was fourth.

	blindfold	vision	shield	cave
first	+	−	−	−
second	−	−	+	−
third	−	−	−	+
fourth	−	+	−	−

SUMMARY:
First: blindfold
Second: polished shield
Third: slip into cave
Fourth: peripheral vision

The Dragon Watch

From statement 1, Har was not the youngest. From statement 3, neither Edvo nor Frer was the youngest. From statement 4, Tolo was not the youngest. Therefore, if these statements are true, Winn must be the youngest. Also from statements 1, 3, and 4, Winn held the fifth watch (since he had a later watch than Edvo, Frer, and Tolo, and Har did not have the fifth watch). However, from statement 2, Winn could not have held the fifth watch and be the youngest. One of these statements must be false (and therefore someone else besides Winn held the fifth watch, or someone else besides Winn is youngest).

Assume that statement 1 is false. If so, Har could be either the youngest or have held the fifth watch. However, from statements 4 and 6, Har was not the youngest, and from statements 3 and 6, Har did not hold the fifth watch. Therefore, the false statement is not statement 1.

Assume that statement 3 is false. If so, Edvo could be either the youngest or have held the fifth watch, as could Frer. However, from statement 2, Edvo was not the youngest, and from statements 7 and 5, since he was younger than Frer, he did not hold the fifth watch. From statement 7, Frer was neither assigned a later watch nor was he younger than Edvo. Therefore, statement 3 is not false.

Assume that statement 4 is false. If so, Tolo could have stood the fifth watch or be the youngest. However, from statement 2, Tolo was not the youngest, and from statement 7, he was not the last watch. Therefore, the false statement is statement 2.

Therefore, Winn stood the fifth watch. Har did not stand the first watch, and Tolo stood an earlier watch than Frer or Edvo. Tolo stood the first watch. Since Har was not the oldest, from statement 8, he was not assigned the second watch. Therefore, Frer, who stood an earlier watch than Edvo (statement 3), stood the second watch and, from statement 8, was the oldest.

From statement 4, Tolo was not the second oldest, the fourth oldest, or the youngest. Therefore, Tolo was the third oldest. Also from statements 3 and 7, Edvo was not the fourth oldest or the youngest. Therefore, Edvo was the second oldest. Since the fourth oldest stood an earlier watch than Edvo, Har must have been the fourth oldest and Winn was the youngest. Since the fourth oldest stood an earlier watch than Edvo, Har had the third watch and Edvo had the fourth watch.

	assigned watch					youngest	4th oldest	3rd oldest	2nd oldest	oldest
	1st	2nd	3rd	4th	5th					
Edvo	−	−	−	+	−	−	−	−	+	−
Frer	−	+	−	−	−	−	−	−	−	+
Har	−	−	+	−	−	−	+	−	−	−
Tolo	+	−	−	−	−	−	−	+	−	−
Winn	−	−	−	−	+	+	−	−	−	−

SUMMARY:

Edvo	fourth watch	second oldest
Frer	second watch	oldest
Har	third watch	fourth oldest
Tolo	first watch	third oldest
Winn	fifth watch	youngest

New Ponies

From statement 1, Tolo was not Son of Fergy or Son of Evel. From statements 1 and 5, since Tolo's new pony was not black, he was not Son of Alfo. Therefore, if both statements 1 and 5 are true, Tolo was Son of Dirk.

However, statements 2 and 3 indicate that Boro was second to acquire a new pony, as was Son of Dirk. Either Tolo was not Son of Dirk, or Boro was not second to acquire a pony, or Son of Dirk was not second to acquire a pony.

From statements 2 and 4, if both are true, Boro's pony must have been eleven hands. From statement 3, if true, Son of Dirk's new pony was not eleven hands. Therefore, the false statement must be 2, 3, or 4.

Therefore, statements 1 and 5 are true; Tolo was Son of Dirk. From statements 1 and 6, Tolo's pony was not ten or twelve hands. Therefore, it was nine or eleven hands. Therefore, statement 3, which states that Son of Dirk's pony was neither nine hands nor eleven hands, is false.

Therefore, Boro was the second to acquire a pony. From statement 1, since Tolo's pony was acquired immediately after Kover's, Tolo was the fourth to acquire a pony, Kover was third, and Jes was first.

From statements 2 and 5, Boro, who acquired the white pony, was the Son of Fergy, and Jes was the Son of Alfo. His pony was black.

From statement 4, Tolo did not acquire the pony that was eleven hands. Therefore, Tolo's pony was nine hands. From statement 2, Kover, Son of Evel, whose pony was not twelve hands or eleven hands, acquired the pony that was ten hands. Boro, whose pony was not twelve hands, acquired the pony that was eleven hands; Jes's pony was twelve hands.

Conclusions, so far:

first name	second name	size	color	order of acquisition
Boro	Son of Fergy	11	white	2nd
Jes	Son of Alfo	12	black	1st
Kover	Son of Evel	10		3rd
Tolo	Son of Dirk	9		4th

From statement 1, Tolo's pony was not palomino; it was gray, and Kover's was palomino.

SUMMARY:

Boro	Son of Fergy	eleven hands	white
Jes	Son of Alfo	twelve hands	black
Kover	Son of Evel	ten hands	palomino
Tolo	Son of Dirk	nine hands	gray

Work and Recreation

If statements 1, 2, 4, and 6 are all true, then the carpenter's favorite activity is singing (statement 1), the cobbler's favorite is dancing (statement 2), the weaver's favorite is instrumental music (statement 6), and storytelling is not the favorite of either the blacksmith or miller (statement 4). That would mean storytelling is no one's favorite activity, which cannot be the case. Therefore one of those four statements is false.

From statement 3, Zett's second-favorite activity must be the same as Winn's favorite, storytelling (statement 5). Since storytelling is the carpenter's second-favorite activity (statement 8), Zett must be the carpenter, and storytelling is not also the carpenter's favorite activity. This means that statement 1 must be true, because if statement 1 were false, clues 2, 4, and 6 would combine to once again leave no profession whose favorite activity is storytelling. Therefore Zett the carpenter's favorite activity is singing.

From statement 5, Winn was not the cobbler or the miller, therefore neither the cobbler nor miller have storytelling as their favorite activity or dancing as their second-favorite activity. This leaves either the weaver or the blacksmith as the one whose favorite activity is storytelling, which means we can narrow the false statement down to 4 or 6. The cobbler's favorite activity, then, is dancing, and his second-favorite is not puzzles. The cobbler is not Winn, Zett the carpenter, Hober (statement 7), or Dok (whose favorite activity cannot be dancing, since, from statement 3, that activity must be Fram's second-favorite, but dancing is Winn's second-favorite activity). Therefore Fram is the cobbler. Conclusions at this point are as follows:

	trade	favorite recreation	second-favorite recreation		trade	favorite recreation
Dok					blacksmith	
Fram	cobbler	dancing			carpenter	singing
Hober					cobbler	dancing
Winn		stories	dancing		miller	
Zett	carpenter	singing	stories		weaver	

We already know Winn is not the miller, and Hober is not the miller either (statement 7), so Dok is the miller. Dancing, storytelling, and singing are already accounted for as favorite activities by others, which leaves instrumental music and puzzles. But since Fram the cobbler's second-favorite activity is not puzzles, that cannot be Dok's favorite (statement 3), so Dok the miller's favorite is instrumental music, and Hober's is puzzles.

Now that we know instrumental music is the miller's favorite and not the weaver's, we can identify statement 6 as the false one. So the blacksmith doesn't enjoy stories (statement 4), meaning storytelling is the weaver's favorite, and

347

puzzles are the blacksmith's favorite (and therefore Hober is the blacksmith and Winn the weaver, whose second-favorite activity is dancing). Hober the blacksmith's favorite activity is solving puzzles, so that isn't also his second-favorite, which must therefore be singing, leaving puzzles as Dok the miller's second-favorite.

SUMMARY:

name	trade	favorite recreation	second-favorite recreation
Dok	miller	instrumentals	puzzles
Fram	cobbler	dancing	instrumentals
Hober	blacksmith	puzzles	singing
Winn	weaver	storytelling	dancing
Zett	carpenter	singing	storytelling

A Giant in the Shire

From statements 2 and 5, Alf was not Son of Rup, Son of Tas, Son of Quin, or Son of Edno. Therefore, if the two statements are valid, Alf's second name was Son of Lor.

From Statement 6, Son of Lor did not raise goats or pigs. Therefore, if true, he must have raised cattle or sheep. However, from statement 7, Alf did not raise sheep, and from statement 1, he must have raised goats. (Since neither of the two who wielded pitchforks raised sheep or goats, one raised cattle and the other raised pigs.) Therefore, either Alf was not Son of Lor, in which case either statement 2 or statement 5 is false; or Alf was Son of Lor and did not raise goats, in which case either statement 1 or statement 7 is false; or Alf was Son of Lor and did raise goats, in which case statement 6 is false.

Assume that Alf was not Son of Lor and statement 2 is false. From statement 5 we can conclude that Alf was Son of Rup or Son of Tas. However, from statement 1, both wielded pitchforks, and from statement 7, Alf wielded an ax. Therefore, statement 2 is not false.

Assume that statement 5 is false. If so, Alf could be either Son of Edno or Son of Quin. However, from statement 7, Alf did not raise sheep, and from statement 3, both Son of Edno and Son of Quin raised sheep. Therefore, statement 5 is not false. Therefore Alf was Son of Lor.

If statement 6 is true, Alf (Son of Lor) must have raised sheep or cattle. However, statement 3 implies that Alf did not raise sheep and statement 2 implies that Alf did not raise cattle. Therefore, statement 6 is false and Alf raised goats.

From statement 1, Son of Rup and Son of Tas raised cattle and pigs. From statement 2, Hon, who was not Son of Tas, raised cattle. Therefore, Hon was Son of Rup, and Son of Tas raised pigs. Both wielded pitchforks. From statement 3, Son of Edno and Son of Quin raised sheep.

Our conclusions, so far, are:

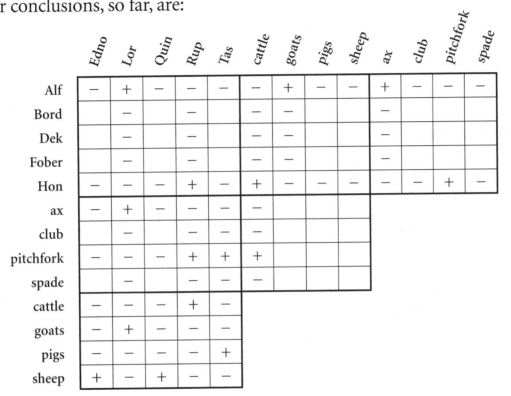

	Edno	Lor	Quin	Rup	Tas	cattle	goats	pigs	sheep	ax	club	pitchfork	spade
Alf	−	+	−	−	−	−	+	−	−	+	−	−	−
Bord		−		−		−	−			−			
Dek		−		−		−	−			−			
Fober		−		−		−	−			−			
Hon	−	−	−	+	−	+	−	−	−	−	−	+	−
ax	−	+	−	−	−	−							
club		−		−	−	−							
pitchfork	−	−	−	+	+	+							
spade		−		−	−	−							
cattle	−	−	−	+	−								
goats	−	+	−	−	−								
pigs	−	−	−	−	+								
sheep	+	−	+	−	−								

From statements 2 and 5, since Dek was one of the leaders in organizing the group, he was not Son of Quin, and, from statement 4, he was not Son of Tas. Therefore, Dek was Son of Edno. Also from statement 4, since Fober wielded a spade, Dek wielded a club. Since Bord must have wielded a pitchfork, he was Son of Tas, and Fober was Son of Quin.

SUMMARY:

Alf, Son of Lor	goats	ax
Bord, Son of Tas	pigs	pitchfork
Dek, Son of Edno	sheep	club
Fober, Son of Quin	sheep	spade
Hon, Son of Rup	cattle	pitchfork

Pony Races

If all four statements in race 1 are true, Lak finished before Pro (statement 2), who finished before Pen, who finished before Ismo (statement 1), who finished before Pir (statement 3). Inserting Adus in third place (statement 4), we get this finishing order: Lak first, Pro second, Adus third, Pen fourth, Ismo fifth, Pir sixth.

Assuming all statements in race 2 and the previous race are true, Pro finished between second place and some other place (statement 6). That means he didn't win, finish second, or finish last. Since Pir finished fifth (statement 7), Pro finished third or fourth. Pen finished before Lak (statement 8), who finished before Ismo, who finished before Adus (statement 5), so there are two possible finishing orders: Pen first, Lak second, Pro and Ismo third and fourth (but we don't know which is which), Pir fifth, Adus sixth.

Assuming all statements in race 3 and the previous two races are true, Lak finished before Pro (statement 11), who finished before Pen, who finished before Pir (statement 9), who finished before Ismo. Since Lak won the first race, he cannot have also won this race, but if Lak finished second, Pir can only finish fifth, which contradicts statement 12 (Pir finished fifth in the second race). So one of the first 12 statements must be false.

In race 4, Pir finished before Lak (statement 16), who finished before Pro, who finished before Adus (statement 14). Pen finished fifth, and we don't yet have enough information to know where Ismo finished. Let's now assume race 2 includes the false statement. Race 1's finish is as above. Lak still cannot have won race 3, so its finish must be Adus first, Lak second, Pro third, Pen fourth, Pir fifth, and Ismo sixth. If statement 7 is true, Pir finishing fifth would contradict statement 12, so statement 7 would have to be false. But statement 6 also cannot be true, because there is no place for Pro to finish between his second-place finish in race 1 and his third-place finish in race 3. Therefore all of race 2's statements are true.

Race 2's possible finishing orders, considered independently of race 1, are similar to what we have already deduced, but Pro could also finish in second place if he wins either race 1 or 3. In all cases, however, Pen finishes first, Pir fifth, and Adus sixth. That means Adus cannot also have finished sixth in race 4. In that race (besides Pen, who finished fifth), the only racer who can have finished after Adus is Ismo, so race 4's finishing order is Pir first, Lak second, Pro third, Adus fourth, Pen fifth, Ismo sixth.

If race 3's statements are all true, then Lak, Pro, Pen, Pir, and Ismo must finish in that order, with Adus finishing in any position. But that means either Ismo or Adus must finish last, which is impossible, since both have finished last in other races. Therefore one of race 3's statements is false, and our conclusions above about races 1 and 2 are correct, though we still don't know Pro and Ismo's final placement in race 2.

We know Pir's finishing position in three races: last in race 1, fifth in race 2, and first in race 4. From statement 13, Pir must have finished in third in some race, so that's where he finished in race 3. Since only two people finished before Pir, either clue 9 or 11 is false; if they were both true, Pro, Pen, and Lak would all have to finish before Pir. Clue 10 is true, then. Since Lak won race 1, he didn't win this race, and finished second. Who did win race 3? Not Pen, who won race 2. Not Ismo, who finished after Pir (statement 10). Not Pro, who must have finished fourth or later (statement 6). That means Adus finished first, and now we know statement 9 must be false. Pro finished before Ismo (statement 11), who we already know did not finish last, so they finished fourth and fifth, respectively, leaving Pen to finish sixth.

Pro finished second in race 1 and fourth in race 3, so Pro must have finished third in race 2 (statement 6), and Ismo finished fourth.

SUMMARY:

	Race 1	Race 2	Race 3	Race 4
1.	Lak	Pen	Adus	Pir
2.	Pro	Lak	Lak	Lak
3.	Adus	Pro	Pir	Pro
4.	Pen	Ismo	Pro	Adus
5.	Ismo	Pir	Ismo	Pen
6.	Pir	Adus	Pen	Ismo

A Visitor to the Land of Liars

From B's second statement we know immediately that it is true. Therefore, B's first statement is also true; A is not a Pemtru. A is an Amtru who has spoken falsely. Therefore, it must be afternoon. Therefore, since B's statement is true, B is a Pemtru.

SUMMARY:

It is afternoon, A is an Amtru, and B is a Pemtru.

En Route to the Valley of Liars

From A's second statement, we can conclude that A is an Amtru. Only an Amtru, true or false, can say it is morning. If it is morning, a Pemtru would lie, saying it is afternoon. If it is afternoon, a Pemtru would truthfully say so. From B's second statement we can conclude that it is morning, whether the statement is true or false. If it were afternoon, a Pemtru would speak the truth, and an Amtru would claim to be a Pemtru. Assume that both A and B are Amtrus. Again, B's statement is impossible because he is referring to a fellow Amtru in the morning and so must lie. Therefore, A's second statement is true, it is morning, and it follows that his first statement must also be true; the road leading East is the correct one.

Since B disagrees, B must be a Pemtru, in the morning, falsely claiming to be an Amtru.

	Amtru	Pemtru
A	−	+
B	+	−

SUMMARY:

The road leading east is the correct one. It is morning, A is an Amtru, and B is a Pemtru.

Two Valley Liars

Assume it is morning. If so, A's statement could be true. If so, A and B would both be Pemtrus. B's statement, however, that A is not a Pemtru, would be false—not possible for a Valley Pemtru referring to an inhabitant in the same group in the morning. If it is morning, assume that A is a Pemtru and B is an Amtru. Again, however, B's statement would not be possible, since B would be an Amtru in the morning referring to an inhabitant not in the same group and, therefore, would have to be truthful. The other possibility, that A is an Amtru and B is a Pemtru, means A's statement could not be made by A, who would have to speak the truth.

Therefore, it is afternoon. A must be an Amtru, since the statement could not be made by a Valley Pemtru in the afternoon. If B is also an Amtru, A would have to truthfully state so. Therefore, B is a Pemtru. B's statement, that A is not a Pemtru, is true.

	Amtru	Pemtru
A	+	−
B	−	+

SUMMARY:

It is afternoon, A is an Amtru, and B is a Pemtru.

Two More Valley Liars

Assume it is afternoon. If so, if A is a Pemtru, his first statement could not be made. A would deny that B is a Pemtru. If it is afternoon, A must be an Amtru. If so, if B were a Pemtru, A would falsely claim that B is an Amtru. If B were an Amtru, A would truthfully confirm this.

Therefore, it is morning. Assume A is an Amtru. If so, if B is an Amtru, A's first statement is false, which is consistent for a Valley Amtru in the morning. However, A's second statement, implying that A and B are both Amtrus, would be true, which is an impossible assertion for a Valley Amtru in the morning. If A is an Amtru, B must be a Pemtru, which would be consistent with his first statement. However, A's second statement would be false, which is not consistent. Therefore, A is a Pemtru. If B were a Pemtru, he would confirm A's statements. Since he rejects them, B is an Amtru, who has told the truth.

	Amtru	Pemtru
A	−	+
B	+	−

SUMMARY:

It is morning, A is a Pemtru, and B is an Amtru.

Three Valley Liars

Consider B's statement, which concerns what time of day C claims it is. If C is a Pemtru (who lies in the morning and tells the truth in the afternoon) C will claim it is afternoon. If C is an Amtru, the reverse will be the case; C will claim is it morning. So B's statement is equivalent to saying "C is an Amtru."

Assume it is morning. If C is really an Amtru, then B's statement is true. But B can't make a true statement about an Amtru in the morning—two Amtrus speaking about each other will lie, as would a Pemtru speaking about an Amtru. The other alternative is that C is really a Pemtru, which means B's statement is false. Again, this is impossible, because B can't make a false statement about a Pemtru in the morning—two Pemtrus speaking about each other will tell the truth, as would an Amtru speaking about a Pemtru.

Therefore, it is afternoon. B's statement is now completely consistent regardless of what B and C are. Now look at C's statement. It can't be true because two Pemtrus lie when speaking about each other. So the statement is false. C can't make a false statement about an Amtru in the afternoon—two Amtrus speaking about each other will tell the truth, as would a Pemtru speaking about an Amtru.

Therefore, B is a Pemtru, C's statement is false, and C is an Amtru. This makes B's statement true (since he's a Pemtru speaking about an Amtru).

Now look at A's statement. If A is an Amtru, his statement is true, but Amtrus can't make true statements in the afternoon when talking only about Pemtrus. Therefore, A is a Pemtru, and his statement is false, which is consistent.

	Amtru	Pemtru
A	−	+
B	−	+
C	+	−

SUMMARY:

It is afternoon, A and B are Pemtrus, and C is an Amtru.

Three Valley Liars Again

From A's statement, we can conclude that, if it is morning, A must be an Amtru who has spoken truthfully, since a Pemtru in the morning would speak truthfully if referring to another Pemtru, and falsely if referring to an Amtru.

From B's statement, we can conclude that B is either an Amtru in the afternoon or a Pemtru in the morning. If B's statement is true, C belongs to the same group. If B's statement is false, C is either an Amtru in the morning or a Pemtru in the afternoon.

From C's statement, we can conclude that C is either an Amtru in the morning or a Pemtru in the afternoon.

Therefore, if it is morning, A has spoken truthfully about another Amtru. However, an Amtru in the morning mentioning another Amtru would not tell the truth. Therefore, it is not morning; it is afternoon.

B, whose statement is false, is an Amtru, and C is a Pemtru. From A's statement, we can conclude that A is a Pemtru, who has made a false statement about two Pemtrus.

	Amtru	Pemtru
A	−	+
B	+	−
C	−	+

SUMMARY:

It is afternoon, A and C are Pemtrus, and B is an Amtru.

Four Valley Liars

Assume it is afternoon. If so, assume B's statement is true; then B is the only Pemtru. If so, D's statement must be false, and D must be an Amtru. If so, A must be an Amtru, and his statement, referring to another Amtru, would have to be true. However, A's statement would be false, an inconsistency.

Therefore, if it is afternoon, B's statement is false; B must be an Amtru. If so, from D's statement, D is an Amtru, since, in the afternoon, a Pemtru referring to an Amtru would speak truthfully. If so, A's statement could not be made. If A were an Amtru in the afternoon, referring to another Amtru, his statement would have to be true. If A were a Pemtru in the afternoon, again, his statement would have to be true. In either case, D would not refer to A as a Pemtru.

Therefore, it is morning. Assume that B's statement is false. If so, B is a Pemtru. If so, D, whose statement is false, must also be a Pemtru. However, in the morning, a Pemtru mentioning another Pemtru must speak truthfully.

Therefore, B's statement is true; B is the only Amtru. D's statement is false, and D is a Pemtru. A is also a Pemtru, whose statement regarding D is true. C is also a Pemtru, whose statement referring to an Amtru is false.

	Amtru	Pemtru
A	−	+
B	+	−
C	−	+
D	−	+

SUMMARY:

It is morning. A, C, and D are Pemtrus, and B is an Amtru.

Who Is the Impostor?

Consider B's statement. The implication is that if it is afternoon, he is an Amtru; if it is morning he is a Pemtru. If it is afternoon, B must be an Amtru who has spoken truthfully. However, in the afternoon, an Amtru would speak falsely, and for the statement to be false, B would be a Pemtru. In the afternoon, a Pemtru would speak truthfully. In either case that would be an impossibility. If it is morning, B must be either a Pemtru who has spoken truthfully or an Amtru who has spoken falsely—again, an impossibility. Therefore, whether it is morning or afternoon, B's statement is not possible. Therefore, B must be the impostor.

Consider that Amtrus and Pemtrus are equally represented.

Assume that it is morning. If so, C's statement could not be made. If C were an Amtru, the inference that A is an Amtru would have to be false, making A a Pemtru; however, if A were a Pemtru, C would speak truthfully and confirm it. If C were a Pemtru, the statement, referring to an Amtru in the morning, would not be possible. If A were an Amtru, C would falsely refer to A as a Pemtru. If A were a Pemtru, C would truthfully indicate so.

Therefore, it is afternoon. A's statement could only be made by a Pemtru. (If A were an Amtru he would claim the same group as C, whether true or false.) C's statement is false; it could be made by an Amtru or a Pemtru.

Since we know that A is a Pemtru, if D were an Amtru, his statement would be true, not possible for an Amtru in the afternoon. Therefore, D is a Pemtru, who has spoken falsely about another Pemtru in the afternoon.

If E's statement is true, E is a Pemtru; if it is false he is an Amtru. Therefore, since there are two Amtrus, we can conclude that C and E are both Amtrus who have spoken falsely.

	Amtru	Pemtru	Impostor
A	−	+	−
B	−	−	+
C	+	−	−
D	−	+	−
E	+	−	−

SUMMARY:

B is the impostor, and it is afternoon. A and D are Pemtrus, and C and E are Amtrus.

Part IV

Mystifying
Logic Puzzles

Educational Accomplishments

From statement 1, if Prince Tal excelled in chivalry, his second subject was horsemanship. However, from statement 3, if he did especially well in horsemanship, he excelled in fencing. From these two statements we can conclude that the hypothesis in statement 1 is invalid. Prince Tal did not excel in chivalry.

From statements 4 and 5, if Prince Tal excelled in fencing, his second subject was chivalry. However, if his second subject was chivalry, he excelled in horsemanship. Therefore, he did not excel in fencing. Therefore, statement 2 is valid.

	chivalry	fencing	horsemanship
excelled	−	−	+
did well	−	+	−

SUMMARY:

Prince Tal excelled in horsemanship and did especially well in fencing.

Battles With Dragons

From statement 2, Sir Aard encountered neither Flame Thrower nor Old Smoky. From statement 4, Sir Bolbo encountered neither Flame Thrower nor Black Heart. Therefore, Sir Delfo encountered Flame Thrower.

From statement 6, Sir Delfo did not encounter Biter nor Old Smoky. Therefore, Sir Bolbo must have encountered Old Smoky.

From statements 3 and 1, since we know that Sir Delfo encountered Flame Thrower, Sir Aard did not encounter Dante, and Sir Delfo did not encounter Black Heart. From statement 5, since Sir Delfo encountered Flame Thrower, he did not encounter Dante. Therefore, Sir Bolbo encountered Dante, and Sir Aard encountered Biter and Black Heart.

	Biter	Black Heart	Dante	Flame Thrower	Ol' Smoky
Sir Aard	+	+	−	−	−
Sir Bolbo	−	−	+	−	+
Sir Delfo	−	−	−	+	−

SUMMARY:

Sir Aard encountered Biter and Black Heart.
Sir Bolbo encountered Dante and Old Smoky.
Sir Delfo encountered Flame Thrower.

Who Tilted With Whom?

According to statement 1, if either Prince Tal or Sir Aard tilted with Sir Keln, Sir Bolbo tilted with Sir Gath. However, from statements 4 and 3, if Sir Gath and Sir Bolbo tilted, so did Sir Delfo and Prince Tal, and then Sir Keln tilted with Sir Gath. Therefore, Sir Keln did not tilt with Prince Tal or Sir Aard.

From statement 6, if Sir Keln tilted with Sir Gath, Prince Tal tilted with Sir Aard. However, from statement 5, if Prince Tal and Sir Aard tilted, so did Sir Bolbo and Sir Gath. Therefore, Sir Keln did not tilt with Sir Gath.

From statement 3, since Sir Keln did not tilt with Sir Gath, Prince Tal did not tilt with Sir Delfo, and from statement 7, since Sir Keln did not tilt with Sir Aard, Prince Tal did not tilt with Sir Bolbo. Therefore, Prince Tal must have tilted with either Sir Aard or Sir Gath. From statements 5 and 4, if Prince Tal tilted with Sir Aard, Sir Bolbo and Sir Gath tilted; this, however, means that Sir Delfo and Prince Tal tilted, an impossibility. Therefore, Prince Tal tilted with Sir Gath. From statement 2, Sir Keln tilted with Sir Delfo.

The remaining knights, Sir Bolbo and Sir Aard, tilted with each other.

	Sir Aard	Sir Bolbo	Sir Delfo	Sir Gath	Sir Keln	Prince Tal
Sir Aard	−	+	−	−	−	−
Sir Bolbo	+	−	−	−	−	−
Sir Delfo	−	−	−	−	+	−
Sir Gath	−	−	−	−	−	+
Sir Keln	−	−	+	−	−	−
Prince Tal	−	−	−	+	−	−

SUMMARY:

Sir Bolbo tilted with Sir Aard.
Sir Keln tilted with Sir Delfo.
Prince Tal tilted with Sir Gath.

Encounter With the Fearsome Beast

According to statement 3, if Sir Aard was prostrate on the ground, Prince Tal and Sir Bolbo were not thrown. If this was the case, Sir Delfo was the one who climbed a tree. However, from statement 2, if Sir Delfo climbed a tree, Sir Aard was not thrown. Therefore, Sir Aard was not the one who was prostrate on the ground.

According to statement 1, if Sir Bolbo climbed a tree, Prince Tal and Sir Delfo were not thrown. If so, Sir Aard was the one who was prostrate on the ground. However, since we know that Sir Aard was not the one who was prostrate on the ground, Sir Bolbo was not the one who climbed a tree.

According to statement 2, if Sir Delfo climbed a tree, Sir Aard and Prince Tal were not thrown. If so, Sir Bolbo was the one who was prostrate on the ground. However, from statement 6, if Sir Bolbo was prostrate on the ground, Sir Delfo was not thrown. Therefore, Sir Delfo did not climb a tree.

According to statement 5, if Prince Tal did not climb a tree, either Sir Bolbo or Sir Delfo climbed a tree. Since we know that neither Sir Bolbo nor Sir Delfo climbed a tree, Prince Tal was the one who climbed a tree. Therefore, Sir Aard must have been one of the two who were not thrown.

Our conclusions so far are:

	climbed a tree	prostrate on the ground	was not thrown
Sir Aard	−	−	+
Sir Bolbo	−		
Sir Delfo	−		
Prince Tal	+	−	−

According to statement 4, if Sir Aard was not thrown, which we know to be the case, Sir Bolbo was not thrown and Sir Delfo was prostrate on the ground.

SUMMARY:

Sir Aard was not thrown.
Sir Bolbo was not thrown.
Sir Delfo was prostrate on the ground.
Prince Tal climbed a tree.

Strange Creatures

From statement 7, since Sir Delfo saw either a basilisk or a monoceros, Sir Delfo did not see a bonnacon, a satyr, or a leucrota. Therefore, from statement 1, Sir Bolbo did not see a monoceros, and from statement 6, Prince Tal did not see a monoceros. From statement 8, Sir Bolbo did not see a leucrota. From statement 4, since Sir Delfo saw either a basilisk or a monoceros, neither Sir Bolbo nor Sir Aard saw a basilisk.

From statement 2, since we know that Prince Tal did not see a monoceros, Sir Bolbo did not see a bonnacon. Therefore, Sir Bolbo saw a satyr.

Conclusions so far are:

	basilisk	bonnacon	leucrota	monoceros	satyr
Sir Aard	−				−
Sir Bolbo	−	−	−	−	+
Sir Delfo		−	−		−
Sir Keln					−
Prince Tal				−	−

From statement 3, since Sir Aard did not see a satyr, Sir Keln was the one to see a leucrota. From statement 5, since Sir Aard did not see a basilisk, Prince Tal did not see a bonnacon. Therefore, Sir Aard is the one who saw a bonnacon, and Prince Tal saw a basilisk. Therefore, Sir Delfo saw a monoceros.

SUMMARY:

Sir Aard saw a bonnacon.
Sir Bolbo saw a satyr.
Sir Delfo saw a monoceros.
Sir Keln saw a leucrota.
Prince Tal saw a basilisk.

Prince Tal and the Enchantress

From statement 5, if the noblemen stormed the castle, Prince Tal was imprisoned for three days. But this contradicts statement 6, so the noblemen did not storm the castle.

If he broke the door, from statement 4, Prince Tal was imprisoned for one week or two weeks. But from statement 6, if his imprisonment was for one week, he did not break the door, so if he broke the door, his imprisonment was for two weeks. This contradicts statement 7, though, so he didn't break the door.

If the ransom was paid, then Prince Tal was imprisoned for one week or two weeks, according to statement 4. However, statement 3 says that it's impossible for an imprisonment of two weeks and a ransom payment, so if the ransom was paid, Prince Tal was imprisoned for one week. This contradicts statement 2, though, so the ransom was not paid.

Therefore, the dungeon keeper left the door open. From statement 1, Prince Tal was imprisoned for one day or three days. But, from statement 2, it couldn't have been for one day, so it must have been for three days.

SUMMARY:

Prince Tal was imprisoned for three days and the dungeon keeper left the door open.

To the Rescue

From statement 1, if Sir Keln rescued Maid Marion or Maid Mary, Sir Aard rescued Maid Muriel or Maid Marie. Following through statements 5, 3, and 7, if Sir Aard rescued Maid Muriel or Maid Marie, Prince Tal rescued Maid Mary or Maid Morgana, Sir Bolbo rescued Maid Matilda or Maid Marion, and Sir Delfo rescued both Maid Muriel and Maid Marie, which is a contradiction. Therefore, Sir Keln did not rescue Maid Marion nor Maid Mary.

From statement 6, since we know that Sir Keln did not rescue Maid Marion or Maid Mary, Sir Aard rescued either Maid Marion or Maid Muriel. From statements 5, 3, and 7, Sir Aard did not rescue Maid Muriel nor Maid Marie. Therefore, he rescued Maid Marion. From statement 8, since Sir Aard did not rescue Maid Marie, but did rescue Maid Marion, Prince Tal rescued both Maid Matilda and Maid Muriel.

Our conclusions so far are as follows:

	Marie	Marion	Mary	Matilda	Morgana	Muriel
Sir Aard	−	+	−	−	−	−
Sir Bolbo		−		−		−
Sir Delfo		−		−		−
Sir Keln		−	−	−		−
Prince Tal	−	−	−	+	−	+

From statement 2, since Prince Tal rescued Maid Matilda, Sir Bolbo rescued Maid Mary. From statement 4, since Sir Bolbo rescued Maid Mary, Sir Keln rescued Maid Morgana. The remaining maiden, Maid Marie, was rescued by Sir Delfo.

SUMMARY:

Sir Aard	Maid Marion
Sir Bolbo	Maid Mary
Sir Delfo	Maid Marie
Sir Keln	Maid Morgana
Prince Tal	Maid Matilda and Maid Muriel

Prince Tal's Encounters With Four Dragons

From statement 8, Prince Tal must not have forgotten his shield during the first and third encounters, since from statements 5, 6, and 7, it is apparent that he did not feign death during his second encounter. Therefore, the encounter in which Prince Tal forgot his shield and left without fighting must have been the second or fourth one. From statements 5 and 7, if the second encounter was with Dante, Quicksilver, or Vesuvius, Prince Tal did not forget his shield at that time. Further, if the second encounter was with Meduso, it was not the time that Prince Tal left without fighting, since we know that Prince Tal fought Meduso using his peripheral vision. Therefore, Prince Tal forgot his shield at the fourth encounter, and that encounter was not with Meduso.

From statements 1 and 4, Vesuvius was not the first or fourth dragon confronted, since Prince Tal's fellow noblemen did not arrive to save him during the fourth encounter, and if they arrived to save him during the first encounter, it was with Quicksilver. From Statement 3, since Prince Tal did not feign death during the fourth encounter, it was not with Dante. Therefore, the fourth encounter was with Quicksilver.

From statement 2, since the fourth encounter was not with Meduso, the first encounter was not with Dante. Therefore, the first encounter was with Meduso.

From statement 6, since the encounter with Meduso was the first one, Prince Tal did not feign death in his confrontation with this dragon. From statement 4, Prince Tal's fellow noblemen did not arrive to save him during the encounter with Meduso. Therefore, the outcome of the encounter with Meduso was that the dragon suffered a coughing fit.

Conclusions so far are:

	coughing fit	feigned death	forgot shield	help arrived	1st	2nd	3rd	4th
Dante	−		−		−			−
Meduso	+	−	−	−	+	−	−	−
Quicksilver	−	−	+	−	−	−	−	+
Vesuvius	−		−		−			−

Either the encounter with Vesuvius or the one with Dante resulted in Prince Tal's fellow noblemen arriving in time to rescue him. From statement 7, the encounter with Vesuvius was not the second one. Therefore, the second encounter was with Dante, and from statement 5, the outcome was that Prince Tal's fellow noblemen rescued him. Therefore, the third encounter was with Vesuvius and the outcome was that Prince Tal feigned death.

SUMMARY:

1st encounter	Meduso	coughing fit
2nd encounter	Dante	help arrived
3rd encounter	Vesuvius	feigned death
4th encounter	Quicksilver	forgot shield

One Dragon

If either part of A's statement is true, the statement is true. A is not blue, as all blue dragons lie. If the statement is true, A is a gray rational; if it is false, A must be a red rational.

SUMMARY:

The dragon is a rational.

Two Dragons

A is not from Wonk, as blue dragons always lie. A's first statement is false, so A is either a red rational or a gray predator. A's second statement is false; at least one of A and B is a rational.

B, who also claims to be from Wonk, has lied. From B's second statement, B is a gray predator. Therefore, A must be a red rational.

	A	B
color	red	gray
type	rational	predator

SUMMARY:

A is a red rational.
B is a gray predator.

Three Dragons

A's second statement is true. If it were false, A would be a red predator, and red predators always tell the truth. A is a gray rational. Therefore, from A's first statement, C is blue.

We know that B's statements are false, since B's first statement claims that A is from Wonk. From B's second statement, since A is a rational, C must be a predator. From C's two statements, which are false, we can conclude that B is a red rational.

	A	B	C
color	gray	red	blue
type	rational	rational	predator

SUMMARY:

A is a gray rational.
B is a red rational.
C is a blue predator.

Two Are From Wonk

Consider that two of the three dragons are blue.

Since blue dragons from Wonk always lie, one of A's and B's first statements, asserting that B and C are from Wonk, must be true, and the other false. Thus, one of B and C is not blue. Therefore, A has lied; he must be one of the two from Wonk. Therefore, B has told the truth. B is a gray rational, and A and C are blue predators.

	A	B	C
color	blue	gray	blue
type	predator	rational	predator

SUMMARY:

A is a blue predator.
B is a gray rational.
C is a blue predator.

One Dragon From Wonk

Consider that one dragon is blue.

Assume A is a gray rational as indicated by his second statement. If so, C must be a gray rational as A's first statement claims. However, from C's first statement, A is not a gray rational. Therefore, A's statements are false, and C's statements are true. C must be a red predator. From C's second statement, B is blue; and, from B's third statement, B is a predator. From B's first and second statements, A is a red rational.

	A	B	C
color	red	blue	red
type	rational	predator	predator

SUMMARY:

A is a red rational.
B is a blue predator.
C is a red predator.

At Least One From Wonk

Consider that at least one is blue.

A must be blue. Only a blue dragon can claim that he is a gray predator or a red rational. B's second statement must be false, since if it were true, C's second statement would be impossible. From B's third statement, B is not gray, and from A's second statement, which is false, B is not red. Therefore, B is blue.

D's third statement correctly asserts that both A and B are blue. Therefore, D is a red predator, as claimed.

C, whose statements are false, is a gray predator. From C's third statement, B is a rational, and from B's first statement, A is a predator.

	A	B	C	D
color	blue	blue	gray	red
type	predator	rational	predator	predator

SUMMARY:

A is a blue predator.
B is a blue rational.
C is a gray predator.
D is a red predator.

Three Dragons Again

If A's first statement is true, A is either a gray rational or a red predator. If his first statement is false, he is either a blue rational or a blue predator. If B's second statement is true, C is blue and from C's first statement, which would be false, A's statements are true. If B's first statement is false, A is red and, again, C's first statement is false. Therefore, in either case, A's statements are true. A is either a gray rational or a red predator.

From A's second statement, C is either gray or red. Therefore, since at least one dragon is blue, it must be B. From B's first statement, which is false, A is a red predator. From A's second statement, C is red, and must be a rational. From C's second statement, B is a rational.

	A	B	C
color	red	blue	red
type	predator	rational	rational

SUMMARY:

A is a red predator.
B is a blue rational.
C is a red rational.

How Many Are Protected?

Assume A's second statement is true. If so, B's statements are false; B is either a red rational or a blue rational. If so, from B's second statement, C could be a red rational or a blue rational. However, C's third statement would be true and first statement would be false, which is not possible. Therefore, A's statements are false.

From A's second statement, at least one of the three must be a predator. From A's first statement, he is either red or blue, and from A's third statement, C is either gray or blue.

Assume that C's statements are true. If so, C is a gray rational, and from C's second statement, A must be a red rational. However, C's first statement indicates that he and A are different types, an inconsistency. Therefore, C's statements are false; A is not red. Therefore, A is blue.

From C's third statement, B is a predator, which is consistent with B's first statement. Therefore, B is a red predator. From B's second statement, C must be a gray predator. From C's first statement, A is a predator.

	A	B	C
color	blue	red	gray
type	predator	predator	predator

SUMMARY:

A is a blue predator.
B is a red predator.
C is a gray predator.

Who Speaks for Whom?

Assume that A's statements are true. If so, from A's second statement, A must be a gray rational. From C's second statement, which agrees with A's second statement, C's statements are also true, and C is either a gray rational or a red predator. If so, from C's first statement and A's third statement, B is a red rational, with all false statements.

However, B's first statement is in agreement with the type that C would claim for A. This statement would not be possible for a red rational. Therefore, A's statements are false.

Therefore, from A's statements, B would claim that C is a rational, A is either red or blue, and B is a predator. C, who asserts that A is gray, is also a liar. From C's first statement, A would claim that B is not red. Therefore, B is red.

B's first statement, that C would claim that A is a rational, is correct. Therefore B is a red predator, and from B's second statement, C is a red rational. A is a predator, and since we have established that A is a liar and is not gray, A is blue.

	A	B	C
color	blue	red	red
type	predator	predator	rational

SUMMARY:

A is a blue predator.
B is a red predator.
C is a red rational.

The First Trial

Consider that at least one of the signs is false.

The two signs agree. Since at least one is false, they cannot both be true. Therefore, they are both false, and path A leads to the next trial.

SUMMARY:

Path A is the correct choice.

The Second Trial

Consider that two signs are true, and one is false.

Assume path A leads to the next trial. If so, the signs at all three paths are false. Therefore, path A is the wrong choice. Assume path C is the one to follow. If so, all three signs are true. Therefore, path C is a wrong choice. Therefore, path B must be the right choice. The signs at paths A and B are true, and the sign at path C is false.

	sign A	sign B	sign C
if path A is correct	F	F	F
if path B is correct	T	T	F
if path C is correct	T	T	T

SUMMARY:

Path B is the correct choice.

The Third Trial

Consider that one of the three signs is false.

Assume A is the path to follow. If so, the sign at path A is false, the sign at path B is true, and the sign at path C is false. Therefore, path A is not the path to follow.

Assume B is the correct path. If so, the sign at path A is true, the sign at path B is false, and the sign at path C is false. Therefore, path B is not the correct path.

C is the correct path. The sign at path A is false, the sign at path B is true, and the sign at path C is true.

	sign A	sign B	sign C
if path A is correct	F	T	F
if path B is correct	T	F	F
if path C is correct	F	T	T

SUMMARY:

Path C is the correct choice.

The Fourth Trial

Consider that two of the three signs are false.

Assume bridge A is the one to cross. If so, the sign at bridge A is true, the sign at bridge B is false, and the sign at bridge C is true. Therefore, Bridge A is not the one to cross.

Assume that bridge B is the one to cross. If so, the sign at bridge A is false, the sign at bridge B is true, and the sign at bridge C is true. Therefore, bridge B is not the one to cross.

The bridge to cross is C. The sign at bridge A is true, the sign at bridge B is false, and the sign at bridge C is false.

	sign A	sign B	sign C
if path A is correct	T	F	T
if path B is correct	F	T	T
if path C is correct	T	F	F

SUMMARY:

Bridge C is the correct choice.

The Fifth Trial

Consider that at least two of the signs are false.

Assume that path B leads to the next trial. If so, the sign at path A is true, the sign at path B is true, the sign at path C is false, and the sign at path D is true. Therefore, path B is not correct. Assume that path C leads to the next trial. If so, the sign at path A is true, the sign at path B is false, the sign at path C is true, and the sign at path D is true. Therefore, path C is not the correct choice. Assume that path D leads to the next trial. If so, the sign at path A is false, the sign at path B is true, the sign at path C is true, and the sign at path D is true. Therefore, path D is not correct.

Therefore, path A is the correct choice. The sign at path A is false, the sign at path B is true, the sign at path C is false, and the sign at path D is false.

	sign A	sign B	sign C	sign D
if path A is correct	F	T	F	F
if path B is correct	T	T	F	T
if path C is correct	T	F	T	T
if path D is correct	F	T	T	T

SUMMARY:

Path A is the correct choice.

The Sixth Trial

Consider that at least three of the signs are false.

Assume A is the path to follow. If so, the sign at path A is true, the sign at path B is true, the sign at path C is false, the sign at path D is false, and the sign at path E is true. Therefore, A is not the correct path. Assume B is the path to follow. If so, the sign at path A is true, the sign at path B is true, the sign at path C is false, the sign at path D is false, and the sign at path E is true. Therefore, B is not the path to follow. Assume that D is the correct path. If so, the sign at path A is true, the sign at path B is true, the sign at path C is false, the sign at path D is false, and the sign at path E is true. Therefore, D is the wrong path. Assume that E is the correct path. If so, the sign at path A is true, the sign at path B is true, the sign at path C is false, the sign at path D is false, and the sign at path E is true. Therefore, path E is the wrong path.

Therefore, path C is the correct path. The sign at path A is false, the sign at path B is false, the sign at path C is true, the sign at path D is true, and the sign at path E is false.

	sign A	sign B	sign C	sign D	sign E
if path A is correct	T	T	F	F	T
if path B is correct	T	T	F	F	T
if path C is correct	F	F	T	T	F
if path D is correct	T	T	F	F	T
if path E is correct	T	T	F	F	T

SUMMARY:

Path C is the correct choice.

The Final Trial

Consider that four of the signs are true.

Assume that B is the path to follow. If so, the signs at paths A, F, and G are true, and the signs at B, C, D, and E are false. Therefore, B is not the correct path. Assume that C is the path to follow. If so, the signs at paths E, F, and G are true, and the signs at paths A, B, C, and D are false. Therefore, path C is not the correct path. Assume that D is the correct path. If so, the signs at paths B, D, and G are true, and the signs at A, C, E, and F are false. Therefore, D is wrong. Assume that E is the path to follow. If so, signs at paths B, D, and G are true, and the signs at paths A, C, E, and F are false. Therefore, E is not the path of choice. Assume that F is the correct path. If so, the signs at paths B, D, and G are true, and the signs at paths A, C, E, and F are false. Therefore, F is not the path to follow. Assume that G is the correct path. If so, the signs at paths B, C, and E are true, and the signs at paths A, D, F, and G are false. Therefore, G is not the correct path.

Therefore, A is the path to follow. The signs at paths A, B, E, and G are true, and the signs at paths C, D, and F are false.

	sign A	sign B	sign C	sign D	sign E	sign F	sign G
if path A is correct	T	T	F	F	T	F	T
if path B is correct	T	F	F	F	F	T	T
if path C is correct	F	F	F	F	T	T	T
if path D is correct	F	T	F	T	F	F	T
if path E is correct	F	T	F	T	F	F	T
if path F is correct	F	T	F	T	F	F	T
if path G is correct	F	T	T	F	T	F	F

SUMMARY:

Path A is the correct choice.

Addition, Six Digits

Each letter above the line represents a digit that has a difference of one from the digit represented by the same letter below the line.
The digits are 0, 1, 2, 3, 4, and 5.

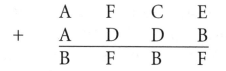

$$
\begin{array}{ccccc}
 & A & F & C & E \\
+ & A & D & D & B \\
\hline
 & B & F & B & F \\
\end{array}
$$

Since the largest available digit is 5, A must be 1 or 2, and B below the line is 2 or 4. From the hundreds column, since F above the line and F below the line must be one number different, D must be 1. Therefore, A is not 1; A is 2. B below the line is 4, and B above the line is 3 or 5. From the tens column, C must be 3, since C plus 1 equals 4. Therefore, B above the line is 5. Considering the digits left, F above the line must be 4. Therefore, F below the line is 5, and E is 0, the remaining digit.

SUMMARY:

A	B	C	D	E	F
2	5	3	1	0	4
	4				5

$$
\begin{array}{cccc}
 & 2 & 4 & 3 & 0 \\
+ & 2 & 1 & 1 & 5 \\
\hline
 & 4 & 5 & 4 & 5 \\
\end{array}
$$

376

Subtraction, Six Digits

The digits are 0, 1, 2, 3, 4, and 5.

```
    F   B   A   C   B
-   D   A   F   E   B
    ─────────────────
        C   F   D   E
```

From the ones column, E below the line equals 0, and E above the line must be 1. From the ten-thousands column, D above the line is one less than F above the line, since the answer disappears in that column. D above the line must be 4, 3, or 2.

From the thousands column, since there was a carry from the ten-thousands column, B must represent a smaller digit than A. Since the largest available digit is 5, the only possibility is that A is 5, B is 0, and C below the line is 5. Therefore, C above the line is 4.

From the tens column, D below the line must be 3. From the ten-thousands column, D above the line cannot be 4, since that digit is taken. Therefore, D above is 2, and F above is 3. From the hundreds column, A minus F equals F. Therefore, since A above is 5 and F above is 3, F below is 2.

SUMMARY:

```
    A   B   C   D   E   F
    5   0   4   2   1   3
    ───────────────────
            5   3   0   2
```

```
    3   0   5   4   0
-   2   5   3   1   0
    ─────────────────
        5   2   3   0
```

377

Addition, Seven Digits

The digits are 0, 1, 2, 3, 4, 5 and 6.

```
      D   G   A   E   C
  +   E   F   B   A   C
  ─────────────────────
  C   F   G   D   G   F
```

C below the line represents a carry from the ten-thousands column. C below the line must be 1. Therefore, C above the line is 0 or 2. Therefore, from the ones column, F below the line is 0 or 4. If F below is 4, from the ten-thousands column, D plus E must equal 14. This is not possible with the available digits. Therefore, F below is 0, and C above is also 0. F above must be 1.

From the ten-thousands column, since F below is 0, D and E are 6 and 4, or 4 and 6. From the tens column, E plus A equals G. Since we know that F below is 0 and C below is 1, there is no combination of digits available in which E could be 6. Therefore, E is 4 and D above is 6. Therefore D below is 5. The only possible digit available to A is 2, and G below is 6. Therefore, G above is 5. B is 3, the remaining digit.

SUMMARY:

A	B	C	D	E	F	G
2	3	0	6	4	1	5
		1	5		0	6

```
      6   5   2   4   0
  +   4   1   3   2   0
  ─────────────────────
  1   0   6   5   6   0
```

Addition, Seven Digits Again

The digits are 0, 1, 2, 3, 4, 8, and 9.

```
      E   D   B   D   D
      E   D   B   D   D
  +   E   D   B   D   D
  ─────────────────────
  C   F   A   B   D   E
```

D above the line, in the tens column, must be 4 or 9. No other available digits above the line will equal D below the line given a carry from the ones column. However, if D above the line were 9, the carry from the ones column would be 2, and D below the line, in the tens column, would be 9, the same as D above the line. Therefore, D above the line is 4 and D below the line is 3. E below the line, in the ones column, must be 2.

Since A represents 4 plus 4 plus 4 plus a different carry than 1, that carry must be 2, and A equals 4.

B above the line must be 9, and B below the line is 8 (9 plus 9 plus 9 plus a carry of 1 from the tens column). Given what's left, E above the line is 3, F is 0 (3 plus 3 plus 3 plus a carry of 1 from the thousands column), and C is 1.

SUMMARY:

A	B	C	D	E	F
	9		4	3	
4	8	1	3	2	0

```
      3   4   9   4   4
      3   4   9   4   4
  +   3   4   9   4   4
  ─────────────────────
  1   0   4   8   3   2
```

Multiplication, Six Digits

Each letter in the problem (above the line) represents a digit that has a difference of one from the digit represented by the same letter in the answer (below the line).

The digits are 0, 1, 2, 3, 4, and 5. (Parentheses indicate row numbers for reference in the solution below.)

```
              C    A    E     (1)
         ×    E    C    E     (2)
              E    C    A     (3)
         D    F    B          (4)
    E    C    A               (5)
    E    B    B    B    A     (6)
```

E above the line can't be 0, since it starts a three-digit number. It can't be 3 or 4, since that would make A below be 9 or 6. It can't be 5, since E below would then be 4, and row 1 times 5 can't start with a 4 since C can't be 0. If E above the line were 1, A below the line would also be 1, making A above the line 0 or 2. If A above the line were 0, C below the line (row 3) would also be 0, making C above the line (row 2) 1, which is already taken. If A above the line were 2, C below the line (row 3) would also be 2, making C above the line 3. This would not fit, since F would be 6. Therefore, E above is 2. Therefore, A below the line is 4.

E (row 2) times C (row 1) equals E (row 3). Therefore, there must be a carry from E times A (since E below must be an odd number). Therefore, E below the line must be 3, and A above the line must be 5.

The remaining letter above the line, C, is 1.

SUMMARY:

A	B	C	D	E	F
5		1		2	
4	2	0	1	3	5

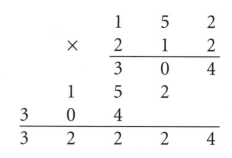

380

Subtraction, Seven Digits

The digits are 0, 1, 2, 3, 4, 5, and 6.

```
    B   D   C   A   B   F   B
-   E   E   B   G   E   A   E
    ─────────────────────────
        G   E   E   F   C   F
```

From the millions column, B is one more than E, since the column disappears in the answer to the problem. Therefore, from the ones column, F below the line equals 1. Therefore, F above the line is 0 or 2. From the hundreds column, it is apparent that no carry to the tens column is required, since the digit in the answer is the same as for the ones column. Therefore, F above the line must be 2, and A is 0 or 1. C below the line must be 2, since 1 is taken. Therefore, A is 0. C above the line must be 1 or 3.

From the hundred-thousands column, considering that a carry from the millions column was required, E above the line must be 5, 4, or 3, and D must be 0, 1, or 2. Therefore, since 0 and 2 are taken, D is 1. Therefore, C above the line is 3, and E above the line is 5 or 4.

From the hundred-thousands column, if E above the line is 4, G below the line must be 6, and B must be 5. If so, however, G above the line must also be 5. Therefore, E above the line is 5, B is 6, and G above the line is 4, the remaining digit above the line. Subtracting yields the rest.

SUMMARY:

```
    A   B   C   D   E   F   G
    0   6   3   1   5   2   4
    ─────────────────────────
            2       6   1   5


    6   1   3   0   6   2   6
-   5   5   6   4   5   0   5
    ─────────────────────────
        5   6   6   1   2   1
```

Addition, Seven Digits Once Again

The digits are 0, 1, 2, 3, 4, 5, and 6.

		F	C	C
	F	A	C	C
B	A	E	C	A
+ A	D	C	F	A	A
A	C	B	A	C	A

From the hundred-thousands column, A below the line represents A above the line plus a carry from the ten-thousands column. Therefore, the sum of B above the line, D, and the carry into the ten-thousands column has to be 10 or more. The carry into the ten-thousands column can be no more than 1, so the sum of B above and D has to be 9 or more, and C below is either 0, 1, or 2. That means that C above is 0, 1, 2, or 3, but looking at columns 1 and 2, the only one that makes a value of A above that works in both columns is C above equal to 0. In this case, A above must be 1, and A below is 2. This makes C below equal to 1. Column 4, with a 1 and a 0, doesn't have enough to carry into the ten-thousands column, so the sum of B above and D is 11, thus one is 5 and one is 6. Looking at the hundreds column, F + 1 + E + F sums to either 2 or 12. The only numbers left for E and F are 2, 3, and 4, and the only combination that works is F = 4 and E = 3. This makes B below in the thousands column equal to 6, which means E above is 5 and D is 6.

SUMMARY:

A	B	C	D	E	F
1	5	0	6	3	4
2	6	1			

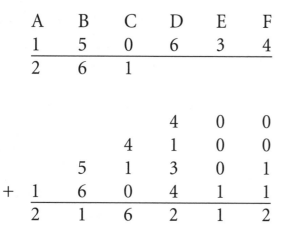

			4	0	0
		4	1	0	0
	5	1	3	0	1
+ 1	6	0	4	1	1
2	1	6	2	1	2

382

Multiplication, Seven Digits

The digits are 0, 2, 3, 5, 6, 8, and 9. (Parentheses indicate row numbers for reference in the solution below.)

	D	E	B	(1)
×		D	G	(2)
	E	E	E	(3)
B	F	G		(4)
A	E	C	E	(5)

There is no digit 1 in the problem. Therefore, 0 must be represented by a letter that is not both above and below the line. The possibilities for 0 are A, C, D, and F. D can be eliminated, since it is located at the left end of lines 1 and 2. A can be eliminated, since it represents a digit one number greater than B below the line resulting from a carry from E below plus F. Additionally, since there is a carry from E below plus F, F must be greater than 0. Therefore, C is 0.

The multipliers D and G above (line 2) must be 2 and 3 or 3 and 2, since neither digit creates a carry that results in a fourth digit in rows 3 or 4. D must be 2, since if it were 3, D times D plus a carry from E above times D would create a fourth digit in line 4. Therefore, G above the line is 3, and G below the line must be 2 since there is no 4 available.

B below the line must be 5 or 8 and A must be 6 or 9. B above the line must be 6 or 9. However, 3 times 9 (B above times G above) would yield 7, a digit not available. Therefore, B above the line is 6, B below the line is 5, and A is 6.

E below the line must be 8 since B above times G above equals 18 (lines 1, 2, and 3). Therefore, E above the line is 9, and F equals 9, since E below plus F plus a carry equals E below (lines 3, 4, and 5).

SUMMARY:

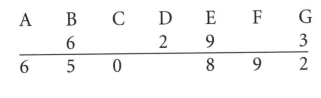

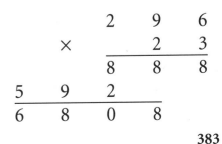

Four Horses

From statement 2, Mary did not own or ride the horse Charger. From statements 1 and 4, Danielle rode Charger, so neither Danielle nor Harriet owned Charger. Therefore, Charger was owned by Alice.

From statements 3 and 5, since Alice did not ride El Cid or Silver, she rode Champ. Since Champ's owner rode El Cid, and El Cid's owner rode Silver, Danielle owned Silver. Then from statement 1, Harriet owned El Cid and rode Silver, and Mary owned Champ and rode El Cid.

	Alice	Danielle	Harriet	Mary
horse owned	Charger	Silver	El Cid	Champ
horse rode	Champ	Charger	Silver	El Cid

SUMMARY:

Alice owned Charger and rode Champ.
Danielle owned Silver and rode Charger.
Harriet owned El Cid and rode Silver.
Mary owned Champ and rode El Cid.

Five Thespians

From statements 4 and 5, Roland did not play the victim, the murderer, the sheriff, or the witness. Therefore, Roland played the magistrate. From statements 6 and 2, we can conclude that Ronald played Roland the murderer. From statements 1 and 8, we can conclude that Raymond's character was Ronald the victim.

Our conclusions at this point are:

	magistrate	murderer	sheriff	victim	witness	character name
Raymond	–	–	–	+	–	Ronald
Rodney	–	–		–		
Roland	+	–	–	–	–	
Ronald	–	+	–	–	–	Roland
Rupert	–	–		–		

From statement 7, Rodney played the part of Raymond. Since the two remaining parts are the sheriff and the witness, and since from statement 3, Rupert did not play the sheriff, it is evident that Rodney played the sheriff and Rupert played the role of Rodney, the witness. The remaining character, Rupert, was the magistrate.

SUMMARY:

Raymond played Ronald, the victim.
Rodney played Raymond, the sheriff.
Roland played Rupert, the magistrate.
Ronald played Roland, the murderer.
Rupert played Rodney, the witness.

Five Authors

From statement 4, Milton writes general fiction. From statements 2 and 3, neither John, Sarah, nor Florence writes mystery novels. Therefore, James writes mystery novels, and uses Montague as his pseudonym (statement 2). From statement 6, John must be the author of travel books.

At this point our conclusions are:

	biography	general	historical	mysteries	travel	pseudonym
Florence	–	–	–	+	–	Montague
James		–		–	–	
John	–	–	–	–	+	
Milton	–	+	–	–	–	
Sarah		–		–	–	

From statement 1, Sarah does not write historical novels. Therefore Florence writes historical novels, and Sarah writes biographies. Also from statement 1, Florence's pseudonym is Blackledge, and from statement 5, John's pseudonym is Williams. Sarah's pseudonym is Quincy, and Milton's pseudonym is Hastings.

SUMMARY:

James Blackledge writes mystery novels under the name Montague.
Sarah Hastings writes biographies under the name Quincy.
John Montague writes travel books under the name Williams.
Milton Quincy writes general fiction under the name Hastings.
Florence Williams writes historical novels under the name Blackledge.

St. Bernards and Dalmatians

From statement 1 we can conclude that Simon's St. Bernard is not named Sidney. Therefore the name is Sam or Smitty, and Sam or Smitty owns the Dalmatian named Sidney. From statement 2, we can conclude that Smitty's Dalmatian is not named Sam. Therefore the name is either Sidney or Simon, as is the name of Sam's St. Bernard. From statement 4, we can conclude that Sam's Dalmatian is not named Simon. Therefore the name is either Sidney or Smitty, and Sidney or Smitty owns the St. Bernard named Simon.

From statement 5, we can conclude that Sidney's Dalmatian is not named Smitty. Therefore, the name is either Sam or Simon, and Sam or Simon owns the St. Bernard named Smitty. From statement 3, we can conclude that the Dalmatian named Sam is not owned by Smitty. Therefore, the owner is Sidney or Simon. Also, Smitty's St. Bernard must be named Sidney or Simon.

From statement 5, we know that Sam or Simon owns the St. Bernard named Smitty. From statement 2, we know that Sam's St. Bernard is named Sidney or Simon. Therefore, Simon must own the St. Bernard named Smitty.

From statement 4, we know that Sam's Dalmatian is named either Sidney or Smitty. Therefore, Sam must own the Dalmatian named Smitty, since the name is not available to any of the other three owners.

From statement 4, we know that Sidney or Smitty owns the St. Bernard named Simon. From statement 2, we know that Sam's St. Bernard is named Sidney or Simon. Therefore, Sam's St. Bernard must be named Sidney. Therefore, Smitty's Dalmatian is named Sidney (from statement 2), and his St. Bernard is named Simon (from statement 3). Our conclusions at this point are:

	Sam	Sidney	Simon	Smitty
St. Bernard	Sidney		Smitty	Simon
Dalmatian	Smitty			Sidney

Therefore, Sidney's St. Bernard is named Sam, Simon's Dalmatian is named Sam, and Sidney's Dalmatian is named Simon.

SUMMARY:

Sam's St. Bernard is named Sidney, and his Dalmatian is named Smitty.
Sidney's St. Bernard is named Sam, and his Dalmatian is named Simon.
Simon's St. Bernard is named Smitty, and his Dalmatian is named Sam.
Smitty's St. Bernard is named Simon, and his Dalmatian is named Sidney.

Islanders' Boats

From statement 2, O'Byrne's daughter is Ophelia. Therefore, his fishing boat is not named *Ophelia*. From statement 4, O'Brien's fishing boat is not named *Ophelia*, and from statement 5, O'Bradovich's fishing boat is not named *Ophelia*. Therefore, that name belongs to O'Boyle's fishing boat. Therefore, O'Boyle's sailboat is not named *Ophelia*.

From statement 4, O'Brien's sailboat is not named *Ophelia*, and, since O'Byrne's sailboat is not named *Ophelia* (his daughter's name), that name belongs to O'Bradovich's sailboat.

From statement 3, O'Byrne's sailboat is not named *Olivia*. From statement 2, O'Boyle's daughter is named *Olivia*. Therefore, O'Brien's sailboat is named *Olivia*. From statement 4, O'Brien's fishing boat is not named *Olga*. Therefore, his fishing boat must be named *Odette*.

Our conclusions, so far, are:

	O'Boyle	O'Bradovich	O'Brien	O'Byrne
daughter	Olivia			Ophelia
sailboat		*Ophelia*	*Olivia*	
fishing boat	*Ophelia*		*Odette*	

O'Brien's daughter, who is not named Odette, must be named Olga, and O'Bradovich's daughter is Odette.

From statement 1, O'Byrne's fishing boat and O'Boyle's sailboat have the same name. Therefore, the name is not *Olivia* or *Ophelia* (their daughters' names). Since O'Brien's fishing boat is named *Odette*, O'Byrne's fishing boat and O'Boyle's sailboat are both named *Olga*. Therefore, O'Byrne's sailboat is named *Odette*, and O'Bradovich's fishing boat is named *Olivia*.

SUMMARY:

> O'Boyle's daughter is Olivia, his sailboat is *Olga*, and his fishing boat is Ophelia.
>
> O'Bradovich's daughter is Odette, his sailboat is *Ophelia*, and his fishing boat is *Olivia*.
>
> O'Brien's daughter is Olga, his sailboat is *Olivia*, and his fishing boat is *Odette*.
>
> O'Byrne's daughter is Ophelia, his sailboat is *Odette*, and his fishing boat is *Olga*.

Writers of Classic Books

From statement 1, the Conrads gave or received a book by Dickens and gave or received a book by Kafka. From statement 2, since the Tolstoys were the ones who received a book by Dickens, it must have been given by the Conrads, who received a book by Kafka. According to statement 4, the Brontës received a book by Conrad from the namesakes of the author of the book given by the Conrads. Therefore, since we know that the Conrads gave a book by Dickens, the Brontës received a book by Conrad from the Dickenses.

Since we know that the Conrads were the couple who received a book by Kafka, from statement 3, a book by Forster was received by the Kafkas. Also, from statement 3, since we know that the Conrads gave a book by Dickens, and that it was given to the Tolstoys, the Forsters received a book by Tolstoy.

Conclusions at this point:

	Brontë	Conrad	Dickens	Forster	Kafka	Tolstoy
Brontës		received	—			
Conrads	—	—	gave	—	received	—
Dickenses		gave	—			
Forsters		—	—			received
Kafkas		—	—	received		
Tolstoys		—	received			

A book by Brontë must have been received by the Dickenses, since this is the only remaining possibility.

From statement 5, since we know that the Dickenses received a book by Brontë, the Brontës gave a book by Forster to the Kafkas. Since (also from statement 5) the namesakes of the book given by the Kafkas (the remaining choices are a book by Brontë or a book by Tolstoy) gave a book by Kafka, the gift given by Kafka must have been a book by Tolstoy, and the Tolstoys gave a book by Kafka. Therefore, the Forsters gave a book by Brontë.

SUMMARY:

The Brontës gave Forster and received Conrad.
The Conrads gave Dickens and received Kafka.
The Dickenses gave Conrad and received Brontë.
The Forsters gave Brontë and received Tolstoy.
The Kafkas gave Tolstoy and received Forster.
The Tolstoys gave Kafka and received Dickens.

Two Inhabitants

From A's statement, we know that A is a Pemtru. Only a Pemtru can, truthfully or falsely, state that it is afternoon.

From B's statement, we know that it is afternoon, whether B's statement is truthful or not. In this case, B has made a false statement.

SUMMARY: It is afternoon, A is a Pemtru, and B is an Amtru.

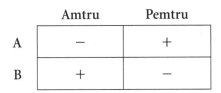

	Amtru	Pemtru
A	—	+
B	+	—

Is A's Statement True?

Consider that two are Pemtrus.

Assume it is morning. If so, and if A is an Amtru, his statement is true, and B is a Pemtru. However, B's statement would be impossible for a Pemtru in the morning. Therefore, if it is morning, A must be a Pemtru. If so, A's statement is false, and B is an Amtru. However, since A's statement would be false, B's statement would be impossible for an Amtru in the morning.

Therefore, it is afternoon. If A is an Amtru, B is also an Amtru. However, since we know that two are Pemtrus, A is not an Amtru. A is a Pemtru, as is B. C, whose statement is false, is an Amtru.

	Amtru	Pemtru
A	−	+
B	−	+
C	+	−

SUMMARY: It is afternoon, A and B are Pemtrus, and C is an Amtru.

Three Inhabitants

Consider that there are two Pemtrus and one Amtru.

Assume it is afternoon. If so, two of the three are Pemtrus, who have told the truth and one is an Amtru, who has lied. If so, since A claims that B is a Pemtru and B claims that C is a Pemtru, one of A and B must be the Amtru. It must be A, as stated by C. This means that B and C are the two Pemtrus. However, this means that A, who claims that B is a Pemtru, has spoken truthfully, an impossibility for an Amtru in the afternoon. Therefore, it must be morning. A and C, who have both lied, are the two Pemtrus, and B, who has told the truth, is the Amtru.

	Amtru	Pemtru
A	−	+
B	+	−
C	−	+

SUMMARY: It is morning, A and C are Pemtrus, and B is an Amtru.

Four Inhabitants

Consider that two are Amtrus and two are Pemtrus.

Assume it is afternoon. If so, if A is an Amtru, A's statement is false and B is a Pemtru. If so, B's statement is true and C is a Pemtru. If so, C's statement is true and D is a Pemtru. However, D's statement would be false. Therefore, if it is afternoon, A is a Pemtru. If so, B is an Amtru, C is an Amtru, and D is a Pemtru. Again, D's statement would be false, not possible for a Pemtru in the afternoon.

Therefore, it is morning. Assume A is an Amtru. If so, B is an Amtru, C is a Pemtru, and D is an Amtru. However, this would mean there is only one Pemtru. Therefore, A is a Pemtru, B is a Pemtru, C is an Amtru, and D is an Amtru.

	Amtru	Pemtru
A	−	+
B	−	+
C	+	−
D	+	−

SUMMARY: It is morning, A and B are Pemtrus, and C and D are Amtrus.

Five Inhabitants

Assume it is afternoon, and assume A's statement is true. If so, A is a Pemtru. If so, D, who claims A is an Amtru, must be an Amtru. If it is afternoon, B's statement must be true, and B is a Pemtru. If so, E who asserts that B is a Pemtru is also a Pemtru. C, who falsely asserts that D and E belong to the same group, is an Amtru. However, this would mean two Amtrus and three Pemtrus. Since we know there are three Amtrus and two Pemtrus, if it is afternoon, A's statement is not true.

Assume it is afternoon and A's statement is false. If so, A is an Amtru. If so, D, who claims A is an Amtru, is a Pemtru. B must be a Pemtru, as is E. If so, C, who truthfully claims D and E are in the same group, is a Pemtru. However, this would mean four Pemtrus and one Amtru. Therefore, it is not afternoon.

It is morning. Assume B's statement is false. If so, B is a Pemtru. E, who truthfully states B is a Pemtru, is an Amtru. A must be an Amtru. D, who claims A is an Amtru, is an Amtru. C, who truthfully asserts that D and E belong to the same group, is an Amtru. However, this would mean four Amtrus and one Pemtru.

Therefore, since we know it is morning, B's statement is true, and B is an Amtru. E, who falsely claims that B is a Pemtru, is a Pemtru. A's statement is true, and A is an Amtru. D, who truthfully asserts that A is an Amtru, is an Amtru. C, who falsely claims that D and E belong to the same group, is a Pemtru.

	Amtru	Pemtru
A	+	−
B	+	−
C	−	+
D	+	−
E	−	+

SUMMARY: It is morning; A, B, and D are Amtrus; and C and E are Pemtrus.

Four Valley Inhabitants

Consider that both groups are represented equally by the four valley inhabitants.

Assume it is afternoon. If so, if C were an Amtru, he would truthfully or falsely assert that B is an Amtru. If C were a Pemtru, again, he would truthfully or falsely assert that B is an Amtru. It would be impossible for C to refer to B as a Pemtru. Therefore, since C claims that B is a Pemtru, it cannot be afternoon.

It is morning. Whether C is an Amtru or a Pemtru, he has truthfully or falsely stated that B is a Pemtru. From B's statement in the morning, that he and A belong to the same group, we know that B is a Pemtru. (If B were an Amtru, truthfully or falsely, he would deny that he and A belong to the same group.)

For the same reason, from A's statement, A is a Pemtru and D could be an Amtru or a Pemtru. However, since both groups are represented equally, D and C must both be Amtrus.

	Amtru	Pemtru
A	−	+
B	−	+
C	+	−
D	+	−

SUMMARY: It is morning, A and B are Pemtrus, and C and D are Amtrus.

Three Valley Inhabitants

Assume it is afternoon. If so, from A's statement we can conclude that A is an Amtru, as a Pemtru in the afternoon could not refer to another valley inhabitant as a Pemtru. If it is afternoon, C must be a Pemtru, as an Amtru would be truthfully referred to as such by A. However, B's statement that he and C are not both Amtrus would be true, not a possible statement in the afternoon.

Therefore, it is morning. A is either a Pemtru who has spoken truthfully or falsely about C, or an Amtru who has spoken falsely in a statement referring to another Amtru (if C were a Pemtru, A would truthfully say so).

Assume A is a Pemtru. If so, if C is a Pemtru, C's statement, which refers to A, must be true: A would say that B is an Amtru. However, as a Pemtru in the morning, A's reference to B as an Amtru must be false. Therefore, B must be a Pemtru. However, this is a contradiction, as A's reference to another Pemtru in the morning must be true.

Therefore, if A is a Pemtru, C must be an Amtru. If so, again, C's statement would be true: A would falsely say that B is an Amtru, which leads to the same contradiction as in the previous paragraph.

Therefore, A and C are both Amtrus. C's statement referring to A must be false: A would not say that B is an Amtru. B must be an Amtru who has spoken falsely about another Amtru.

SUMMARY: It is morning, and A, B, and C are Amtrus.

	Amtru	Pemtru
A	+	−
B	+	−
C	+	−

Does C Live on the Hill?

Consider that the hill inhabitant will speak the truth only if none of the other speakers are truthful. Otherwise, he will lie. Also consider that it is afternoon.

If C is the hill inhabitant as claimed, B has spoken falsely and, therefore, must be an Amtru. A, who truthfully confirms this, must be a Pemtru. As the hill inhabitant, C could not have spoken truthfully. Therefore, C is not the hill inhabitant.

C, who has spoken falsely, must be an Amtru. B, who falsely claims C is a Pemtru, could be an Amtru or the hill inhabitant. If B is the hill inhabitant, A's statement is false and A is an Amtru. D, who falsely states that A is a Pemtru, must be an Amtru. Therefore, since A, C, and D all make false statements, B, if the hill inhabitant, would speak truthfully. Since B falsely claims C to be a Pemtru, B is not the hill inhabitant.

Therefore, the hill inhabitant must be A or D. Assume D is the hill inhabitant. If so, since A truthfully states that B is an Amtru, he is a Pemtru. If D is the hill inhabitant his statement would be false. However, it is not. Therefore, A, who has spoken truthfully, is the hill inhabitant. B, C, and D have spoken falsely; all three are Amtrus.

SUMMARY: A is the hill inhabitant, and B, C, and D are Amtrus.

	Amtru	Pemtru	Hill
A	−	−	+
B	+	−	−
C	+	−	−
D	+	−	−

One From the Hill

Consider that the hill inhabitant will speak the truth only if none of the other speakers are truthful. Otherwise, he will lie.

Assume that A is the hill inhabitant. If so, if it is morning, D's statement is true, and A's statement about D is also true. But a hill inhabitant lies if others speak the truth, so if A is the hill inhabitant, it must be afternoon. If so, B's statement is true, so A's statement must be false. This means D is a Pemtru and his statement is true. But since C's statement is not true, C is an Amtru, which contradicts D's statement. Therefore, A does not live on the hill.

Assume that B is the hill inhabitant. If so, B's statement about C must be true. But C's statement is also true. Therefore, B is not the hill inhabitant.

Assume that C is the hill inhabitant. If so, C's statement is true, and D's statement is true, also. Therefore, C is not the hill inhabitant.

Therefore, D lives on the hill. B's statement is true, so D's statement must be false. Since C's statement is false, from D's false statement C must be an Amtru and it must be afternoon. So B is a Pemtru, and A, whose statement is true, is also a Pemtru.

	Amtru	Pemtru	Hill
A	−	+	−
B	−	+	−
C	+	−	−
D	−	−	+

SUMMARY: It is afternoon, D is the hill inhabitant, A and B are Pemtrus, and C is an Amtru.

Index

Note: *Italicized* page numbers indicate clues, and **bold** page numbers indicate solutions.